JOHN

736 -

f22 -283F

WATER FLYING CONCEPTS

An advanced text on wilderness water flying.

by Dale De Remer, Ph.D.

Second Edition
1990

Published by:

IAP, Inc.,
A Hawks Industries Company
P.O. Box 10000
Casper, WY 82602-1000
307-266-3838
800-443-9250
FAX: 307-472-5106

Third Printing

Cover photo by Mr. Bob Lundberg, UND Aviation student.
Computer graphics by Mr. Jim Piazza, UND Aviation student.
Cartoons ably illustrated by Mr. Bart Taylor, UND Avation student.
Photographs credited to Bill McCarrel are copyrighted by him.
Other photos by author unless otherwise credited.
Printed in the United States of America.

Library of Congress Catalog Card Number: 89-091576.
ISBN Number: 0 89100-374-6.

Young person, hopeful pilot,
learn well your many lessons
from classroom, airplane
and the world about you
so that, one day,
you can become
that silver tipped,
venerable, command aviator
you aspire to be.

Learn well, and beware!
For there are many who
drive airplanes about the sky
yet know little of what they do.

Learn well, and be alert
for yours can be a life
of incredible vistas,
beautiful experiences,
and occasional moments
of nearness to God.

TABLE OF CONTENTS

About the Author(s) aa
Foreword
Author's Statement as

Chapter 1
About this Book and Water Flying

Chapter 2
More About this Book and Water Flying

Chapter 3
Seaplane Takeoff Performance

Chapter 4
Seaplane Takeoff Technique Studies

Chapter 5
Seaplane Flight Performance

Chapter 6
Center of Gravity Effects

Chapter 7
Reducing Water Drag

Chapter 8
External Loads

Chapter 9
Stability on the Water

Chapter 10
Flight Planning and Decision-Making

Chapter 11
Flight Planning for the Wilderness

Chapter 12
Fuels and Fueling

Chapter 13
Mooring

Chapter 14
Wilderness Operations

Chapter 15
Seaplane Camping - Light and Comfortable

Chapter 16
Survival!

Chapter 17
Reflections of a Seaplane Examiner

Glossary of Terms G

Bibliography B

Index I

About the Author(s)

Dale De Remer was raised in Southern California and received his Bachelor of Science degree from California State Polytechnic University at San Luis Obispo, California. While completing his Master of Science and Doctor of Philosophy degrees at Utah State University, he learned to fly. Flying became a part of everyday life. It opened doors of opportunity as it provided quick, far-reaching transportation for his businesses. He served as corporate pilot, agricultural pilot, and chief pilot for various companies, while logging over 18,000 hours total time in general aviation aircraft of many types. He holds ATP, CFI and CFI-I licenses with single and multiengine land and sea, rotorcraft-helicopter and instrument ratings. He has over fourteen years experience teaching aviation to young men and women at the university level. He is presently teaching his eighth year for the Center for Aerospace Sciences, University of North Dakota. Each summer he conducts advanced wilderness seaplane pilot courses which take his students as far north as the Canadian Arctic tundra. Dr. De Remer was appointed Field Director, Central Northwest Region, for the Seaplane Pilot's Association in 1987. In 1989, he was promoted to full professor and received the UND Foundation - Lydia and Arthur Saiki - UND Student Government Outstanding Faculty Advisor award.

Anders Christenson, who contributed chapter 17, holds a Bachelor of Arts degree from Macalester College and Master of Arts from the University of Minnesota. He holds the ATP license and Flight Instructor: Single and multiengine land, single engine sea and instrument ratings with over 22,600 total hours experience. Of this, over 20,000 hours is flight instruction given! Total seaplane instruction time exceeds 2,000 hours. He is a designated pilot examiner for the FAA for private, commercial and ATP licenses and flight instructor certification. He has written for Air Progress and is a regular contributor to the Minnesota Flyer and at the Minnesota Seaplane Pilot's Safety seminars.

Paul Johnson, who contributed chapter 16, has been active in survival education and ground search and rescue for over 15 years. He currently works as a volunteer with the Canadian Red Cross Search and Rescue program, as well as with the National Association for

Search and Rescue in the U. S. He has several teaching accreditations in wilderness rescue, first aid, search management and mountain rescue. Paul is a pilot. He flew the Canadian North and High Arctic for many years before starting his consulting practice, specializing in aviation and remote worksite safety.

Malcolm Joyce, who contributed the Foreword, earned a Bachelor of Commerce degree from Mount Allison University. He holds an airline transport license as well as a helicopter license. He is a former Canadian military jet fighter pilot and served three years flying with the USAF on pilot instruction duties. In 1983 he was appointed Regional Manager for Transport Canada's Aviation Safety Programs Branch where he is responsible for aircraft accident prevention in Central Canada. In his position he flies the Beechcraft Kingair and the DHC-2 Beaver on wheels, floats and skis. He conducts aviatin safety presentations, workshops, and conferences in his safety work. He is also responsible for identifying and investigating any safety deficiencies in the National air transportation system, and participates regularly in national and international aviation safety seminars. He has written a number of articles for aviation safety publications..

Foreword

Water flying, either on floats or with a boat hull, has been the real pioneer in air transportation. The covered wagon opened up the West but the water-borne aircraft moved back the northern frontiers. The float aircraft is still the workhorse of commercial air transportation and communication in Northern Canada, Alaska and other areas of the world where a suitable runway is not always available.

Recreational float and boat flying provides access to the final wilderness frontiers for its pilots and passengers. However, because of the residual pioneer aspects of seaplane flying and its associated hazards, this type of aviation requires more than the usual pilot decisions and judgements. Furthermore, it has been well established that most aircraft accidents are caused by some type of human behaviour failure. These failures are usually within the decision-making range and capability of the pilot. It is not surprising, therefore, that seaplane flying has a somewhat higher incidence of aircraft mishaps.

As one who flys the DHC-2 Beaver on wheels, skis and floats as well as having logged many hours on the DHC-3 single Otter on floats, I have been impressed with the research in this book. Dr. De Remer has opened up and examined many technical aspects of water flying and conducted studies into the reasons for current procedures and techniques.

There are many experts in the basic techniques of water take-offs and landings as well as on how to get there and how to survive in the 'bush'. There are also a number of 'how to fly' books with which beginning float pilots are familiar. Dr. De Remer's research builds on this basic knowledge. He flexes his enquiring academic mind which is continually asking "why" and "how".

Dr. De Remer has combined his enthusiasm for flying with his desire to fill in the knowledge gaps. It has been my pleasure and eduation to co-sponsor annual aviation safety seaplane seminars with Dr. De Remer both in Canada and in the USA. The highlight of these meetings has been the presentations by Dr. De Remer based on academic, scientific and practical research using his own aircraft on floats, plus crews of dedicated University of North Dakota aviation students. These lectures always have universal appeal, from the minimum hour impressionable pilot to the tough, multi-houred "I've been there" career bush pilot. With his research material now committed to this book, I have no reservations in recommending it to any level of seaplane pilot. There is something in this book for the pilot spouse, the pilot offspring (who knows everything) and for the bush pilot who makes his/her living on floats. Float and flying facts at this level will be a natural and welcome challenge for pilots of all levels of knowledge and experience. Work yourself through the mathematical formulae or, if your specialty has been maintaining and perfecting your flying proficiency, and your math skills have slipped, trust the numbers and skip over the calculations. The information package comes through either way.

In the aircraft accident prevention business at Transport Canada, we emphasize the critical importance of sound and thoughtful decision making, decision making which is based upon good judgement. But judgement and decision making are greatly enhanced by the pilot's knowledge base. Hazardous pilot attitudes also detract from safe decision making. Dr. De Remer's concepts may very well take some of the thrill and guess work out of flying for you, particularly those short lake take-offs. But, if your thrill is wondering if you are going to clear the trees after you lift off the water, then you definitely have a dangerous attitude profile, and well may be destined to become one of my accident prevention failure statistics.

Aviators are sometimes fooled by thinking that if their flying is in compliance with the regulations, then they are entitled to enjoy a safe flight. Government standards are in place to provide protection, but our success and pleasure in flying is enhanced, and even determined, by our preparation for pilot decision making. All risk factors will never be removed from an activity which has a thrill, a challenge, or is worth doing. There are government standards with which all must comply but in water flying, the pilot is much more the chief executive in risk management. As the pilot, you are in control, and luck plays a very small part in your success. I like the expression 'the harder you work, the luckier you become'. This applies to all aspects of aviation but, when the seaplane pilot is engaged with the beauty we call the Wilderness, the work that has been done and the attitude and knowledge taken into the wilderness will be the pilot's greatest asset, protection and insurance. It can be said that being familiar with the work accomplished in this book will definitely increase a pilot's luck factor by decreasing the risk factor.

Look at it this way: expanding your knowledge will take some of the mystery out of float flying but it will never remove the mystique!

The survival content in this book (Chapter 16) features the expertise of Paul Johnson. Mr. Johnson is a regular guest lecturer at Transport Canada's Company Aviation Safety Officer course. He beautifully demonstrates his competence on these occasions by being able to condense a survival briefing into a most challenging and information packed 50-minute lecture. I have been exposed to briefings on survival by people who achieve less in two days. His succinct, state of the art survival composit is here to be enjoyed.

Reflecting with Anders Christenson (Chapter 17) can be humbling as well as informative. He has some key rules which accentuate the positive aspects of water flying.

Flying off and onto the water from convenient, well-serviced areas and into the remote wilderness is one of the most challenging and demanding of all flying skills. Because it is not easy, and because it continually presents the pilot with a variety of data which must be integrated into sound decision-making and precisely coordinated physical inputs, it has the potential for extreme peaks of self-satisfaction and down-right fun. But, to **keep** it pleasant, the many natural hazards that seaplane pilots are exposed to must be either reduced, avoided or managed. To accomplish this we owe it to ourselves, our loved ones and our passengers to keep our information gaps to a minimum.

In these pages will be found information which compliments and augments this need of all seaplane pilots. For these reasons, I commend this book to all who have an interest in flying and/or seaplanes.

Malcolm S. Joyce
Regional Manager
Aviation Safety Programs
Transport Canada
Central Region

Author's Statement

(Supplement to the Second Edition)

The First Edition presented me with a problem I didn't anticipate. It sold out too soon -- in less than a year! I have had to steal time from other projects in order to make the necessary revisions and additions so the Second Edition could go to print.

I simply could not abide with the idea of reprinting the first edition with the knowledge that there were some errors, so in this Second Edition I have concentrated on clearing up those errors that have been found, adding a few more hints and some clarifications. Chapter 9 has been expanded with information developed from a paper submitted to the Flight Safety Foundation. That paper was written by myself and Dr. Lonny Winrich, UND Computer Science Department, and is the result of further thinking inspired by the error in the original Chapter 9 which provided us with the world's biggest Beaver, so nicely pointed out by Dave Wiley when he said "boy, they sure grow big Beavers back in your country". Thanks for all the other good comments you made as well, Dave.

Most of the errors have been found by the wonderful and knowledgable people who are seaplane affectionados. To them goes my deep appreciation. My sincere thanks to George Evelin, a retired British engineer whose years of experience includes doing stress analysis on many of the european large monohull seaplanes, for his exhaustive response to the First Edition. Also, on this side of the big pond, thanks to all of you who have written or called with suggestions for changes and improvements.

I will be pleased if this volume adds to seaplane pilot personal knowledge, and therefore, safety.

By the way, I have heard not a word in response to my request on the page facing page 1-1. This might lead one to the erroneous (I hope) notion that there are currently no living seaplane pilot-poets. What do all you pilots do on the long, boring cross-country flights if you don't compose poetry or limerics about seaplane lore? Let me hear from you! It is too late for this Second Edition but there is a good chance that you can be published in WATER FLYING.

Dale De Remer

Author's Statement

Over the years of development of materials for this book, many have helped. Although I can't begin to mention the names of all who have helped, I would like to thank each of you, from my beginning instructor to those from whom I am still learning about seaplane flying.

This book, with the exception of Chapters 16, 17 and the foreword were written solely by myself. The manuscript was prepared on a desktop publishing program by myself or under my direct supervision. In order to be able to achieve complete control over the content of this book, it was necessary that I also publish it, which I have done. Although it is not yet considered a collector's item, you are reading from one of only 1,000 copies of the first edition.

Cruising sailboat skippers have a saying which goes, "If you put off starting that long cruise until the boat is 100% ready to go, you will never leave the dock". The same applies to this book. It is not 100% perfect, nor even 100% as I would like it to be, but it is time to cast off its docklines and hope that you, its reader, won't be too critical. When you are critical, I hope that you will let me know about this book's shortcomings.

Whenever two seaplane pilots meet, all of the ingredients are present for a disagreement about some seaplane subject. Some excellent learning discussions are the result. It is my hope that this book will generate some of the same sort of discussions, in the interest of furthering individual knowledge.

The final pages dealing with the subject of this book have not been written. I hope that they will never be written for that would mean that all the learning about seaplane operation had already taken place.

So the learning goes on for all of us. It is my hope that you will find this book to be of help to you, in this wonderful, fun-filled endeavor.

Dale De Remer

Oh, the working class
can kiss my ass,
For I'm a floatplane pilot.

My days are long
'til my work is done
and the wilderness is my home.

I work o'er a land
where the wolf and the loon
join at evening to sing a littany.

I live, like the wolf,
by my wits to be sure
and a machine called Pratt & Whitney.

I come and I go
from the wilderness far
and leave there not a trace.

I've been lost and most bitten,
scared, sorely smitten, yet
there's a smile upon my face.

For I'm a floatplane pilot.

Author's note: The first three lines are from floatplane lore. The rest is by the author, last revised near 63N., 101W. If anyone knows the original or other versions with the same beginning lines, please let me hear from you!

CHAPTER 1

About This Book and Water Flying

It is a beautiful afternoon. You are flying at 5500 feet MSL across the center of Lake Superior, eastbound. This is something you never felt comfortable doing in an airplane equipped with wheels. But, this trip, you can look down and see those big floats beneath you. Looking south you can just barely see the south shore of the lake. To the north, the water below fades into the haze - the north shore can't be seen. Looking down, it is hard to focus your eyes because the surface of the lake is so calm and smooth, only the white cumulus clouds above you can be seen in the mirrored surface of the lake. What a fabulous cross-country!

Your reverie is interrupted by your passenger-flight instructor saying: "O.K., the engine just quit. Now what are you going to do?". What would your answer be? Think about it for a moment before you read on, and answer the flight instructor's question to the best of your ability.

Your answer, done properly, should lead you to a safe, power off (unless your re-start procedure is successful) landing on a large lake. If the procedure is done correctly but all the cards are stacked against you, you should still be able to accomplish the landing with only some structural damage to the seaplane, but with a happy outcome for the occupants.

Your answer should contain at least the following components:

Pilot: "First, I would start to establish best glide speed"

Flight Instructor: "Which one? How do you determine what speed is correct? Does this speed vary with altitude or aircraft weight?". The answer, of course, depends on whether you are most interested in best glide distance (best distance glide speed) or staying aloft the longest and having the slowest rate of descent (minimum sink glide speed). In this instance, you may want to use either or both speeds, depending on whether you spot a boat you want to land near (for rescue and depth perception purposes) and need to glide some distance to it, or if you want to stay aloft the longest (time for a mayday, long prayer or lowest rate of descent so the buoyant materials you grabbed from their planned locations within reach of the pilot's seat can beat you to the water, to help with depth perception).

"What do you carry those weights for?", your flight instructor asks. "They have many uses, including marking, and helping me know for sure if I can make it out of a short lake.", you say.

"I suppose you are going to ask me about that roll of toilet paper back on the hatrack, too", you say to your instructor. "Besides the obvious use, I can use it to help me determine the height of the obstacles I must take off over." (There's more to read on this in chapter three).

As for the questions about glide speeds, see chapter five. It will tell you how to determine minimum sink glide speed, because it is probably not to be found in your POH (pilot's operating handbook).

A part of this scenario that started over the "big lake" on the first leg of this advanced seaplane pilot's course is a good discussion with your flight instructor about the fine points of loading (chapter 6) and its effect on performance in the air (chapter 5) and on the water (chapters 3 and 4), high density altitude operations (chapter 3), short lake departures (chapter 3), carrying external loads (chapter 8), landing and surviving (chapter 16), fast water and rocky shore operations, wilderness navigation (chapters 10, 11, 14), rough water operations and other topics that become day-to-day encounters when using the floatplane to its fullest.

This is the sort of learning experience that you might expect in an advanced course in float flying -- something you might like to do someday if you are the kind of pilot that takes a lot of pride in doing things well. If you took such an advanced course, this might be the textbook, so you can start the course here and now -- by reading whatever you care to, from these pages.

Then maybe one day you will be the one in the left seat, over Lake Superior, putting to the test what you have read about.

If you can't take an advanced course, please consider doing a bit of it each year. . . . get some recurrent or refresher training . . . lots of good seaplane pilots I know do each year. Besides, it's another great excuse to go flying!

Chapter two explains about why this book was written, and how to use it.

CHAPTER 2

More About This Book And Water Flying.

Not so very long ago, I finished my seaplane add-on rating. I was very enthused with this fabulous new way to fly, and winter was coming on, so I asked for ALL the reading materials about water flying. To my great surprise and disappointment, I had already read everything! I searched the university and community library systems. The libraries searched further for me, without success.

"It's not fair", I said to myself, "I have so much more to learn!"

Now you know how this book came to be. After more than 17,000 hours of general aviation flying in everything from cubs to turboprops, and 90,000 miles of skippering my own 46 foot sailboat over the oceans of this hemisphere (we lived aboard for 6 1/2 years), I was ready to combine flying and sailing.

I had a piece of paper in my pocket that said I was a Commercial seaplane pilot (and seaplane flight instructor as well). But I knew that I had a great deal more to learn before I would be the confident, experienced seaplane pilot I wanted to be.

I wanted answers to questions that seemed as numerous as the wavelets on the lake: How many compartments must fill on one side before you tip over? How heavy can the seas be, and still operate safely? What is the effect of loading on performance? How do I know if I can take off, fully loaded, from this short lake (I don't even know how long the lake is!)? In the bush, how do I make emergency patches on the floats? How do I know if I am properly prepared to take my plane into the bush? How do I navigate with no radio nav-aids when all the lakes look alike? What else do I need to know?

If I go off into the bush, I will be responsible for the comfort and lives of those who go with me -- am I prepared for that? What tools and survival gear should I take with me? What else do I need to know about my engine? How do I repair cables if they break? What are the consequences of a broken flying wire? The questions seemed endless.

I have talked to many seaplane pilots who love to fly their seaplane and really enjoy fishing, camping and exploring the wilderness. But these same people hesitate to fly their own seaplane into the bush or cross-country across dryland or otherwise 'unfriendly' country because they feel inadequate to the task. And well they may be. I am sure that I was, with only seven hours total time-seaplane, and a new commercial seaplane pilot ticket. I had several things going for me, though, including a new found love for flying floats, a lot of flying and water experience, and a strong intuitive feeling that I still had a lot to learn.

All new seaplane pilots suffer from a handicap. The training we get, in preparation for the seaplane rating, only really qualifies us to fly around the pond at the home seaport and do some 'lite' cross-country flying. Yet the seaplane rating in our pocket doesn't restrict us. We find that insurance rates for seaplanes are much higher than for our airplane when it is on wheels. Is seaplane flying more dangerous? No, I don't think so, as long as we don't exceed our capabilities, and do take advantage of recurrent training on a periodic basis, to refresh us. Mostly, we need to improve our pilot skills to match the capability of our seaplane!

But how? There are many ways. That is what this book is about -- learning more about seaplanes and seaplane flying. This is not a book about "How to" fly floats. There are already several such good books (Bibliography, items 2.1, 2.2, 2.3, 2.4). There are also one or two that are not very good, so be careful what you read.

This is a book about knowing more about your seaplane, and about yourself as a seaplane pilot. This book is intended for the seaplane pilot who is probably new, but possibly an 'old salt', who wants to know more. Keep in mind, however, that as we learn more, new and different questions are raised, so don't expect to put this book down with all your questions answered. You may be provoked to thought that leads to new questions. Rather, revel with me in the joy of learning something new and in the pride of knowing that, as you learn, you become a better seaplane pilot.

How to use this book, and other sources

If you are a new seaplane pilot, be sure you refer often to the **glossary** of terms at the back of the book. It is important that you speak the 'lingo', and aren't confused by terms such as 'windward' and 'leeward'.

The **bibliography** section has in it only books and publications that have the kind of information on seaplanes that you are probably looking for. It is "where to go" for other sources of information on seaplanes. Numbers without words in parenthesis, such as (5.2) are **references** to the bibliography section.

Figures and **tables** are numbered consecutively within each chapter, so (table 5.2) refers to the second figure or table in chapter five. Separate numbering is not used for figures and tables, so you won't find a figure 5.2 and a table 5.2. Figures are either graphs, diagrams or photographs. All **photographs** were taken by the author unless credit is given.

Also, I recommend that you join the Seaplane Pilot's Association so that you can read the only periodical that is devoted entirely to seaplanes. The articles in that periodical, WATER FLYING, are a

Figure 2.1. The seaplane is a fishin' boat. Note trolling motor.

great source of seaplane knowlege (2.5). Attend the Seaplane Safety Seminars and fly-ins that occur all over the country, too (you can find out about them in Water Flying). You don't need to own your own seaplane to attend. If you do own your own, take advantage of seaplane refresher training from a senior seaplane instructor when you go to these affairs. Ask one of the people who are arranging the fly-in to set you up with one of these senior instructors. At the Minnesota seminar, it is a tradition...a free service, in the interest of safety, provided by the Minnesota Department of Aeronautics and a few senior flight instructors.

THE FUN EXPERIENCE-

I rarely pass up an excuse to go flying, because its so darn much fun! There are those who consider an airplane to be only a tool to get from point A to point B as quickly and safely as possible. For some of us, however, an airplane is the most fun way to get where we are going. It is also the most fun way to go nowhere in particular!

Figure 2.2. The seaplane is a speedboat, and perhaps an antique, like this Curtis Robin on Edo 3430's. Courtesy Edo Corporation.

Figure 2.3. The seaplane can take us to the real wilderness.

Figure 2.4. Or to a fancy resort.

But the seaplane is the funnest of the fun! Why? The seaplane is a boat and an airplane. Its a fishin' boat, a speedboat, a cargo boat and a sailboat, all-in-one. It is an airplane that is capable of taking us places that no other type of vehicle can take us.

It can take us to the fanciest resorts (they are almost always on a lake and almost always thrilled to have a seaplane parked on the beach out in front -- it adds to the resort's image of affluence and adventure). The seaplane can also take us back in time to the most primeval wilderness.

Going cross-country in a seaplane is a fun challenge and a unique experience. When you land, you may be the first seaplane the people there have ever seen up close. Instantly, you are the star attraction (or the chief villian!).

Figure 2.5. Cross country to Colorado. Refueling stop at Down's Marina, Pierre, SD., on the Missouri River.

So, come with me on an armchair adventure, into the fun of learning more about seaplanes and seaplane flying.

CHAPTER 3

TAKEOFF PERFORMANCE

Perhaps more than any other type of aircraft, the seaplane presents opportunities for making takeoffs from strange, uncharted locations, each with its own set of problems. I have heard many "high time" seaplane pilots say, "every takeoff and landing is different, so how do you write about the subject?" It is true that each takeoff is somewhat different, and the principles of good airmanship and seamanship must be correctly applied. It is not the intent of this book to cover the basic "how to" principles that are already well covered in other publications. Rather, lets look at the factors which affect takeoff performance so that a sound understanding of what your seaplane will and won't do exists, then let's explore how you can easily deal with any takeoff performance problem in a professional, worry-free way.

FACTORS AFFECTING TAKEOFF PERFORMANCE

When you ask your aircraft to perform for you, the following factors will determine how quickly your craft will become airborne, and how much distance is needed to get off the water and clear an obstacle.

1. **Pressure Altitude** - the altitude that would exist if atmospheric conditions were equivalent to a standard pressure day. It is easy to determine pressure altitude. Just set your altimeter's Kollsman window reading to 29.92 inches of mercury and read the indicated altitude.

Every pilot knows that, with a higher altitude, the air is less dense. There are less air molecules in each cubic foot of air for your airplane to use to develop lift. More important, there are less oxygen molecules available in each cubic foot of air to combine with fuel to produce power in the engine. The result: poorer performance, which translates into a longer water run and a greater distance to clear that proverbial "50 foot obstacle".

This won't be a major factor if flying from waterways of nearly equal elevation, but you will see a very significant change in performance if much of an altitude change occurs. Typically, you can expect about a 12% increase in takeoff distance for each 1000 feet of altitude increase.

Most POH's (pilot's operating handbook) provide data which permit the pilot to estimate the effect of altitude on the length of water run and distance over the 50 foot obstacle. The data is given in feet of distance, which is all very fine, but do you know the length of water run available to you? Probably not, even at your home base, let alone that wilderness lake you are thinking about departing from. That's OK, we will show you a way to determine if there is enough room BEFORE you land, then we will show you how, once down on the water, to be sure you have enough performance to make the takeoff work, even without knowing the length of the water run you have. But first, a good basic knowlege of the factors that will affect your craft's takeoff performance is valuable, so let's continue.

2. **Temperature** - As the air (a gas) warms up, this elevated temperature manifests itself in the form of greater molecule velocity. The particles of air (mostly nitrogen and oxygen molecules), when heated, have acquired energy which causes them to speed up. The effect of this is that they occupy a larger volume, so, like higher altitude, higher temperature causes our aircraft to develop less lift and power because there are less molecules of air and oxygen in a given volume. The net effect is less performance when the temperature is higher.

In case your POH doesn't provide you with the takeoff run performance for altitudes above sea level, you can compute approximate values using the following formula: For each 1000 feet of pressure altitude above sea level, add 12% to the sea level takeoff run. Then, for each 15 degrees F. or 8.5 degrees C. ABOVE standard temperature (for that altitude), add 12% of the newly computed takeoff run found by applying the pressure altitude rule-of-thumb. See the standard temperature table, table 3.1.

Or, using your whiz-wheel (E-6B flight computer or equivalent), compute the density altitude (pressure altitude corrected for non-standard temperature) and apply the rule-of-thumb: For each 1000 feet above sea level, increase sea level takeoff distances by 12%. These figures will be found to be close approximations for aircraft of power loadings of 12-17 pounds per horsepower.

Table 3.1. ICAO Standard Atmosphere temperatures.

Altitude, feet	Temperature, degrees F.
Sea Level	59
1000	55.4
2000	51.9
3000	48.3
4000	44.7
5000	41.2
6000	37.6
7000	34
8000	30.5
9000	26.9
10000	23.3

Note: add .35 degrees per 100 feet, to interpolate between 1000 foot levels.

Example: Today we expect to have a departure to do from lake Tufluk, which is not a large lake at all. The lake's elevation is 2516 feet ASL (above sea level) and at 2 P.M. today we estimate the temperature will be 80 degrees F. at the lake. From the POH, we know that our Cessna 180 on 2870 floats has a takeoff water run at SL, calm wind, of 1145 ft. and the total distance over that 50' obstacle is 1860 ft. Weather pressure charts for the area indicate that high pressure will exist in the area, with 30.10 inches of mercury expected over lake Tufluk this afternoon.

Our calculations should look like this:

PRESSURE ALTITUDE: 30.10 - 29.92 = 0.18 inches higher than standard pressure. Therefore, pressure altitude will be about 180 feet lower (1" Hg of pressure equals about 1000 feet of altitude) than the actual lake elevation. So, 2516' - 180' = 2336' (when you land on the lake, your altimeter should read 2516' with an altimeter setting of 30.10; if you reset the Kollsman window reading to 29.92", your altimeter should read 2336 feet, the pressure altitude).

According to our rule-of-thumb, we need to add 2336'/1000' x 12% to the sea level takeoff distance, or add 28%.

TEMPERATURE CORRECTION: Standard day temperature at 2516' should be:

59° F. - (3.5° F./1000 ft. x 2.336 thousand ft.) = 50.8° F., or
15° C. - (2° C./1000 ft. x 2.336 thousand ft.) = 10.3° C.

Today's 2 P.M. temperature of 80° F. is (80 - 50.8) = 29.2 or about 30 degrees F. ABOVE standard day temperature. By our rule, we need to add 30 degrees F./15 degrees F. = 2 x 12% to the takeoff run.

Therefore, we need to add the following corrections to the SL takeoff run:

28% for pressure altitude of 2336 feet ASL.
24% for 30° F. warmer than standard day.
52% must be added to the published sea level standard day performance:

Takeoff run: 1145 ft. x 1.52 = 1740 ft.
Total distance over 50' obstacle: 1860 x 1.52 = 2827'

CALCULATION BY DENSITY ALTITUDE METHOD: Since density altitude is pressure altitude corrected for temperature variations from standard day conditions, and since a 1000' altitude correction is equivalent to a 15° F. or 8.5° C. variation from standard, the density altitude at lake Tufluk at 2 P.M. today will be:

Pressure altitude: 2336 ft.
Temperature: 80° F. or 27° C.

To closely approximate density altitude, add to pressure altitude one thousand feet for each 15 degrees F. or 8.5 degrees C. that the temperature is above standard atmosphere temperature.

To compute the temperature variation from standard, subtract the standard temperature at the pressure altitude from the ambient (actual) temperature.

To compute standard temperature at any altitude, subtract 3.5 degrees F. or 2 degrees C. per 1000 feet of pressure altitude from 59 degrees F. or 15 degrees C. (sea level standard temperature). For example, the standard temperature at 2336 feet is:

Farenheit: 59 - (3.5 degrees x 2.336 thousand feet) = 50.8°F.

Celsius: 15 - (2 degrees x 2.336 thousand feet) = 10.3° C.

Result: The standard atmosphere temperature at 2336 feet is 50.8 degrees F. or 10.3 degrees C. and the temperature variation from standard is 80° F. minus 50.8° F. = 29.2° F. or about 30° F. The density altitude calculation should look like this:

Pressure altitude	=	2336 ft.
Temperature correction	=	30 F. variation from standard day / 15 F. variation per 1000'
	=	2 x 1000', or 2000' correction
Density altitude	=	2336' + 2000' = 4336 ft.

(My E6-B shows the density altitude to be about 4300 ft., what does yours say?)

The correction of takeoff water run and distance over 50' is:

Water run: SL water run + (4.336 x 12% of SL water run)
Total distance: SL T.D. + (4.336 x 12% of SL T.D.)

This, of course, results in the same answers we computed in the sections above.

3. **Gross Weight.** - Most modern day POH's provide takeoff data for variations in weight of the aircraft. If this information is not available but you do have the sea level, gross weight takeoff conditions available, it is possible to approximate the takeoff distances by the following:

Takeoff performance is affected approximately by the square of the weight change. The formula you can use to determine a distance multiplier for the effects of weight on takeoff performance is:

$(\text{Actual weight/Gross certificated weight})^2 = \text{multiplier}$

For example, let's say we figured our actual weight for the takeoff from lake Tufluk to be 2750 pounds. Our takeoff distances would be:

$(2750/2820)^2 = .951$

Then: .951 x 1740' = 1655' water run

.951 x 2827' = 2688' total over 50' obstacle

For those who choose to load their seaplanes above the maximum certificated (legal) weight, the above method underestimates the distances required. Should you choose to load above the legal limit, you should be reminded that, when you do so, you have entered the realm of 'test pilot', and many factors enter into the prediction of the outcome of the flight. If you insist on loading over gross, up to about 10% over gross, book figures indicate that if you add 10% to the answers from the method shown above, the results will be conservative estimates, however, no one but you can be held responsible for the results of your choice to overload. For clarity of methodology only, and not in recommendation of overloading, here is an example:

Say we find that our aircraft gross weight totals up to 2950 pounds. Certificated gross is 2820. The overload is within 10%.

Then: $(2950/2820)^2 = 1.094 + 10\% = 1.204$

1.204 x 1740 = 2095 ft. water run

1.204 x 2827 = 3404 ft. total over the obstacle

Aircraft weight has a serious effect on all factors of aircraft performance. Increased weight will decrease climb and cruise performance and increase landing distances. Usually, we seaplane pilots are most affected by takeoff performance. Thus, the detailed treatment of that subject here.

WHERE the weight is placed in the aircraft will determine the location of the plane's longitudinal center of gravity (fore and aft). The location of C.G. is also very important as it has a sizeable effect on your plane's performance, stability and control. More about that in Chapters 5 and 6.

4. **Wind** - On takeoff, wind is usually considered to be the seaplane pilot's friend. Five to ten knots is usually ideal because it provides the

water conditions which reduce hydrodynamic drag by allowing float cavitation but doesn't cause waves so large that there is a possibility of structural damage to floats or airframe. The small wavelets that are created in sheltered water at these wind speeds are ideal because as the float passes over these wavelets, air is trapped between float bottom and water (cavitation). This lessens the wetted area of the float and decreases water drag, resulting in more rapid acceleration to liftoff speed than can be expected with glassy water conditions where more of the float bottom is wetted. Modern float designs provide channels on the bottom of the float that are meant to entrap air under the float for the same purpose.

Wind speeds greater than 10-12 knots increase wave size, except in very sheltered water, to the point where some pounding takes place during the takeoff run. The positive side of the increased wind speed is that the water run is shortened so that you and the aircraft are subjected to the pounding for a shorter period of time.

Just how rough can the water be and still accomplish a safe takeoff without damaging the aircraft? I wished that I had known the answer to that question one day when we awoke to find the wind freshening. By the time we were ready to go, the wind speed was 35 knots gusting to 42. Waves in the harbor had been building all morning and now appeared to be 2 to 2 1/2 feet. The launching ramp was located such that, when the aircraft was placed on it, we faced directly into the wind with plenty of water in front of us for a takeoff. I deliberated for a long time before deciding to go. Had the aircraft been smaller than the Cessna 180 I was flying that day, or had it been heavily loaded, or had I needed to maneuver, turn downwind or taxi any distance before departing, I surely would not have made the decision to go. Positive factors in the decision-making-process were the fact that I only needed about 10 knots of acceleration to reach flying speed and the lee shore (where the waves were breaking) was sand with friendly help available.

The aircraft was warmed up and the pre-takeoff check completed on the ramp. Power was fully applied and the nose lowered to a flat running attitude as soon as the aircraft came off the hump onto the step to make the step run smoother. The aircraft was 'helped' into the air at the lowest possible flying speed then leveled in ground effect until Vx plus ten was achieved, to provide for gusty conditions. It all happened very fast. I only remember 'bumps' from three waves. I suspect our water run was less than 100 feet. The takeoff didn't seem rough at all. Landing in those conditions would have been a different story, though.

At first consideration, one would think that a headwind would help the seaplane more than the landplane because of the decrease in water drag that occurs from calm wind conditions to wind speeds of 5-10 knots. For the landplane, the wind has little effect on rolling drag. However, the hydrodynamic drag on the seaplane is so much greater than rolling drag is for the landplane (except in deep mud or snow conditions), even when the water is ruffled by ideal wind conditions, the data shows us that the landplane has a greater proportional decrease in takeoff distance with a given headwind. For example, the Cessna 180 seaplane enjoys about a 24% decrease in water run and a 20% decrease in total distance over a 50' obstacle for each 10 knots of headwind component, while the 180 landplane of comparable weight has its ground roll reduced 31% and over-the-obstacle distance reduced 24% by the same wind.

The seaplane's great advantage lies in the fact that usually the seaplane is able to takeoff directly into the wind where the landplane is restricted to the direction of the runway which, in my experience, is not often directly into the wind. The exception to this is operations from narrow canals and rivers where crosswind takeoff techniques and special water rudder handling methods are invoked by the pilots operating there.

Yes, there is a rule-of-thumb that can be used to estimate the effect of wind on takoff distance. First, however, we better review the concept of headwind and crosswind components, just in case you cannot depart directly into the wind.

As can be seen in figure 3.2, the headwind component of the wind is the velocity of a wind coming from the direction of takeoff that would have a force equivalent to the force exerted by the crosswind in a direction opposite the direction of takeoff. It is that portion of a crosswind that will help or hinder your plane's takeoff effort, expressed as a direct headwind. The trigonometric functions are utilized to solve the wind vector diagram of figure 3.2. All you have to do, to estimate headwind component, is be sure you solve correctly for the angle between direction to the wind and takeoff heading. In figure 3.2, the wind is coming from 140 + 180 = 320 degrees. Takeoff direction is 360 degrees. Angle alpha is 360 - 320 = 40 degrees.

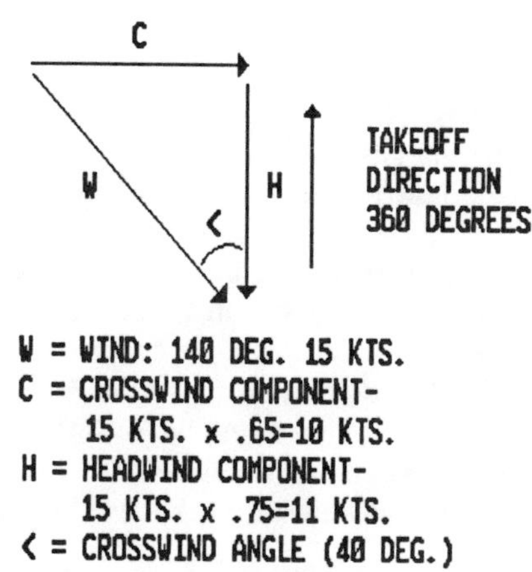

Figure 3.2. The headwind/crosswind component triangle.

Now take a look at table 3.3. Choose the nearest crosswind angle and find the headwind component multiplier. You can interpolate between values if you wish. In the case of 40 degrees crosswind angle, the headwind component multiplier is .75, and when multiplied with the given wind velocity, the headwind component is about 11 knots.

Table 3.3. Headwind Multipliers

Angle between wind and takeoff heading	Multiplier
0^0	1.00
10^0	0.95
20^0	0.90
30^0	0.85
45^0	0.70
60^0	0.50
90^0	0.00

Now that you know how to find the headwind component, here is the rule of thumb, which assumes you have been able to determine your takeoff water run and distance over the obstacle, corrected for all other factors except wind. This rule requires that you know your lift-off speed. Lift-off speed and wind speed must both be in the same units of velocity. Determine the ratio of wind speed to lift-off speed and subtract it from .93 to find the wind effect multiplier for water run.

Example: Indicated lift-off speed: 52 mph
Headwind component: 15 mph

Multiplier =.93 - 15/52 = .93 - .288 = .642

With a 15 mph wind, you will use .642 or 64% of the distance for your water run that you would under no wind conditions.

To estimate total distance over a 50' obstacle, with winds of 10 mph or more, double the water run distance figured with the method above.

Caution. The above discussion has provided rules of thumb for estimating performance. They must be considered just that - - only estimates. If POH values are available, use them. If not, use of these rules of thumb should be with the knowledge that they are only close approximations.

Water (hydrodynamic) Drag

Drag is usually defined as being a force which acts in a direction opposite to the flightpath or to the water run path. The in-flight dragforms are discussed in Chapter 4.

Hydrodynamic drag first becomes apparent to the new seaplane pilot during the takeoff run when the flight instructor demonstrates finding the "sweet spot" where the aircraft continues to accelerate well. If too much or too little back pressure is applied to the elevator control while on the step, hydrodynamic drag is increased, probably to the point where drag is greater than thrust, and the aircraft decelerates! At that point, the new pilot learns that it is important to keep drag to a minimum, so that thrust will always be greater than drag, resulting in a NET ACCELERATING FORCE (NAF). If drag is great enough to be equal to thrust, there will be no NAF, and the aircraft will not accelerate.

Anything the pilot does to increase drag at any time during the takeoff run will increase the takeoff distance. Thus, a good understanding of water drag can be useful to the pilot.

This is a complex subject, to be sure. Water drag is affected by the pilot's loading of the aircraft (see weight effect in this chapter and C.G. effect in Chapter 7), and the pilot's technique (Chapter 4). Some new materials can be used to decrease drag (Chapter 7).

The seaplane takeoff is a very complex maneuver. The aircraft's attitude and the rate of acceleration are always changing, as is drag and thrust.

The amount of drag which occurs during the seaplane's takeoff run varies with speed and other factors, but can be estimated from table 4.2, the takeoff time-speed curve. Just as computations of the area under that curve produce distance traveled at any time-point on the curve, the slope of the curve is an indicator of the rate of acceleration that is taking place. The steeper that curve is, the faster the aircraft is accelerating.

Rate of acceleration (slope of the curve) is an indicator of the amount of NET ACCELERATING FORCE (NAF) present. The amount of NAF present tells us the amount of excess thrust, so THRUST AVAILABLE - NAF = DRAG.

Let me say it another way:

THRUST AVAILABLE - DRAG = NAF

or, if thrust equals drag, there will be no accelerating force present. The aircraft will not accelerate.

Since we know that propeller thrust is highest at low airspeed, and that it decreases as airspeed increases, and NAF can be derived from the slope of the time-speed curve, total drag can be estimated. Figure 3.4 shows this derived drag curve for the Cessna 180. Most floatplanes today should have a drag curve that is similar to this, except that hump-step and liftoff speeds will vary somewhat with different models.

The drag curve of figure 3.4 shows what most pilots already know, that periods of minimum NAF occur twice during the properly done takeoff run: during the hump phase just before the hump-step transition and at high speed on the step, just before liftoff.

If there is any increase in drag (heavy loading, improper technique, weeds in the water rudders, floatbottom damage, etc.) or decrease in thrust (high density altitude, prop or engine damage, etc.) , NAF will be decreased. If NAF is decreased to zero, the aircraft will not accelerate. If drag is greater than thrust, a negative NAF will result and the aircraft will slow down.

Time becomes an important factor. If the pilot increases drag for any amount of time during the takeoff run, takeoff distance will be increased.

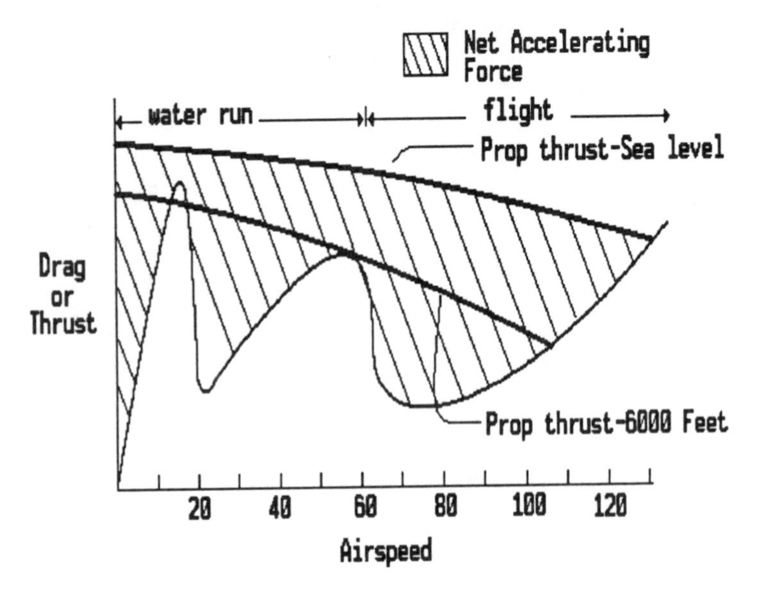

Figure 3.4. The derived drag curve for the Cessna 180.

The effect of high density altitudes becomes apparent with a look at the thrust available curve for 6000 feet. This aircraft at 6000 feet would accelerate to speeds of the hump phase but would be unable to make it over the hump onto the step.

OTHER FACTORS AFFECTING TAKEOFF PERFORMANCE

There are numerous other factors that affect takeoff performance that are not considered in your aircraft's POH. These would include such things as:

1. Deterioration in engine performance due to wear, poor plugs, ignition system, improper mixture, etc.

2. Deterioration in propeller efficiency due to erosion, pits, damage, wrong propeller installed, etc.

3. Deterioration of lift due to dents in airfoils, improper rigging, etc.

4. Increased drag due to improper rigging, rough skin surface condition, damage, etc.

5. Improper pilot technique, or pilot technique different than that used when the POH performance numbers were determined.

6. A factor I call 'old age' which includes performance decreasers such as skin and airfoil damage, increased empty weight due to dirt, dust and grease accumulations, and additions to the aircraft that were never added to the weight and balance computations.

7. Humidity. Water molecules weigh less than molecules of oxygen or nitrogen. So, when water molecules are present in the air there is less weight per unit of volume. Humid air is less dense. Very few light aircraft POH's deal with humidity in their performance tables, but the effect of humidity is significant. The Mooney POH indicates that high humidity may increase takeoff distances by 10%. Keep the humidity factor in mind, as it may add to your troubles just when you don't need it (that glassy water takeoff from a short lake early in the morning when the fog is just dissipating, for example). I don't have any rules of thumb for humidity to amaze you with, but later in the chapter we will see how to deal with all of these factors in a much easier way.

It could be argued that, because of these performance degrading factors, one should treat the POH performance figures as not being sufficiently conservative. I suppose that those thoughts would run through my head if I was faced with a takeoff from a short lake on a warm day with a full load (we might as well add 140 ft. tall pine trees all the way around the lake to our list).

Besides, I don't even know exactly how long the darn lake is, so what good are the POH numbers, anyway?

If you are already down on the lake, and are now contemplating that difficult takeoff, the POH numbers aren't much good for the reasons listed above. It is best if you don't allow yourself to get into this mess in the first place! Remember, it is the pilot in commmand who is ultimately responsible for the fate of his aircraft's operations.

O.K., lets first look at how we can keep ourselves out of this kind of a problem, then we will learn a method whereby you can attempt that takeoff with very little risk or worry. Interested?

Let's go for it!

A Piper and canoe, goin' for it. Photo by Bill McCarrel.

A float pilot by the name of O'Jaque
who tried to depart a short lake

pulled back on the stick
but large tree limbs did nick

'cuz Airspeed!, he found, is a must
as he peered out from LARGE clouds of dust.

Lake Assessment

We should probably call this 'landing and takeoff area assessment'. The habit and technique of evaluation of a prospective landing and takeoff area is one which must be developed to near perfection by the seaplane pilot who is venturing into undeveloped areas and areas that are strange to him, even if they are close to civilization. It is very important that the takeoff area be surveyed and assessed, noting the best departure path, its magnetic heading and the terrain over which the departure will be flown, because this information cannot possibly be obtained once you are down on the water.

There are many questions the pilot should answer before attempting a landing in strange waters. They include all the questions you ask yourself while flying over or on final to familiar waters, such as: wind direction? velocity? gusts? surface traffic? deadheads? (floating or partially submerged debris in the water) airborne traffic? landing and taxi path to approach the dock? and others. They also include numerous other questions you need to answer BEFORE committing yourself to a landing. Most of these are discussed elsewhere in this book. We will deal only with one in this chapter on takeoff performance, and that is: What will be my takeoff path out of there and is it long enough?

The wisdom of determining that the takeoff path is long enough before landing is easily seen. How is it done? First, we need to know how much distance we will need to accomplish the takeoff.

This must be computed using the numbers in the POH, and, if necessary, supplementing the POH numbers with the rules-of-thumb given earlier in this chapter (best done as a preflight planning step, before the flight). Also, you may wish to take into consideration some of the factors that influence performance that are not considered in the POH numbers and add a 'conservatism factor'.

Now that you know approximately the distance needed for takeoff, let's determine if the takeoff path you selected is long enough. For this you will need a timer, stopwatch or clock aboard. Your wristwatch second hand will do.

Let's assume you have determined that, under the conditions you expect to have at the time you want to takeoff, you will need 2600' for a takeoff over that 50' obstacle. You can determine the effective length of lake available by flying low along the takeoff path and note the number of seconds it takes to fly the course.

Will the wind be blowing in the right direction for this path tomorrow, when you want to depart? If departing this afternoon or tomorrow, we can get a good idea of the forecast wind direction then by looking at the pressure pattern prognostic charts before leaving civilization, but probably we would be better off assessing more than one possible takeoff direction on this short lake as well as deciding which direction is most appropriate if the wind is calm at takeoff time.

If you fly the course at 70 mph or 60 Kts. (Indicated airspeed is close enough), each second is equivalent to 100 feet. If 70 mph is too slow to be safe in your aircraft, 90 Kts. or 100 mph will give you about 150 ft. per second. If you need 2600 ft, you need 26 seconds of lake along the takeoff path at 70 mph IAS. What if there is a wind while you are doing this? As long as it is a headwind, it will cause your measurement to indicate that the lake appears to be longer than it really is. If the wind appears to be about the same down on the water, then probably your measurement is equivalent because you will need less distance for your takeoff. If the trees appear to be keeping the wind from the lake, you can fly the takeoff path in both directions and average your readings, to get a more accurate estimate of the length of the takeoff path.

Now you know, approximately, the length of the takeoff path and you can decide before landing, if it is long enough. The final decision about whether or not the takeoff path is long enough will be made at the time and under the conditions of the actual takeoff, and will be done using a method that takes ALL factors into consideration. Please be sure to spend some time with the next section, as it tells you how to do this, using the "No-go Flag".

The No-go Flag Method.

Let me ask you this question: Have you ever made a takeoff where you weren't absolutely sure you could make it? What would you have given, then, to have the outcome of the takeoff never be in doubt? Well, there is a way you can make that next tight takeoff a sure thing. There isn't much measuring or weighing and very little figuring involved. If it is a short lake, you can do what needs to be done while warming up the engine.

Here is the typical scenario: heavy seaplane, short and narrow lake, hot day (sound familiar?). You can add tall pine trees, a rocky shore and 200 miles to civilization, just to make the problem interesting.

Let me stop here for just a moment to remind you that if you are over gross weight and/or haven't determined that you are within the C.G. limits, you are definitely back in the realm of not being able to predict the outcome of the takeoff -- in short, you are a test pilot, flying an untested bird. Now, assuming you know that you are within C.G. limits (loading toward the aft C.G. limit will improve takeoff performance -- more on that in chapters 4 and 5), let's take a look at how this can be done.

The Go, No-Go Flag Concept

There is one very interesting, very reliable fact that shows up in an analysis of any seaplane's takeoff performance figures. Take the takeoff performance figures from the manual, for any condition of density altitude, wind and aircraft weight. Divide the takeoff water run distance by the total distance over the 50 foot obstacle, to obtain a ratio of water run distance to total distance. This ratio I call the Delta ratio. Multiply the Delta ratio by 100 and you have the percentage of total distance that will be "water run".

The interesting thing is that this ratio (or percentage) is nearly constant, regardless of conditions of weight, wind and altitude. De Havilland has known this for years, but shows it as a small footnote to a massive chart of curves and lines that are the takeoff performance tables for the Beaver and Otter. That table is enough to chill the sharpest bush pilot's enthusiasm for figuring takeoff performance.

Perhaps the De Havilland engineer that composed the takeoff performance chart inserted that small footnote, saying "takeoff run is 68% of total distance" as a sort of apology to pilots for the complexity of the chart.

The De Havilland POHs (manuals) say that about 68% of the total distance for the Beaver and 53% for the Otter is water run. You can verify the percentage above for your seaplane by referring to your POH. Divide the water run distance by the total distance over the 50 foot obstacle. For example, for the Cessna 180 on 2870 floats, figure 3.5 shows the ratio of water run to total distance over a 50' obstacle.

Note that the ratio doesn't change much regardless of altitude or gross weight.

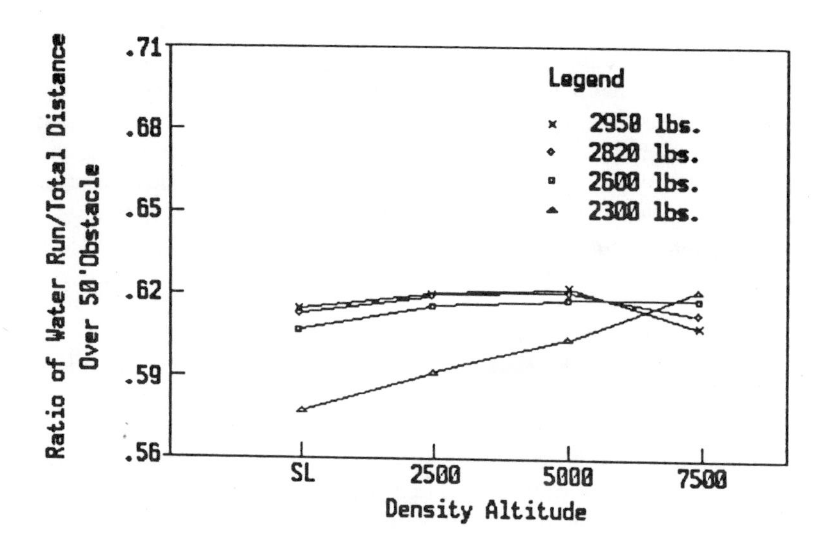

Figure 3.5. Delta Ratios for the Cessna 180 on Edo 2870s.

From figure 3.5, it takes 62% of the total takeoff distance to get a loaded Cessna 180 airborne. If we place a marker at 62% of the total length of the available water run, then that marker becomes a 'Go, No-go' flag. (See Figure 3.6.)

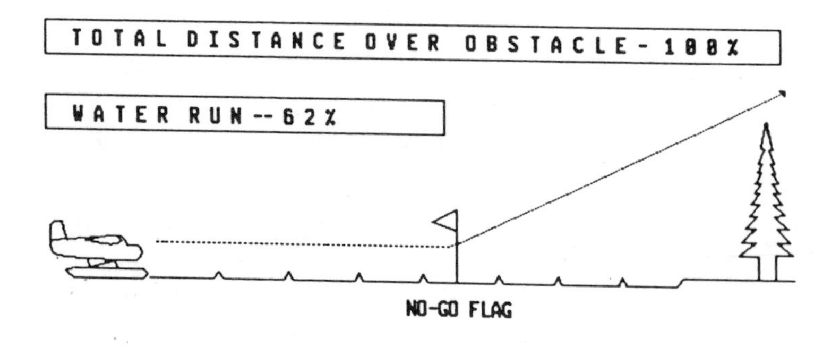

Figure 3.6. The No-go flag concept.

The concept is simply this: Regardless of ANY of the factors that affect performance, if the seaplane-pilot combination has enough performance to get off the water, loaded, within 62% (in the case of the 180) of the available distance, it will also have the capability to make it over the obstacle, assuming the pilot displays a competence level for the rest of the takeoff that is equal to what has been done so far in the water run. If the aircraft is not off the water by the time it reaches the flag, then the combination of factors (altitude, temperature, wind, lake length, humidity, etc.) present at that moment will not allow the successful completion of the takeoff. With this method, the pilot will know for certain, before leaving the water, if the takeoff can be made successfully.

The pilot must predetermine that there is sufficient room to decelerate, in case the no-go flag is reached with the aircraft still on the water. All that has been ventured is some fuel, not anyone's neck!

Should the takeoff be attempted again? Perhaps. The aircraft is lighter now, by the amount of fuel used and perhaps the pilot noticed part of the takeoff technique that could be improved next time. The pilot may elect to wait until conditions improve, such as a better breeze or cooler temperatures. The option of returning for part of the load, or shuttling it to a nearby, longer lake should also be considered.

To reiterate, if we are airborne by the time we get to the flag, there will be sufficient distance left to climb over the obstacle. If the airplane is not airborne by the time it reaches the flag, abort and decelerate because it is unlikely that the obstacle can be made. It is as simple as that! (In this discussion so far, we are assuming that the obstacle at the end of the takeoff run is 50' high. How to deal with higher obstacles will be discussed shortly).

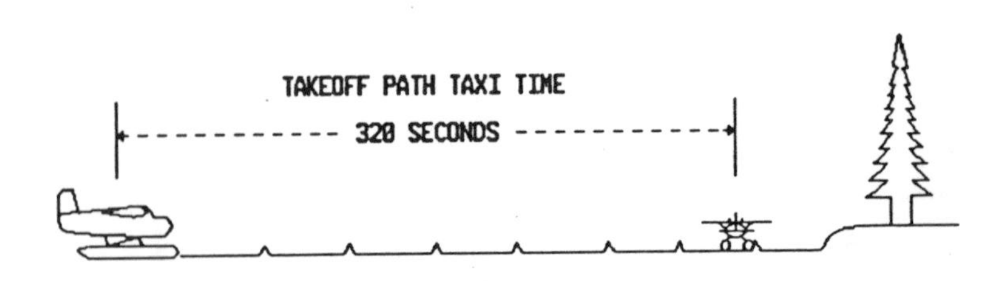

Figure 3.7. Determining where to place the No-go flag.

Placing the Flag

That's easy. Do it while warming the engine up. Just time how long it takes to taxi at constant rpm along the takeoff path, into the wind, from one end of the takeoff run to the other end (See Figure 3.7). Lets say for example that it takes 5 minutes and 20 seconds (320 seconds). While taxiing back, multiply 320 seconds times 62% (for a Cessna 180) = 198 seconds. Now, start at the takeoff point, taxiing into the wind again at the same constant rpm, for 198 seconds. When the time is up, throw the flag out the window (See Figure 3.8). Your peace-of-mind marker is in place, 62% of the way down the takeoff run!

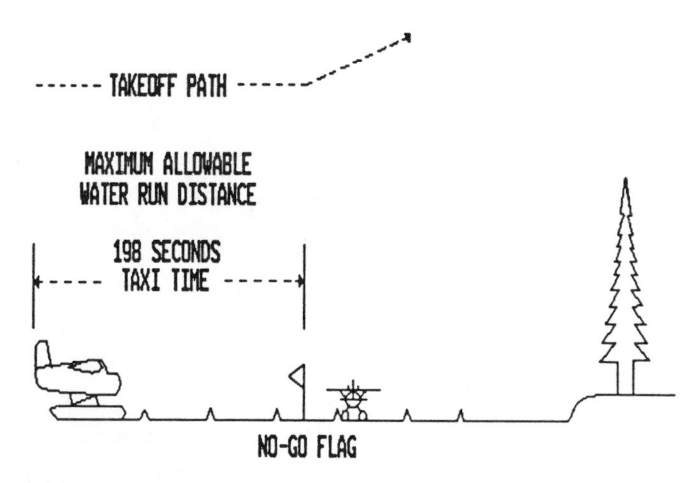

Figure 3.8. Placing the No-go flag.

Making the Flag

Making the No-go flag is easy. Obtain a few 3 or 4 ounce fishing sinkers, some cotton string and some large (16") colorful balloons. The Canadian red weather balloon is perfect. That's all you need. The items are light weight and take little space. I carry them in a small sack that's stuffed in the back of the pilot's seat. If the water is deep, 30 feet of string will keep the balloon stationary long enough to accomplish the takeoff if the water is not moving. Don't use the ready made fish locator markers (float, string and weight) that are for sale at the tackle shop. You can't see them well enough from a distance and they don't bio-degrade.

If you can't see the no-go flag easily at the beginning of and all during the takeoff run, abort the takeoff. You need to be concentrating on making "the perfect takeoff", not looking all over the lake for a marker you can't see.

A word of caution: One should never trust the location of a marker that was placed at an earlier time. Check its location with the taxi-time method.

Figure 3.9. The author, testing No-go flags (balloons) and flag colors, near Fairbanks, Alaska.

DECELERATION DISTANCE

The whole idea with the no-go flag method is to know for sure whether or not the takeoff can successfully be made over the given obstacle. The flag becomes the decision point. If the aircraft is not airborne at the flag, the pilot must abort and decelerate. The pilot has predetermined that there is sufficient distance, from the flag to the obstacle, to climb over the obstacle if he is airborne at the flag. He must also be sure that there is sufficient distance from the flag to the windward shore (where the obstacle is), to decelerate the aircraft and turn without contacting the shore.

The determination of deceleration distance for each aircraft need be done only once, and the results noted. Deceleration distance may be defined as the total distance needed to (1) decide that the takeoff in progress is a "no-go", (2) throttle back to idle power, (3) flare (pitch-up) and raise flaps (optional -- depends on the aircraft), (4) "walk" the rudders to increase drag, and (5) when slowed, lower water rudders and make a 90 degree turn to parallel the near shore.

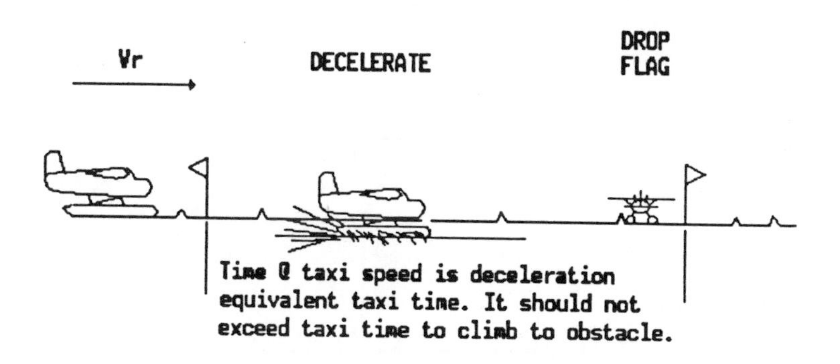

Figure 3.10. Determination of deceleration distance

This distance is easy to determine. Place one of the newly made flags out in a large lake. Enough distance is needed on the leeward (downwind) side of the flag to be able to accelerate, in takeoff mode, to liftoff speed. Be sure there is enough distance on the windward (up-wind) side of the flag to be able to decelerate according to the five steps listed above, or your own best technique. Load the aircraft to gross weight. Accelerate to near liftoff speed toward the flag. When passing the flag, decelerate using your best technique. When slowed and turned 90 degrees, throw out a second flag. (See Figure 3.10.)

Then, while taxiing into the wind at a constant taxi rpm, note the number of seconds needed to taxi between the two flags (deceleration taxi time). Write this number in your little black book, as it should be close enough to use in a reasonably wide variety of situations.

The longest deceleration run will occur with minimum wind but not glassy water conditions. It would be well to conduct your test under these conditions, if possible. Under these conditions, my Cessna 180 decelerates in less than 650 feet, which is 90 seconds taxi time at 500 rpm (deceleration taxi time). *Caution:* use figures for your aircraft and your deceleration techniques, not someone else's.

You may want to add a few seconds for a little extra safety margin. WHEN USING THE NO-GO FLAG METHOD, THE DECELERATION TAXI TIME (IN SECONDS) MUST BE EQUAL TO OR LESS THAN THE NUMBER OF SECONDS IT TOOK TO TAXI FROM THE NO-GO FLAG LOCATION TO THE SHORE YOU PLAN TO DEPART OVER. (See figure 3.11).

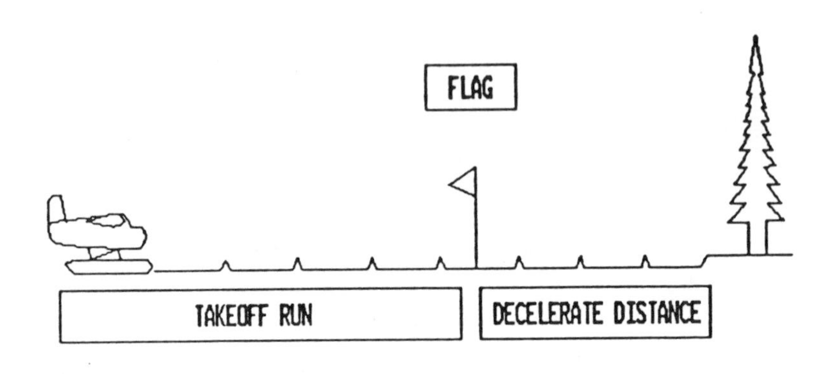

Figure 3.11. Be sure there is sufficient deceleration distance.

There is one more thing! Just before starting the takeoff run, PROMISE YOURSELF that you will NOT violate that takeoff no-go marker flag -- not even by one second!

OBSTACLES HIGHER THAN FIFTY FEET

First, are you sure that you chose the correct takeoff path? If so, it is easy to calculate the added distance you will need for the higher obstacle. We will do an example of that in a moment.

The hardest part is to determine the height of the obstacle. If the obstacle is near the lake edge, you can quite accurately determine the height of the obstacle by the following method:

1. Go to the shore that you will depart over.

2. Mark a tree so you can see the mark out on the lake (toilet paper works well -- it is biodegradable and should be on board).

3. Pace off 100 feet (about 34-40 paces) perpendicular to the takeoff run and mark a tree there.

4. Taxi back out into the lake until the marks can just be seen. With a straight-edge at arms length, mark the distance between the marks on the straight-edge. For the straight-edge, a ruler works well or the scale on a chart. Even your thumb will do, or a pencil.

5. While still the same distance out in the lake, compare the length of the 100' measurement on the rule to the distance from the shoreline to the top of the obstacle.

6. That measurement, compared to the 100' measurement, will allow the pilot to closely estimate the obstacle height. (See figure 3.12.)

Now, taxi back to the location of the no-go flag. From the vantage point of the no-go flag, look at the obstacle. If other obstacles appear in the background, behind the immediate obstacles, it is important to know that the aircraft may not be able to climb over those further, higher obstacles if the performance is such that, on the takeoff run, you aren't off the water until near the no-go flag.

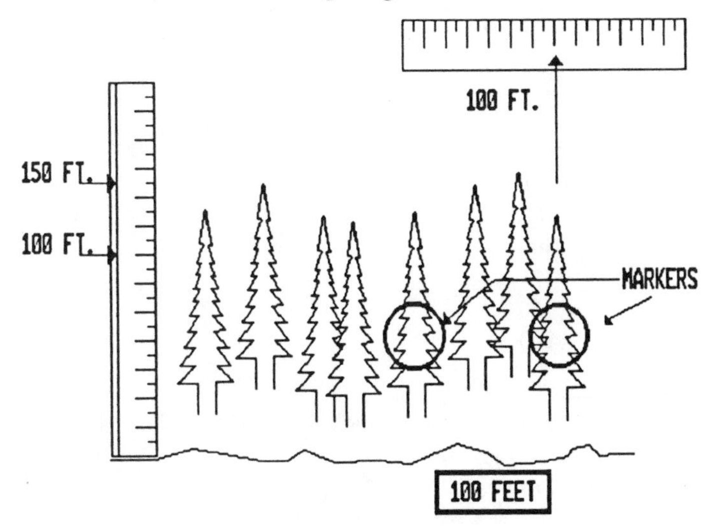

Figure 3.12. Determination of obstacle height.

In that case, the pilot must plan a turn toward lower ground before reaching those further obstacles (or abort the takeoff at the no-go flag). (See figure 3.13.)

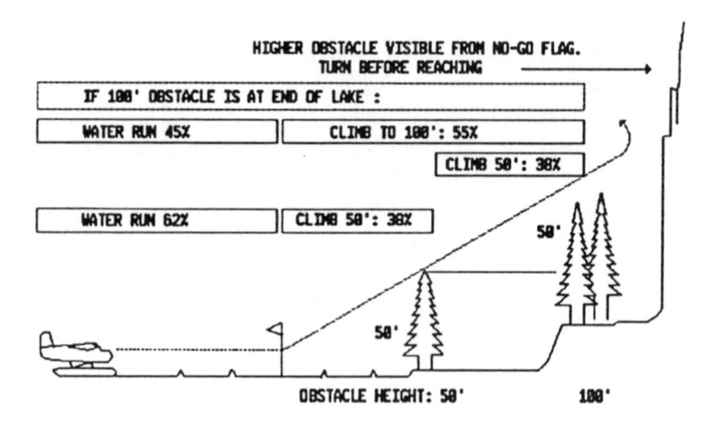

Figure 3.13. Evaluation of obstacles farther from the shoreline.

Table 3.14. Water run multipliers for various obstacle heights (Cessna 180).

Obstacle Height, feet	Multiplier
50	1.00
75	0.84
100	0.73
125	0.63
150	0.56
200	0.47

Based on some simple geometry, table 3.14 shows the multipliers needed for various obstacle heights greater than 50'. For example, if the aircraft's water run is 62% of the total distance to clear a 50' obstacle, then its water run will be .73 times 62%, or 45% of the total distance to clear an obstacle at water's edge that is 100' tall.

So, to be assured of being able to clear that 100' obstacle, set the no-go flag 45% of the available distance down the lake, along the takeoff run. (See figure 3.13.)

Table 3.14 is appropriate only for a Delta ratio of .62. Using it for other Delta ratios may introduce an error in the newly computed Delta ratio for an obstacle other than 50 feet. It is suggested that the Multiplier be determined by using the formula:

$$M = \frac{50}{h-(h-50) \times D.r.}$$

where: M = Multiplier
h = obstacle height, ft.
D.r. = Delta ratio @ 50 ft. (expressed as a decimal)

Or, the Delta ratio for an obstacle height other than 50 ft. can be calculated directly by using the formula:

$$D.r._h = \frac{D.r. \text{ for } 50 \text{ ft.}}{(h/50) \times (1 - D.r. \text{ for } 50 \text{ ft.}) + D.r. \text{ for } 50 \text{ ft.}}$$

Where: $D.r._h$ = Delta ratio for height [h], in decimal form.
h = Obstacle height, ft.

SOME TAKEOFF PERFORMANCE TECHNIQUES FOR THE NOVICE.

If you have used the no-go marker idea, your takeoff technique is not as important. If you don't make it, you can decelerate, taxi back and try again. So, by placing the marker, you have eliminated the stress and worry of: "I have to do it right the first time, or I'm dead".

The more pilots you talk to, the more techniques you will hear about. The trouble is, the really experienced pilots don't talk much, or openly, because the techniques they use in a tight spot may be too advanced for the pilot who is just learning his airplane. Since that experienced pilot hasn't flown with you, he can't judge whether you should know his advanced "tricks-of-the-trade". So, he keeps quiet when hangar flying sessions occur.

To tell you the truth, I never learned a worthwhile seaplane performance improving technique at a cocktail party, hangar flying session or, for that matter, from a book. All those I have learned were either taught to me by a more experienced pilot, observed while riding with other pilots, or figured out for myself. Most of the techniques I have learned happened when I had a chance to ride with a pilot in another geographical location. Techniques that don't seem to be used at all in one area are in common use in another part of the continent where seaplanes are flown. So, if you can talk someone into letting you ride with them when you are travelling in another area, do so -- and keep your eyes open!

If you hear of a technique that sounds interesting to you, try it out very carefully somewhere with a lot of room. The cocktail party tale of the circling takeoff from a tiny lake, you will find out when you try it, is just a tale because most airplanes don't have enough power, when fully loaded, to accelerate in a tight turn.

Probably the most positive technique that can be used is to concentrate on doing everything "just right". There are some fancy techniques that can be used to get a seaplane on the step.

One that is seen too often is that of causing the aircraft to porpoise by fore and aft forces on the elevator. Some recent field (lake) tests by some interested pilots showed that, unless the aircraft was under very high power loading conditions (loaded very heavily), fore and aft elevator control movements significantly increased the time and distance needed to get on the step. Most modern floatplanes will accelerate nicely onto the step, if not over gross weight, with standard techniques of full aft elevator at power application. Some models prefer much of the aft elevator force to be relaxed early with a little forward elevator pressure to finish the process of getting over the "hump" and onto the step. See (2.2, 2.3, 2.4) for a description of the "how to", since it is not the intent of this book to deal with "how to fly seaplanes".

There is considerable technique, however, in the simple process of getting on the step. You may want to practice with your airplane, to determine that "just right" technique of getting your bird on the step as quickly and smoothly as possible.

If you regularly "pump" your aircraft up onto the step, you might want to go out somewhere, where your fellow pilots aren't watching, and practice getting your bird smoothly and quickly onto the step by finding the "just right" method. Then go back and bet your buddies, who are "pumping" their light aircraft up, a beer on who can get off the water quickest. If you happen to be on the dock sometime when a floatplane departs using the "pump" method, don't watch the airplane, watch the wake! You will see alternate areas of very high "roostertails" (imagine the energy put into throwing that heavy water into the air).

LIFTING ONE FLOAT OUT OF THE WATER.

Sure looks pretty, doesn't it? However, studies have shown that, for most modern floatplanes, lifting one float out of the water on takeoff will cause the aircraft to travel further on the water and be on the water for a longer period of time, due to the additional aileron drag and the drag caused by the need to generate more lift than required if wings are level.

The exceptions to this are two: glassy water takeoffs and takeoffs when the aircraft is in a very high power loading condition (heavily loaded). If this maneuver is to be done on a short lake, drag can be further reduced by keeping the ball centered (minimum rudder) which will result in a left-turning takeoff that is accomplished in less distance than if right rudder is used to maintain a straight takeoff track.

Lifting one float should never be done on rough water, where all the pounding forces are concentrated on one side of the airframe. High speed running on rough water, you will find, can be done with a smoother ride and less stress on the airframe if the attitude of the seaplane is kept slightly flatter (nose down) than the run is normally made. For a smoother ride after landing on rough water, put the nose down slightly more than you ususally do (careful -- not too much!), and note how the ride smooths out during deceleration.

THE HIGH ALTITUDE TAKEOFF

Planning a trip to a part of the country where the density altitude is significantly higher? A while back, I had the opportunity to fly out of a lake in Colorado where the density altitude was about 7200 feet. I sure was glad it was a very long lake! You can build your confidence in your ability to handle a takeoff like this (under conditions you have never encountered) by simulation. You can closely simulate the performance your aircraft will exhibit at that higher altitude this way:

1. Compute the expected density altitude by correcting the published (or estimated) elevation of the lake for temperature. For example: elevation of Lake Sweaty: 4800 ft.; expected temperature: 85 degrees F.

From Figure 3.1, standard temperature at 4800' = 42° F.; 85° F. - 42° F. = 43 degrees warmer than standard. Remember the rule: for each 8.5^{o} C. or 15° F. temperature increase, add 1000 ft. Our approximate density altitude is now:

43° F./15° F. = 2.86 x 1000' = 2860' + 4800' = 7480'

2. To simulate power available at that altitude, decrease the takeoff manifold pressure (MAP) setting by .75 inches for each 1000' of density altitude. For example, if your MAP at full throttle is 27" at your home lake at 1000' elevation, then the altitude change will be 7480' - 1000' = 6480 ', and the decreased MAP should be 27" -(6.48 x .75) = 22".

If you want to know approximately what that high altitude takeoff will feel like, go out to your lake, load your aircraft up to gross weight and try some takeoffs using 22" as the maximum available manifold pressure. You may find that you need to develop some new techniques to get your usually peppy bird up on the step! If one is available, it would be a very good idea to take an experienced flight instructor with you. You will probably learn a lot more a lot faster.

There is a lot of fun, joy and pride in accomplishing a well done takeoff. The vast majority of seaplane takeoffs can be accomplished in areas where there is lots of water surface distance. So, for the average takeoff, performance data need not be considered. Don't let the everyday takeoff condition cause you to be unskilled when you find yourself needing to make that short-lake departure. Practice with your plane and your no-go flag, moving it gradually closer, in small increments, to the point where you start your takeoff run. This will improve your skills and technique as well as your confidence. Besides, these practice sessions make a great excuse to "go flying"!

Please Note:

The Delta ratio and No-Go flag concept was first published in the Water Flying Annual, 1987, pages 30-35. It was later republished by the FAA General Aviation News, July-August, 1988. As it is a new concept, it is not (at this writing) endorsed by the FAA. I believe it to be sound and have used it myself, but it is presented here only as a concept, with no guarantees or warranties. If you use it, you do so at your own risk. I welcome any inquiries on the subject and especially would appreciate hearing from anyone who has reason to suspect any of the concepts discussed herein.

CHAPTER 4

Seaplane Takeoff Technique Studies

A note to the reader: This chapter describes the results of research to determine the effects of type of takeoff technique on takeoff distance. It also further refines the Delta Ratio concept and describes how this sort of research is done. This chapter is quite technical in nature, so it might best be read when you have the time and mental energy needed to "do it justice". If you are not now in the mood, perhaps it would be best to look at the pictures, read the Conclusions section, and save the innards (which really are interesting) for a cold, windy day when you can put your feet up by the fire and really get into it. A more technical version of this chapter was published in the Journal of Aircraft of the American Institute of Aeronautics and Astronautics (4.1).

Nomenclature

Delta Ratio = R_D = D_{wr}/D_t, where

D_{wr} = Takeoff water run distance

D_t = Total distance over a 50 foot obstacle

Introduction

Seaplane takeoff performance research is notably rare, partly due to the small numbers of seaplanes in the general aviation fleet and partly due to the difficulty in measuring the takeoff performance perameters over water. This chapter presents a method of instrumentation for accomplishing such measurements with current available technology.

Seaplane takeoff performance information available to pilots in aircraft operating manuals isn't much help to the pilot when (s)he is confronted with a problem of determining whether it is possible to takeoff from a short lake. Unlike the land plane, it usually isn't possible to know the available takeoff distance for the seaplane. Also, many other factors affecting takeoff performance aren't known to the pilot, nor are they addressed in the performance tables in the operating manual.

A method, utilizing Delta ratios, was described in chapter 3, whereby the pilot can determine, before leaving the water, whether or not the takeoff can be made. Furthermore, this method does not require the pilot to have knowlege of lake length, density altitude, engine and propeller condition or aircraft weight. The method does, however, assume (and there seems to be a good case for the concept) that the Delta ratio remains relatively constant over a wide range of flight conditions. The study described below looks at the effect of aircraft weight and takeoff technique on the Delta ratio in an attempt to determine if the Delta ratio is actually constant under these varying conditions.

Instrumentation and Methodology

The following is a description of the instrumentation and methodology used to determine the actual distance of the takeoff water run (the distance the aircraft is on the water during the takeoff) and the total distance over the "standard" 50 foot high obstacle (total distance from the beginning of the water run to the point on the surface under the aircraft when the lowest part of the aircraft is 50 feet above the surface).

A lake was selected which was large enough to provide more than adequate takeoff distance, but not so large as to become rough with windy conditions. The selection required rising ground near the shore to an elevation of 50 feet above the water, both at the departure end of the takeoff run and at the opposite end of the lake. At the shore nearest the start of the takeoff run, a video camera (with 1/100th second lapse time capability) was set up so that 'height of eye' was 50 feet above water level. Near the video camera, an aircraft VHF receiver was set up in order to record on the audio portion of the video tape the comments and called out indicated airspeeds from the test pilot. Below the video camera, a narrow beam traffic radar was set up, with operator who placed the radar readout values verbally onto the audio portion of the video tape. The result was a video tape which contained a photo record of the takeoff, with elapsed time, indicated airspeed. Since the video camera was at an elevation of 50 feet above the water, and the 50 foot elevation mark on the far shore was known, the video easily showed the point in time when the aircraft cleared the 50 foot 'obstacle'. Fig. 4-1 visually describes the instrumentation layout.

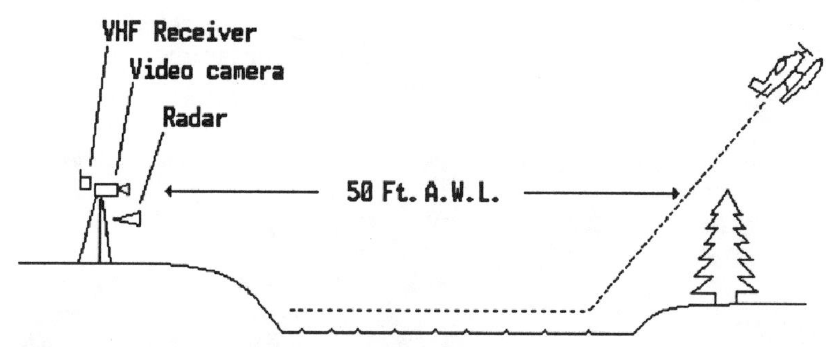

Figure 4.1. The instrumentation layout.

From the video tapes, time vs. speed curves were generated. Figure 4.2 is an example of this. The area under the curve(s) (distance) was computed to produce plots of time vs. distance. Thus, the distance at any point in the takeoff process became available.

The match of speed determined by radar and indicated airspeed as called by the pilot was very good in nearly all cases. Where readings differed, values that appeared not to be representative of the curve line were discarded.

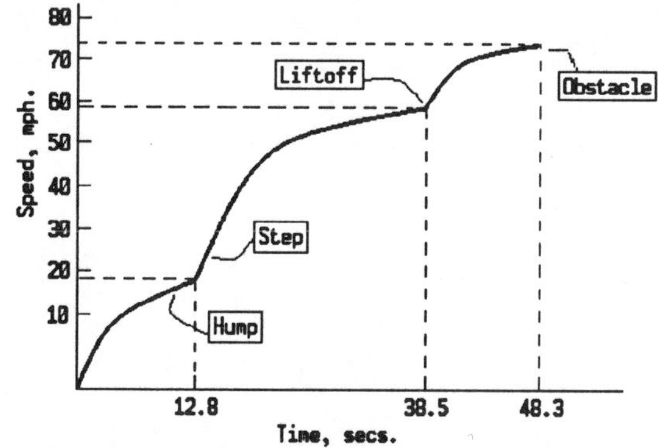

Figure 4.2. Time - speed curve for Cessna 180 at gross weight, conventional takeoff (mean of five takeoffs). The area under the curve represents distance traveled.

Experimental Design

To study the effect of aircraft weight and takeoff technique on the Delta ratio, three aircraft weights, three takeoff techniques and five replications were utilized. A common twin float aircraft (Cessna 180 on Edo 2870 floats) was utilized. Weights chosen were gross weight (2820 lbs.) , gross weight less 14.5% and gross weight plus 14.5%. Weight was adjusted by adding or removing measured amounts of water from the float chamber that was most directly under the aircraft's center of gravity.

Figure 4-3. Test aircraft weight was established by the use of measured amounts of water added to specific float compartments.

Takeoff techniques were: (1) conventional, where the aircraft was allowed to fly off the water from the step attitude; (2) float lift, where the right float was lifted out of the water as soon as aileron effectiveness permitted (after which the aircraft quickly accelerated and lifted off); and (3) flap change, where the pilot, at the appropriate speed, simultaneously changed the flap setting from the normal takeoff setting of 20 degrees to 40 degrees and pitched up slightly in order to

Table 4.4. Takeoff Performance-Mean of 5 Replications

Weight	14.5% Under Gross Weight	Gross Weight	14.5% Over Gross Weight
Procedure	Time to Liftoff-seconds		
Conventional*	30.8	38.5	48.6
Float Lift**	31.6	33.9	43.1
Flap Change***	25.1	29.8	39.6
	Time to 50 Foot Obstacle @ 75 SMIAS		
Conventional	39.9	48.3	57.9
Float Lift	41.2	44.1	54.7
Flap Change	37.0	45.7	57.4
	Water Run Distance-Feet		
Conventional	1346	1810	2724
Float Lift	1392	1516	2140
Flap Change	982	1438	2027
	Total Distance to 50 Foot Obstacle		
Conventional	2223	2767	3639
Float Lift	2304	2533	3314
Flap Change	1897	2746	3854

Table Notes:

* V rotate, SMIAS	48	52	62
** V rotate, SMIAS	fly-off	fly-off	fly-off
*** V rotate, SMIAS	43	47	58
Hump to step transitions, SMPH	17-20	19-21	24-26

'unstick' the aircraft from the water, after which flaps are decreased to the normal obstacle clearance climb setting of 20 degrees while the aircraft is still near the water.

The day that the experimental data was gathered, temperature remained between 23 and 24.5 degrees C. due to an overcast sky, wind varied from 2 to 4.5 knots from zero to 20 degrees left crosswind. Density altitude was approximately 1250 feet. 47 takeoffs were accomplished while these essentially ideal and constant conditions existed.

Takeoff performance with time and distance as the measured parameters, at three aircraft weights is shown in Table 4.4.

Table 4.5 indicates values of the Delta Ratio computed from data in table 4.4.

Table 4.5. Computed Delta Ratios for three takeoff procedures at three aircraft weights.

	AIRCRAFT WEIGHT		
TAKEOFF PROCEDURE	GROSS-14.5%	GROSS	GROSS + 14.5%
Conventional	.605	.654	.748
Float Lift	.604	.614	.646
Flap Change	.518	.524	.526

Conclusions

The flap change procedure was an effective technique for reducing water run time and distance at all weights, but is negatively effective for reducing distance over an obstacle when the aircraft is heavy. In that case, the float lift procedure was most effective.

Although a strong correlation exists, time measurements are not always a good indicator of distance covered, when attempting to measure seaplane takeoff performance.

Delta ratio values differ little with weight and takeoff technique except when the flap change technique is used. The flap change technique decreases Delta ratio sufficiently that Delta ratios derived from aircraft flight manuals cannot be used safely with the No-go Flag technique described in chapter 3. However, there is very little change in the Delta ratio values for the flap change technique with aircraft weight. The Delta ratio for the flap change takeoff technique is consistant and could be used if the pilot knew the correct values.

The Delta ratio continues to appear to be consistent over a wide range of conditions, except that Delta ratio values are significantly lower when the pilot uses the flap change technique for takeoff. An unsafe condition could exist if the pilot used the flap change takeoff technique in conjunction with Delta ratio values that were taken from the aircraft operating manual, and applied them in a departure from an obstacled short lake using the No-go Flag method.

Based on this study, the flap change technique is useful to the experienced pilot who is skilled in the use of this technique when the water run distance or time on the water should be shortened. This technique is appropriate, if used correctly, for rough water takeoffs, short lakes with NO obstructions, water with unavoidable deadheads, etc. This technique should NOT be used when obstructions must be cleared, especially if the aircraft is heavy.

The float lift takeoff is most appropriate for crosswind takeoffs, glassy water takeoffs and takeoffs when heavy, especially when the takeoff is obstacled. This method is not appropriate in rough water due to the fact that all impact forces are applied to only one side of the aircraft instead of being distributed evenly to both sides.

Lifting the upwind float will result in a slightly shorter takeoff run (better performance) but is a very dangerous manuever because the aircraft comes out of the water drifting quickly downwind, as both the wind and the horizontal component of the lift vector are accelerating the aircraft downwind. If the engine should quit after takeoff, the pilot is faced with a touchdown while drifting sideways, and a probable upset. Therefore, lifting the downwind float is the only proper procedure, in my opinion, resulting in liftoff while banked into the crosswind, and little or no drift. All of the testing described herein utilized the downwind float lift.

CHAPTER 5

SEAPLANE PERFORMANCE

Aircraft performance is an interesting subject. Everyone would like to be able to get the best performance from their airplane, so an understanding of the subject has considerable value, even if that understanding requires the effort of some serious study. If you find some points in this chapter to be unclear, it is probably because the author has assumed a level of understanding of performance which you have either forgotten or haven't been exposed to. In that case I suggest you have a look at the performance chapters in Kershner(5.1), then come back to this chapter. Also, REMEMBER, the best source of information on how your airplane will perform IS your airplane! For that reason, this chapter tells how to use your airplane to determine the best speeds and configurations for maximum performance.

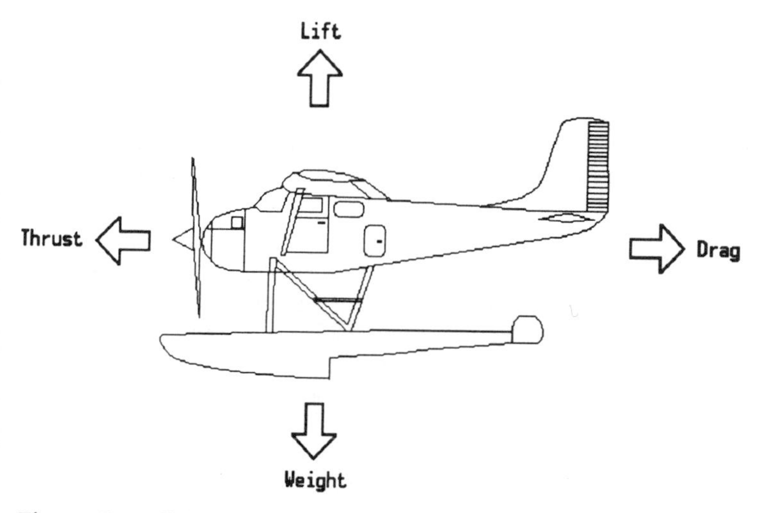

Figure 5.1. Flight Equilibrium.

You have no doubt seen figure 5.1 before (maybe the airplane didn't have floats?). At any rate, the diagram was intended to convey to you several concepts, which were:

1. The aircraft doesn't fall out of the sky because the lift produced equals the weight (actually, W, in the diagram, signifies Total Effective Weight which is the actual weight of the aircraft plus the tail-down force (see the section on C.G. effect on performance, in chapter six). So, lift produced must equal the total effective weight.

2. The aircraft moves through the air at a constant speed because T (thrust) equals D (drag). More accurately, *the thrust component acting parallel to the flight path* equals drag.

3. Under the conditions of the diagram above, the aircraft is said to be in equilibrium, or STEADY STATE, which means there is no acceleration in any direction. Whatever the aircraft is doing, it continues to do, in steady state flight. The aircraft can be in steady state flight in straight and level flight, a climb, a dive or a turn. In steady state flight, the aircraft is not accelerating in any dimension. Airspeed, rate of climb (vertical speed), rate of turn and "g" forces are all constant.

For purposes of our discussions of performance in this chapter, we can greatly simplify the process of understanding if we limit our discussions to the aircraft in steady state flight. Therefore, this chapter deals only with the aircraft in steady state flight. No chandelles, takeoffs, etc.

Let's first review some basics of the horizontal components of performance: Thrust and Drag.

THRUST

Reciprocating engines must employ a propeller to convert engine power into thrust. The power output of the engine is measured in horsepower (H.P.). The actual power available at the shaft is called brake horsepower (B.H.P.). The propeller converts engine B.H.P into another form of power called thrust horsepower (T.H.P.) according to the relationship:

T.H.P. = engine B.H.P. X propeller efficiency (%)

Propeller efficiency is rarely much better than 80-82%, and decreases from there if the propeller is not in tip-top condition. There are at least three good reasons for the sea plane pilot to learn how to keep the erosion (roughness) of the leading edge of the propeller dressed out properly. They are: (1) decrease the danger of propeller blade cracking and failure, (2) keep propeller efficiency as high as possible so that the best conversion of available engine power to thrust horsepower will occur, and (3) a propeller with a smooth leading edge is less susceptible to erosion by small water droplets, so the erosion process will be slowed.

Fixed pitch propellers have a very narrow range of airspeeds at which they produce maximum efficiency (see figure 5.2).

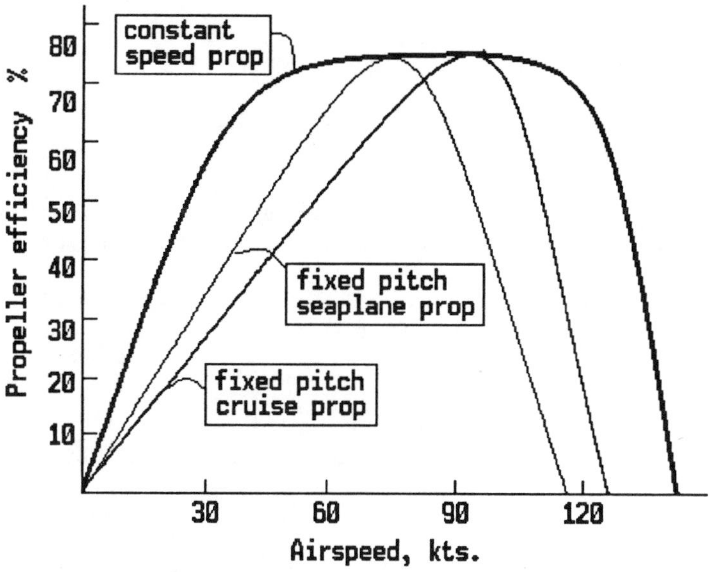

Figure 5.2. Propeller efficiency vs. airspeed.

Seaplanes often are equipped with a propeller of larger diameter than a similiar landplane would have because the larger diameter propeller is more efficient at lower airspeeds.

Most discussions about reciprocating engine aircraft performance talk about thrust horsepower rather than thrust because it is easier for the pilot to relate to the horsepower term. However, it is thrust, not T.H.P., that offsets drag. The two terms are not the same but are related to each other according to the relationship:

$$T = \frac{325 \times T.H.P.}{V}$$

where: T = Thrust, pounds
V = true airspeed, Kts.
T.H.P. = Thrust horsepower

For the reciprocating engine aircraft, the amount of thrust produced by the engine-propeller combination depends on (1) the engine output, (2) the efficiency of the propeller, and (3) the true airspeed!

This relationship is not an easy one to visualize. Perhaps it will help if we plot an example of a 260 H.P. engine running at 75% power using a constant speed propeller with a maximum efficiency of 80%.

Engine output = 260 B.H.P. x 75% = 195 B.H.P.

Engine-propeller output = 195 B.H.P. x 80% =
156 T.H.P.(maximum)

Since the relationship of T.H.P. and thrust varies with airspeed, the values of each, at various airspeeds, are shown in table 5.3.

Table 5.3. Thrust vs. Power

True Airspeed Kts.	Propeller Efficiency %	T.H.P.	Thrust, Pounds
20	42.5	83	1347
40	63	123	998
60	75	146	792
80	79	154	626
100	80	156	507
120	80	156	423
140	80	156	362
160	78	152	309

As can be seen from the example, thrust drops off rapidly with increasing airspeed. Since it is thrust that offsets the effect of drag, it is easy to see why propeller driven airplanes don't fly faster. Since floatplanes have higher parasite drag than their wheeled counterparts, they fly slower. The highest airspeed for level flight will occur at the highest power setting, where the highest T.H.P. and the most thrust is being produced. The airplane will accelerate until the ever increasing drag just equals the thrust being produced. Then the aircraft will achieve steady state flight at its maximum airspeed. Perhaps the relationships described above can be more clearly seen if the data from table 5.3 is plotted, which has been done in figure 5.4.

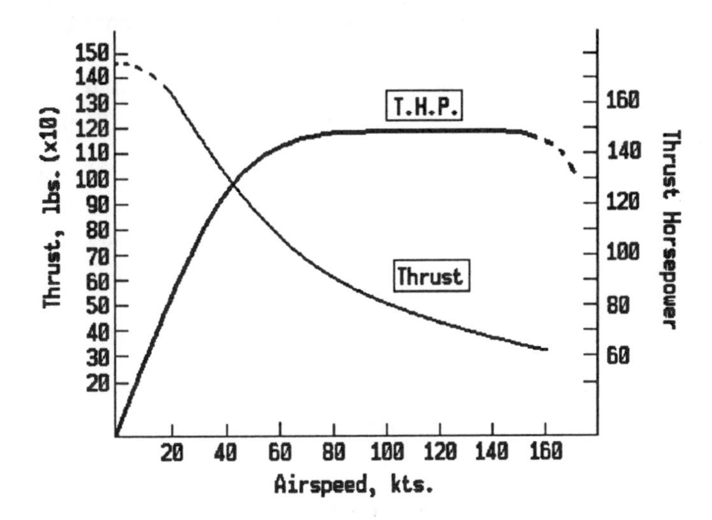

Fig. 5.4. The Thrust-T.H.P. Relationship. Plotted values from Table5.3

Since the relationship of T.H.P. and thrust varies with airspeed, it is not an easy one to keep track of, so we will use T.H.P. for the rest of our discussions, or, more properly, we will use THP required. THRUST HORSEPOWER REQUIRED is a term used which refers to the amount of thrust horsepower required to offset drag and keep the aircraft in steady state (unaccelerated) flight. So, now, for steady state flight, the relationship becomes:

THP required = Power required to overcome DRAG

DRAG

There are several different kinds of drag. We won't go into them all, but a brief discussion of the main drag forms is appropriate. While the seaplane is airborne, the two main types of drag acting on it are PARASITE DRAG and INDUCED DRAG. Both of these are AERODYNAMIC drag forms, which means that the drag is caused by air flow, as opposed to HYDRODYNAMIC drag which is caused by direct contact with water flow.

The float plane wins the dubious prize of having the most parasitic drag of today's light aircraft. PARASITE DRAG includes form drag, skin friction drag, interference drag and other smaller contributors. See Aerodynamics for Naval Aviators (5.1) and Kershner (5.2) for more complete descriptions of the drag forms. PARASITE DRAG is the total of all forms of drag except induced drag. Pick up a 4 x 8 foot sheet of plywood and walk into the wind with the 4 x 8 side exposed to the wind. That's parasite drag!

As airspeed increases, parasite drag increases by the square of the velocity. You will have FOUR times as much force opposing your forward progress with that 4 x 8 sheet of plywood if you walk into a 20 mph wind as you had walking into a 10 mph wind!

INDUCED DRAG is a byproduct of lift. If lift is produced, induced drag is produced. Induced drag increases as angle of attack increases (airspeed decreases), while producing lift.

Figure 5.5 is a plot of induced and parasitic drag on a typical airplane. The two drag forms are added together to produce the TOTAL DRAG curve, which is also plotted.

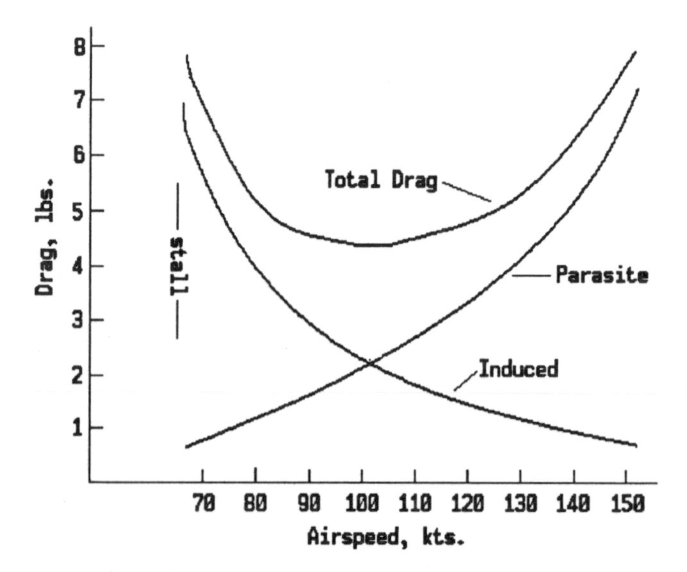

Figure 5.5. The Drag Curve.

Take a moment to study figure 5.5, because it tells the pilot several things:

1. Parasitic drag increases with an increase in airspeed. The increase is exponential (drag quadruples when airspeed doubles).

2. Induced drag increases with an increase in angle of attack of the wing (decreased airspeed). This dragform is responsible for the rapid increase in drag and power required at very low airspeeds, hence the term: "behind the power curve". Consider for a moment that you are flying at a constant altitude over the trees with enough power to hold altitude at 80 KIAS. If you pull back on the elevator control slightly, what will happen? Elevator controls airspeed, so the aircraft will slow down. There will be a momentary slight increase in altitude while slowing THEN THE AIRCRAFT WILL DESCEND!

Look at the total drag curve. As we went from 80 KIAS to 75 KIAS, the drag increased because induced drag increased much more rapidly than parasitic drag decreased. Thus, more power is required at the slower airspeed. If it is not added, or can't be added because we are already at full throttle, the aircraft will descend. The term "region of reverse command" applies to this airspeed region on the backside of the power curve. Even today, some pilots believe that the elevator of an airplane controls altitude. It does, but only at airspeeds above the airspeed for minimum drag (minimum power required). Below that airspeed, aft elevator pressure will cause the aircraft to descend, hence the term "reverse command". The modern day pilot does well to remember that the elevator ALWAYS controls airspeed and that power, or throttle, controls altitude.

3. There is one intermediate airspeed where total drag is least. Since the least power is required to maintain level flight at this airspeed, it is called MAXIMUM ENDURANCE AIRSPEED, or the airspeed at which the aircraft can remain aloft for the longest time, with whatever fuel remains in the tanks.

4. Through much of the speed range of the aircraft, there are TWO airspeeds for any given amount of total drag (except at maximum endurance airspeed). Therefore, there are two airspeeds for any given power setting.

Note that in figure 5.5, drag or thrust required was plotted. For reciprocating engine aircraft, it is more common to use power required or, more properly, THP required. Again, the relationship between thrust required and power required (algebraically rearranged to compute power instead of thrust), is:

$$\text{Power required} = \frac{\text{Thrust required x Airspeed}}{325}$$

For aircraft that are equipped with constant speed propellers (which have a relatively constant propeller efficiency over most of the speed range) there is justification to simply use "power required" as it is so much easier for the pilot to think in this term, as most POH figures are given in "horsepower" or "percent power".

Making a Drag Curve for your airplane.

It is quite easy to develop the drag curve for your own airplane. Why would you want to? Because:

1. Once you have developed the curve for your own airplane, you can determine your airplane's maximum endurance speed and best range (distance) cruise speed for any headwind or tailwind condition.

2. It's another great excuse to go flying!

Here is how it is done: Load your airplane up to a typical cross-country gross weight. Select a morning when the air is smooth. Select a typical cruising altitude (or develop two curves, at low and high altitudes). Maintaining a constant altitude, set up 75% power and note the indicated airspeed when it stabilizes. Determine the power setting (rpm and manifold pressure or just rpm for the aircraft equipped with a fixed pitch propeller) required to give incrementally lower airspeeds, down to an airspeed that is just above stall speed.

While doing this experiment, your airplane will require less and less power as you decrease speed. But, when you reach Maximum Endurance Speed, more and more power will be needed as you approach stall speed. When you plot power required (or rpm) vs. airspeed, your airplane will confirm a curve that has a shape similiar to figure 5.7, which is a plot of the data I determined for my Cessna 180F on floats (table 5.6).

The values of table 5.6 were determined at gross weight and 2500' density altitude. Percent power was determined by interpolating from the cruise performance tables in the POH. If your aircraft is equipped with a fixed pitch propeller, your job is easier. Just plot rpm vs. airspeed.

From figure 5.7 we can see that the use of 42% power will result in one of two airspeeds, either 50 kts. or 80 kts. The maximum endurance airspeed is 60 kts. (the least amount of power needed to overcome drag occurs at this airspeed. Thus, the aircraft can remain aloft for the longest time with whatever fuel is remaining).

Table 5.6. Power Required Data for Cessna 180F.

IAS, mph	MAP, Inches	RPM, 100's	% Power
40	20.25	22	56
45	19	21	47
50	18.25	20.5	42
55	18	20	39
60	17.75	20	38.6
65	18	20	39
70	18	20	39
75	18.5	20	40
80	18.25	20.5	42
86	18.75	20.5	43.5
90	18.5	21	45.2
94	18	22	47.4
97	18.5	22	49
103	19.3	22	52
110	19.5	23	57
120	21.75	23	66
128	23	24	75

Determining Maximum Range Speed

Maximum range (greatest distance covered with fuel remaining) with zero wind can be determined by drawing a line from the zero airspeed line to a point tangent to the power required curve and from that point down vertically to determine the airspeed.

Caution: the horizontal axis of your graph must be linear from zero to maxumum airspeed - do not change the scale. See Figure 5.8, which is figure 5.7 with the tangent line drawn to determine best range speed.

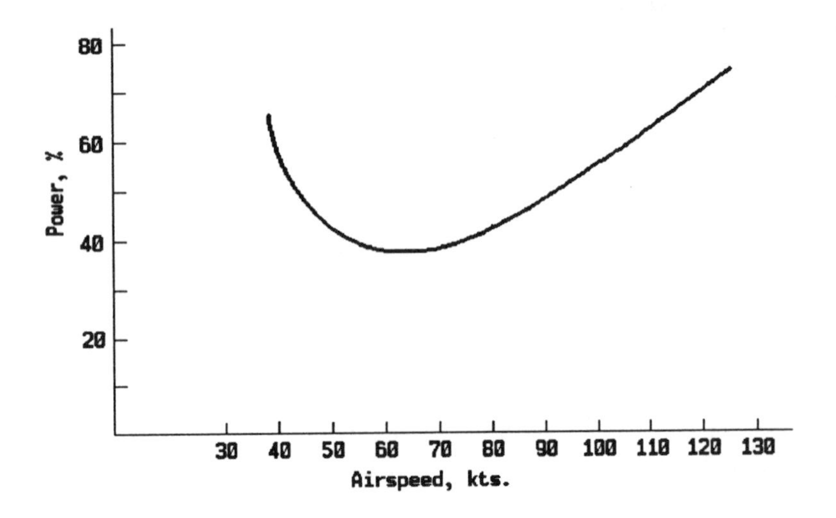

Figure 5.7. Power required curve for Cessna 180F on Edo 2870A floats. Density altitude 2500'. Source: author.

From figure 5.8, the best range airspeed with no headwind or tailwind is determined to be 83 kts.

Determining best range speed with a headwind or tailwind is also easily done. With a 20 knot tailwind component, the aircraft will travel 20 nm. farther in an hour so range will be better, but the best range speed changes, too. With a tailwind, best range speed decreases. Imagine a tailwind of infinite strength. With this infinitely strong tailwind, all we have to do is be airborne and the wind will carry us to our destination. Whoever stays aloft the longest will be carried the farthest. Therefore, with an infinitely strong tailwind, maximum endurance speed will also be maximum range speed.

Take another look at figure 5.8. Maximum endurance speed is significantly less than the no-wind maximum range cruise speed. Between those two points lie all values for maximum range speed for tailwinds from zero tailwind (maximum range speed-no wind) to infinite tailwind (maximum endurance speed).

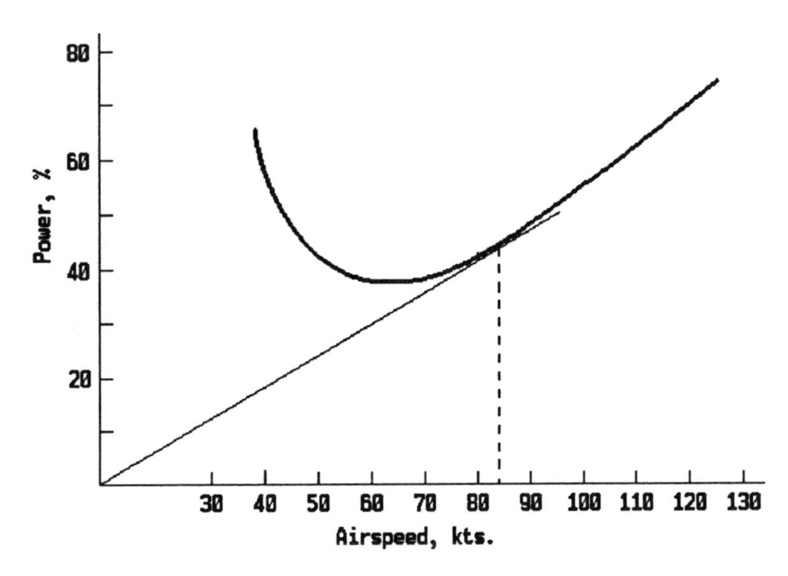

Figure 5.8. Determining Maximum Range Speed.

To determine maximum range airspeed with a 20 knot tailwind component, draw the tangent line starting 20 units of speed to the left of the zero airspeed mark (you will have to extend the horizontal axis to the left of the zero airspeed mark). With a 20 knot headwind, start the line 20 units (knots) to the right of the zero airspeed point, and draw the tangent line. See figure 5.9.

Now you know some performance parameters of your aircraft that weren't in the POH! You will also note that the speeds for maximum range and endurance are far slower than your usual cruise speed.

CLIMB

Why does your airplane climb? I hope you didn't answer "because I pointed the nose up more". At many airspeeds, that just isn't true, is it?

If you had time to take a good course in aerodynamics, your instructor would probably develop the proof for you that the elevator controls airspeed and the throttle controls altitude (or vertical speed). If you think that way, I believe you are a safer pilot.

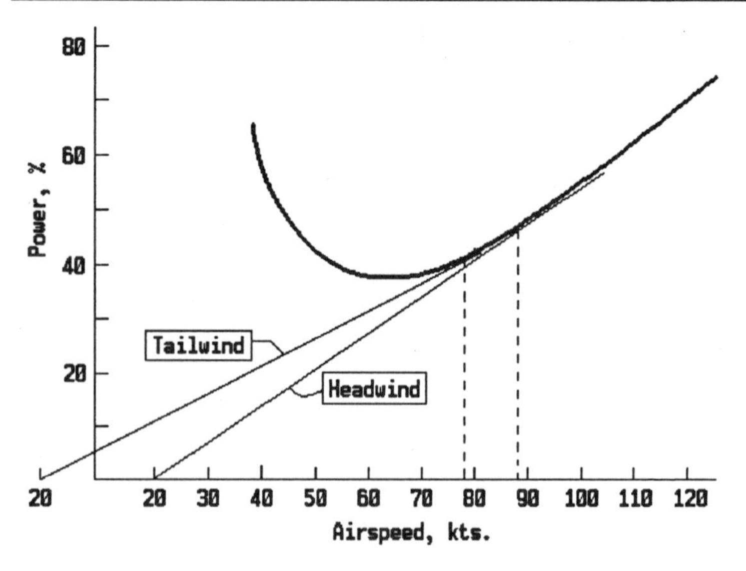

Figure 5.9. Determining Maximum Range Speed with a headwind or tailwind.

Try this: keeping the airspeed constant (elevator, right?) you will find that the throttle controls rate of climb or descent. True, you can trade airspeed for altitude by "zooming", as in the Chandelle, but that is not steady state flight.

The answer to the question about what makes the aircraft climb is actually: the aircraft climbs because there is an excess of THP, over that needed for level flight, at any given airspeed. Take a look at the power required and power available curve of figure 5.10. We can see that there is a region of airspeeds where there is more power available than is required. That extra power is called Excess Thrust Horsepower (ETHP), or sometimes, Net Accelerating Force (Thrust Horsepower available for acceleration or climb).

Climb performance or rate of climb is described by the formula:

$$\text{ROC} = \frac{33{,}000 \times \text{ETHP}}{\text{WEIGHT}}$$

Where: ROC = rate of climb, fpm
WEIGHT = effective wt. of the aircraft.

Aha! The factors that effect rate of climb will be the amount of excess thrust horsepower and the total effective weight of the aircraft. Since airspeed has an effect on ETHP, we have to add airspeed as a very important member of the group of factors that affect climb performance.

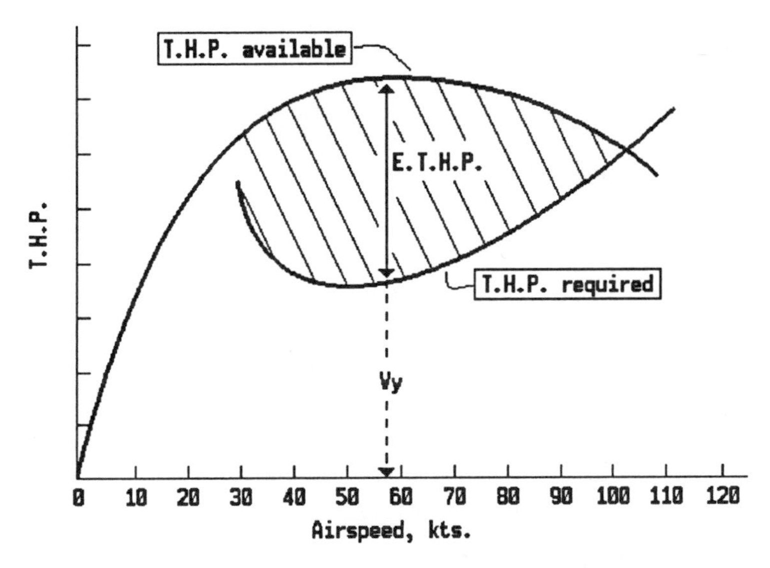

Figure 5.10. THP Available minus THP Required = ETHP.

Figure 5.10 also shows us how the amount of ETHP varies with airspeed. The airspeed where ETHP is maximum is Vy (best rate of climb airspeed). If we were to convert THP to Thrust, and develop a Thrust vs. airspeed curve, then the airspeed where the most excess Thrust occurred would be the aircraft's Vx (best angle of climb). Incidentally, Vx is an often misunderstood V speed. Vx is defined as that speed where the best angle of climb for the airplane occurs, in whatever configuration (of flaps and gear position) results in the best performance. Usually the best angle of climb performance occurs with gear and flaps up. Therefore Vx should not be confused with the speed used on takeoff to clear that famous '50 foot obstacle'.

The Climb Speeds.

Practically speaking, the seaplane pilot has several climb speeds to sort out and remember. Let's list and describe them, in order from low to high airspeed, for review:

Vobs.cl. - Obstacle clearance climb speed in takeoff configuration. This is the speed you want to use to clear that 50 ft. obstacle. Not to be confused with Vx, unless your aircraft has fixed gear and no flaps. Then Vobs.cl. will be nearly equal to Vx (probably a little slower because aircraft acceleration is a factor in any problem dealing with departures over an obstacle). For example, Vx is 70 mphIAS and Vobs.cl. is 60 for the Cessna 180 on floats.

A WORD OF CAUTION- A climbout at Vobs.cl. speed is very definitely an AT RISK maneuver. An engine failure at 50 to 150 feet AGL will require a very fast pitch-down to a very precise attitude. If not done quickly, with precision, the aircraft will impact the water at a very high sink rate. If not done quickly enough, a stall-spin or stall-high sink rate situation will develop. May I suggest this maneuver be practiced at a safe altitude by climbing to 3000 ft. AGL, using that altitude as simulated ground level, decelerate to Vobs.cl., apply full power and climb at Vobs.cl. to 3150 ft. AGL, throttle back and practice recovering quickly to the precise attitude that will give a slow acceleration towards Vmin. sink.

Note how low the airspeed gets before acceleration. Not more that 2-3 knots below Vobs.cl. should be your goal. Find the right attitude for slow acceleration. Also note the rate of sink at 50 feet above the water (3050 ft. AGL). It should not be more than the aircraft's vertical velocity when gliding at Vmax glide. Finish the maneuver with a rotation (flare) and application of full flaps for landing when back down to 3000 AGL (simulated ground level). Practicing the *complete* maneuver will help the pilot remember to use the flaps, and establish the reaction time and correct attitude sight picture that will be needed for survival of this high risk emergency.

Vx - Best angle of climb speed. Used for obstacle clearance when the aircraft is clean (flaps up).

Vy - Best rate of climb speed (usually refers to clean configuration).

Vnc - Normal climb speed. Usually refers to the speed used with the power available after the first power reduction. Often this is the airplane's Vy speed at 75% power.

Vcc - Cruise climb airspeed. An airspeed which results in a good rate of climb but at a higher airspeed which offers the advantages of better engine cooling (very important with most seaplanes), better visibility over the nose for safety and a greater forward distance traveled.

Many older POH's don't provide the pilot with all of these useful airspeeds. Often the pilot uses airspeeds told him by another pilot or determines them by trial and error. Here are some rules of thumb for determining these airspeeds for your aircraft.

Determining Climb Speeds

Vy

Most POH's at least list the best rate of climb speed at sea level standard conditions. Vy speed decreases with increase in altitude. To determine best rate of climb, subtract 1% from the indicated airspeed for each 1000 ft. increase in density altitude.

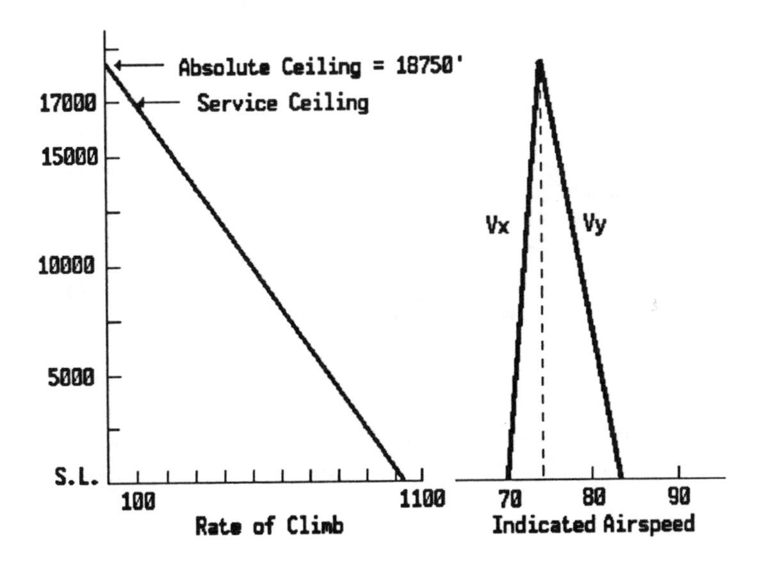

Figure 5.11. Effect of Altitude on Climb Speeds.

Vx

As can be seen from Figure 5.11, best angle of climb speed increases with altitude until it is the same as best rate of climb speed at absolute ceiling. It can be closely approximated by adding 1/2% to the indicated airspeed for each 1000 feet increase in density altitude.

Normal climb

Usually, the POH recommends an indicated airspeed to use with its recommended climb power setting. This speed will be close to Vy airspeed unless the aircraft experiences cooling problems at that airspeed. If only the speed at sea level is given, you can add 1% per 1000 feet density altitude increase.

Cruise climb

With a little experimentation, you will find an airspeed at which the aircraft climbs well (probably not more than a 10-20% decrease in rate of climb), provides good visibility over the nose, has minimum vibration, has adequate (or, at least, best) engine cooling and provides a good speed. For a speed to start experimenting with, take the difference between the published Vx and Vy speeds and add it to the Vy speed. For example, the Cessna 180 speeds are: Vx = 70, Vy = 84, so (Vy - Vx) + Vy = Vcc or 84 - 70 = 14 + 84 = 98. I find that 100-110 indicated is a good cruise climb, depending on the conditions.

GLIDES

There are two glide speeds that are important to the pilot, with power off. They are MAXIMUM DISTANCE GLIDE SPEED and MINIMUM SINK GLIDE SPEED. These two speeds would be used appropriately depending on whether the pilot was most interested in gliding the greatest distance or staying aloft longer.

Believe me, sometime if you find yourself over a large lake that is glassy smooth and your engine quits, you WILL want to know the minimum sink glide speed so that the objects you throw out of the airplane have the best chance of beating you to the water so that you will have some depth perception references for that power off, glassy water landing.

Many older POH's don't give any glide speeds. Those that do (even the new ones) give only the maximum distance glide speed. These glide speeds are quite easy to determine. Here's how: On a calm morning (no vertical development or turbulence yet), climb to 3000 feet or more above ground level, establish a power off glide (propeller control to low rpm for least drag, cowl flaps closed) at an indicated airspeed you believe to be 10-15 knots/mph above what you will find to be the correct glide speed.

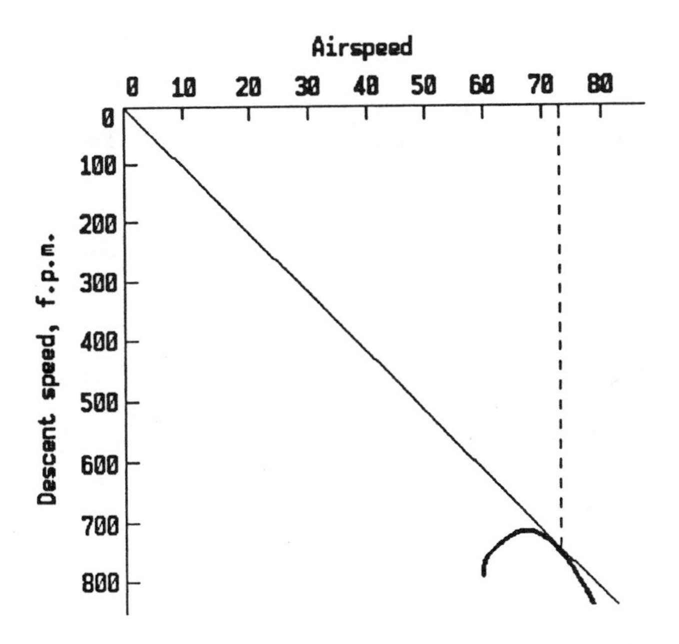

Figure 5.12. Glide speeds for Cessna 180 Floatplane determined by flight test. Source: author.

Once the aircraft stabilizes (trimmed out) at that airspeed, note the altitude and time, then note the altitude one minute later. The altitude lost in one minute will be a better indicator of rate of descent than is available from the VSI. repeat, using an airspeed that is 10 kts/mph slower, and again until you are within 10 kts/mph of stall.

You should probably repeat the speed that gave you the least altitude lost, and one or two slower speeds, using one notch of flaps, as you may be surprised to find the altitude loss to be less with a touch of flaps. Back at home, plot the figures you came up with.

The plot should look very much like Figure 5.12, which I did for my Cessna 180. If you come up with something that is weird at one or more airspeeds, don't despair -- test pilots aren't made in one day -- try those speeds again another day. You may have been in a vertical gust that was so mild that you didn't notice it, but it caused your test to be off.

Once the curve plots out properly, you have all the data you need to determine the two glide speeds. Minimum sink speed is the speed that resulted in the lowest rate of sink. Maximum distance glide speed can be found by drawing a line from the zero airspeed, zero rate of descent (point of origin), to a point that is tangent to the performance curve, then up vertically to find the airspeed. The tangent line is drawn in on figure 5.12 to show the maximum distance glide speed.

Stall Speeds

Most POH's provide the stall speed for gross weight and clean configuration. If not, it is easily determined by flight test. Don't forget to convert it to Calibrated Airspeed before doing any computations with it, if a conversion chart for your model airplane is available. If the conversion chart is not available, use the indicated airspeed (IAS) as a close approximation.

Stall speed increases with an increase in gross weight, and decreases as the aircraft becomes lighter. Stall speed at any weight can be approximated by applying the formula:

$$V_{S2} = V_{S1}\sqrt{W_2/W_1}$$

Where: V_{S1} = Stall speed at gross weight
V_{S2} = Stall speed at new weight
W_1 = Gross weight
W_2 = New weight

Stall speed decreases as amount of power applied increases, but should not change with changes in density altitude. Stall speed increases with an increase of angle of bank. At 60 degrees angle of bank, the load factor (weight of the airplane) is double that of level flight, so stall speed in the 60 degree bank will be 1.4 times the level flight stall speed.

$$V_S\text{ (60 degree bank)} = V_S\text{(level)}\sqrt{2} \quad \text{and} \quad \sqrt{2} = 1.414$$

An aft C.G. loading will decrease stall speed, and a forward C.G. will increase the stall speed since a forward C.G. requires a greater tail down force which increases the effective weight of the aircraft (see figure 6-2 in the next chapter).

Effect of Center of Gravity on Performance

Most pilots know that loading the aircraft so that the center of gravity is near the rear limits, improves performance but decreases stability about the lateral axis (pitch), however there is a bit more to it than that. Chapter six discusses this subject in more detail.

CHAPTER 6

CENTER OF GRAVITY EFFECTS

Most modern seaplane operator's manuals provide us with some data with which to estimate our aircraft's takeoff performance. For example, the Cessna 180 on Edo 2870's (when it was shiny new and all tuned up) requires a water run of 1145 feet and 1860 feet is needed for the total distance to clear the proverbial "50 foot obstacle", provided the wind is calm, it is a "standard day" (sea level pressure altitude and 59 degrees F.) and the aircraft is at gross weight.

Many assumptions are hidden in this data, however. Too many assumptions for this pilot to want to risk using the data in the manual for determining whether I can get out of a short lake. For a more complete discussion of this subject, see chapter three.

One of the factors that is not considered in any seaplane flight manual performance tables (that I know of) is the effect of Center of Gravity on takeoff performance. All it took was for one of my students to ask me, "is the takeoff water run longer or shorter with the aircraft loaded to near the aft C.G. limit?".

The search for knowledge began! I looked in every book about seaplanes I knew about. I looked in every seaplane model manual I could get my hands on. Nothing. I still suspect that there are some manuals out there somewhere, particularly on some of the larger hull model aircraft, which deal with the C.G. effects on takeoff, but I haven't been lucky enough to get my hands on one.

Airborne Effect of C.G.

Aircraft (except Canard types) are designed so that the center of gravity is forward of the center of lift in order to make the aircraft pitch stable. This causes a nose pitch down tendency which requires that the horizontal tail produce a taildown force (TDF). The TDF is added to the real weight of the aircraft to arrive at the effective weight of the aircraft, which is the weight the wings must lift. See figure 6.1.

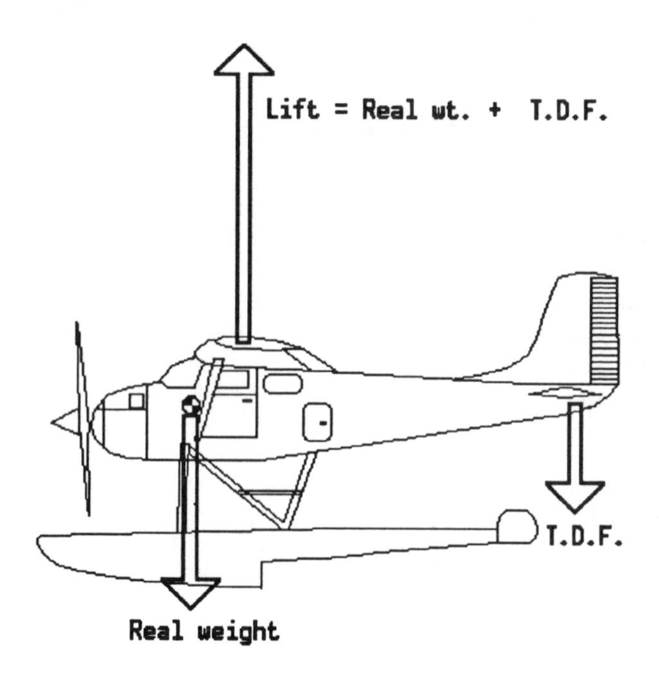

Figure 6.1. Real Weight plus Tail Down Force equals Effective Weight.

If the pilot loads the aircraft so that the C.G. is forward, causing more nose down tendency, more TDF is required, which makes the aircraft effectively heavier. This decreases all aspects of flight performance, slows cruise speed, decreases rate of climb, and increases stall speed (see figure 6.2). So, we know that an aft C.G. improves flight performance (it also decreases pitch stability and may increase flat spin tendencies if the aircraft is loaded beyond the aft C.G. limits). For a more detailed discussion of this subject, see (5.1).

But, what about the effect of C.G. location on performance during the water run portion of the takeoff? No information was readily available on this subject, so during the summer of 1987 a research aircraft which was heavily instrumented to measure takeoff performance was used with an experiment designed to have the airplane provide some answers to this matter.

STALL SPEEDS

CESSNA
MODEL 172RG

CONDITIONS:
Power Off
Gear Up or Down

NOTES:
1. Altitude loss during a stall recovery may be as much as 230 feet.
2. KIAS values are approximate.

MOST REARWARD CENTER OF GRAVITY

WEIGHT LBS	FLAP DEFLECTION	ANGLE OF BANK							
		0°		30°		45°		60°	
		KIAS	KCAS	KIAS	KCAS	KIAS	KCAS	KIAS	KCAS
2650	UP	46	54	49	58	55	64	65	76
	10°	42	52	45	56	50	62	59	74
	30°	39	50	42	54	47	59	56	71

MOST FORWARD CENTER OF GRAVITY

WEIGHT LBS	FLAP DEFLECTION	ANGLE OF BANK							
		0°		30°		45°		60°	
		KIAS	KCAS	KIAS	KCAS	KIAS	KCAS	KIAS	KCAS
2650	UP	50	57	54	61	59	68	71	81
	10°	46	54	49	58	55	64	65	76
	30°	42	51	45	55	50	61	59	72

Figure 6.2. Center of Gravity location changes stall speed and other performance parameters, as evidenced by this Cessna 172RG performance chart.

The Experiment

A Cessna 180 with Edo 2870 floats was instrumented with a cockpit chart recorder which recorded water pitot pressure and water speed transducer output. The airspeed indicator was calibrated using a narrow beam Doppler traffic radar. Takeoffs were recorded on video tape which showed elapsed time to 1/100 seconds. Indicated airspeeds and other pertinent conditions transmitted by the pilot were recorded on the audio portion of the video tape.

Figure 6.3. Loading the test aircraft to gross weight and the aft C.G. limit. Note water pitot assembly on rear spreader bar.

Conventional takeoff technique was used (the aircraft was rotated at Vsf20[1] with wings level). Five takeoffs were done at both forward and

1. Vsf20 = power off stall speed, flaps 20 degrees, at the actual effective weight, in mph indicated airspeed. In this case it was 55 for aft loading and 63 at the forward C.G. limit.

aft C.G. locations. Water run time and distance was determined by producing time-speed graphs from all data sources. Distance of water run was acquired by determining the area under the time-speed curve. The aircraft was loaded to gross weight at the forward and aft limits by placing measured amounts of water in the first, third and eighth float compartments, as needed to produce a gross weight condition and place the C.G. at the proper locations. See figure 6.3.

Also, the minimum manifold pressure needed to get onto the step was determined for the forward and aft C.G. locations. This was done by trimming to the exact center of the takeoff trim range, holding full up elevator until the completion of the second nose rise then releasing all pressure on the elevator. This was done at various manifold pressure

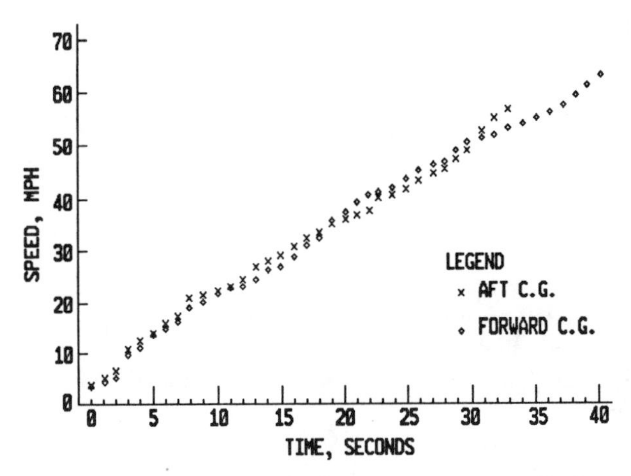

Figure 6.4. Time-speed data. Average of five takeoffs in the forward and aft C.G. conditions.

settings, which the co-pilot kept constant throughout the takeoff run, until a manifold pressure was achieved which would bring the aircraft over the hump onto the step.

The Results

Figure 6.4 shows the time-speed data for the average of five takeoffs in the forward and aft C.G. conditions. It appears that C.G. doesn't have much of an effect on acceleration of the aircraft on the water until a speed of 45 mph is reached. Then there appears to be more rapid acceleration of the aft C.G. loaded aircraft as aerodynamic effects increase at higher speeds.

Table 6.5 shows the distance data for the average of five takeoffs in the forward and aft C.G. conditions. The aft loaded aircraft required only 70% of the water run distance that was needed for the forward loaded aircraft.

Table 6.5. Distance data. Average of five takeoffs in the forward and aft C.G. conditions.

	Center of Gravity Location	
	Forward Limit	Aft Limit
Water Run Distance, Ft.	1956	1386

Conditions for table 6.5:

Density Altitude: 1250 feet
Wind: 20 degree left crosswind, less than 4 knots
Water surface: very slight ripple
Weight: within 20 pounds of gross weight of 2820 pounds
Flaps: 20 degrees
Technique: conventional (see text description)

While the aircraft was loaded at the forward and aft C.G. limits at gross weight, the minimum manifold pressure needed to get the aircraft onto the step was determined. The aircraft was able to make it onto the step quite consistently with 1/4 inch less manifold pressure when loaded in the FORWARD C.G. condition.

Conclusions and Discussion

There is apparently little effect of C.G. location on takeoff water run acceleration until reaching speeds which produce significant aerodynamic lifting forces, at which time the aft loaded aircraft, having the lower effective weight (same real weight), will accelerate faster.

For aircraft that are not power limited (don't have much of a problem making it up onto the step), the aft loaded (effectively lighter) aircraft will accelerate somewhat faster at high speeds and will leave the water at a lower speed, and therefore will have a shorter water run.

For aircraft that are power limited to the extent that they are unable to make it from the hump phase of the takeoff run onto the step, reloading near the forward C.G. may enable the aircraft to be able to make it onto the step, given a sufficiently long takeoff path. Once on the step, the takeoff run will be longer than it would be if the C.G. location were aft, but it may be possible to get airborne if the takeoff pathway is sufficiently long.

If the pilot is having difficulty getting the aircraft onto the step, the causative factors are probably one or more of the following:

1. The aircraft is over gross weight.
2. The density altitude is very high.
3. The pilot is using incorrect technique.
4. The aircraft is mechanically deficient (not producing normal power).

Solutions to problems 1, 2 and 4 are quite apparent. To solve problem 3, the pilot needs to be technique proficient AND the pilot needs a solid understanding of the factors affecting takeoff performance. Technique proficiency is usually best acquired by seeking out a flight instructor who is proficient in teaching seaplane operations which explore the limits of the aircraft's performance envelope. In other words, find a highly experienced flight instructor and get some serious refresher training!

CHAPTER 7

REDUCING WATER DRAG

The America's Cup Trophy was brought back home by the sailing vessel Stars and Stripes because, in each of four separate races, she was faster than the Australian challenger by about 1.5 minutes. She had a top notch skipper and crew but so did the Australians. What was the difference? Perhaps it was the low drag tape that covered her hull below the water line.

NASA has been conducting research for some time on low drag tapes. These are thin layers of material with minute grooves running parallel to the flow. The tape is applied to aerodynamic and hydrodynamic surfaces for the purpose of drag reduction. An eight percent reduction in drag has been produced in NASA tests. 3M Company has perfected a method to manufacture, in vinyl plastics, these special geometric shapes. They call their product RIBLET.

The possibility of using this tape to improve the takeoff performance of floatplanes was recognized shortly after the America's Cup race cast attention on this new product. Mr. Anders Christenson, well known seaplane pilot-examiner from the Minneapolis-St. Paul area was the first person I know of to try it. Reported at the Minnesota Seaplane Fly-in and Safety Seminar in May, 1987, his results were encouraging, although admittedly a "rough test". This early work was hampered by the tape not adhering well to the float bottoms due to being applied on top of a questionable paint job. The tape adhered well enough to the paint, but the paint just couldn't hang on. A "high speed" tape was used, effective at 40-60 mph. Height and width of the tape's grooves determine the speed at which it is most effective, so each tape is most effective only within a narrow speed range.

Much was learned from this early test. First, it was apparent that the tape should be applied directly to the bare metal, unless it can be applied over a very good paint job. Secondly, since each dimension of tape has a limited speed range within which it is effective, it appears that tape of more than one dimension should be used to cover the wide range of speeds encountered by the float hull and each tape dimension must be properly located on the float bottom.

With this knowlege, and in cooperation with the 3M Company, an experimental evaluation was designed in two phases. In the first phase, the float bottoms received a coating of tape on the area from the step to a point six feet in front of the step. In the second phase, completed a year later, the heels (area aft of the step) was covered as well.

Low drag tape of two speed ranges was used in the first phase. 40-60 mph tape was used near the step, with 20-33 mph tape used for the rest of the bottom, to a point six feet forward of the step. In phase two of the study, tape with a speed range of 14- 19 mph was used to cover the heels as well.

Underwater Tufting Study

To be effective, it is important that the grooves of the tape be aligned with the direction of water flow over the float bottom surface. Before application of the tape to the float bottoms, a study was accomplished to determine the actual flow pattern.

Fifteen inch long strands of white yarn were glued (at one end) to the bottom of one float at several locations. The aircraft was then taxied at various speeds over a scuba diver who video taped the passage from three feet below the surface. These tests were hampered by poor water visibility and air bubbles caused by cavitation at the higher speeds, but review of the videos did confirm that the flow direction is essentially parallel to the keel of the float.

Application of the Tape

In the first application, the tape was installed in patches between each row of rivets, starting at the step and going forward six feet. This portion of the float was covered due to the assumption that, once on the step, only this much of the Edo 2870 float, which is 20 feet long overall, would be in contact with the water. Sections of tape were cut to fit each section of float bottom, with 1/4-3/8" of space from the edge of the tape to the rivets. Corners of the tape were rounded with a 1/2" radius. On each float, approximately 1415 sq.in. (9.83 sq.ft.) of tape was used. No tape was used on the heels of the floats. Tape was not applied over the rivets because of 3M Company's experience that predicted poor adhesion and wear characteristics, with time of use. Also discouraging to this practice were reports of poor handling characteristics resulting from the use of flush rivets on float bottoms. A different covering technique was tested and found to be superior, in the author's opinion.

Application was easy, with only directions received over the telephone. The patches of material can be moved after application, for exact placement. Once cut out, actual application of the tape took the author, with an assistant, about 2 hours. None of us had previous experience working with the tape. Cutting the material is time consuming but can be done ahead of time, and elsewhere, if careful measurements are made and recorded. A paper cutter would facilitate this process.

As is the case with painting, preparation of the surface is the most difficult part of the job. All paint was stripped from the bottom of each float in the areas which were to receive the tape. The bare metal was cleaned as if it were to be repainted.

Just before application, the tape is peeled from its plastic backing and sprayed with a detergent and water solution. Then the backing strip is replaced on the tape. The area of the float which is to receive the tape is also sprayed. The tape is separated again from its backing and placed in position. The spray between the tape and the float surface permits the tape to be positioned and aligned so that it's grooves are parallel to the keel of the float. Once the tape is properly located, a squeegee is used to remove the water. The installation is allowed to dry for 24 hours or more. A polyurethane spar varnish is then applied to the edges of the tape and the areas of the float that are bare metal. This is done to seal any small gaps into which water could work it's way. The leading edges received a second application of varnish.

On subsequent installations of low drag tape, the tape was installed in the longest possible lengths, being cut only if there was a seam in the metal of the floatbottom, or if a different speed range material was called for. The tape was laid over rivet rows, and holes cut out of the tape for the rivet heads. Then the tape was squeegeed down, allowed to dry, then spar varnish applied to all edges and to each rivet hole. This resulted in a faster application, with fewer edges and fewer 'endings and beginnings' of the tape, providing better continuity and probably more effective drag reduction. See figures 7.1, 7.2.

Figure 7.1 Applying the low drag tape.

Flight Observations

The first takeoff seemed significantly quicker, but there was no doubt left in the pilot's mind that something was different after the first landing. Rather than decelerating quickly to displacement taxi after the landing, the aircraft slid along the top of the water. It was much like deceleration of the first wheel landing after a summer of flying floats!

There were no adverse handling characteristics. The aircraft went where it was pointed. There was no skidding or yawing. Application of aft elevator control helped decelerate the aircraft more quickly to displacement taxi.

The most noticeable visual difference made by the tape was a significant change in the angle at which water was sprayed from under the float while on the step. Before application of the tape, water was ejected from under the float at a 70-80 degree angle. With the tape, the ejection angle was 25-30 degrees further aft. See Figure 7.3.

Figure 7.2 Treatment of rivet heads.

Application of the tape was made late in the summer, so there were only 6-7 weeks of flying time before the water became hard and white. However, it was enough time to become accustomed to the differences and accomplish the comparative research on takeoff performance that is described below. Once in awhile there was a surprise, though, as different conditions were encountered.

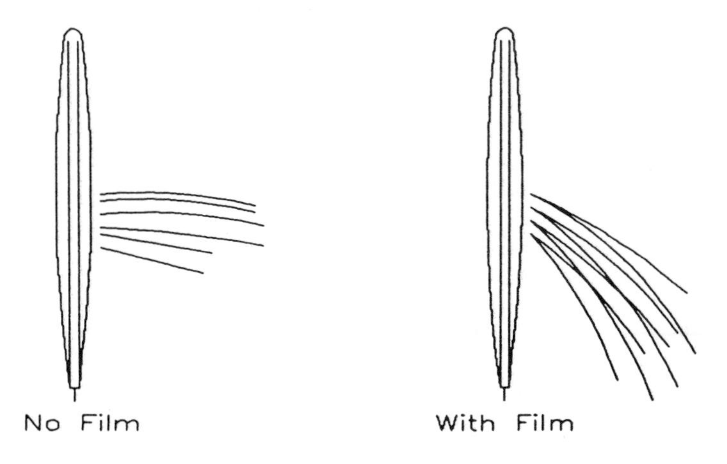

Figure 7.3. Float spray patterns.

Probably the biggest surprise came one glassy calm morning when departing from the home lake, which is really not much more than a pond - about 2500 by 3000 feet. (Leaving this pond heavily loaded when it is glassy is NOT one of my favorite things to do!)

This particular morning (the first glassy takeoff with the tape installed) the airplane accelerated briskly and flew off the water with none of that heavy "suction" feeling usually associated with glassy conditions. I could really sense the improvement that day!

Performance Data Results

Before installing the low drag tape, a series of takeoffs were made at gross weight, using two different takeoff techniques. This was done to provide a control or standard of comparison with which to evaluate the effectiveness of the low drag tape. The conventional takeoff was done with wings level, both floats leaving the water at the same time. Twenty degree flaps were set before power application. Rotation was at 57 miles per hour indicated airspeed. Density altitude was 1250 feet and wind was 4-5 mph on the nose. The flap change takeoff differed only in that the pilot changed the flap setting from 20 to 40 degrees at the moment of rotation, which was done at 52 mph IAS.

Table 7.4. Time and Distance of Water Run - Conventional Takeoff.

Float Bottom	Painted		Low Drag Film	
Takeoff	Time, sec.	Distance, ft.	Time, sec.	Distance, ft.
1.	38.0	1736	31.6	1416
2.	35.2	1800	38.8	1748
3.	38.0	1877	30.3	1356
4.	43.2	2028	32.1	1444
5.	38.0	1610	32.8	1457
Average	38.5	1810	33.1	1484

Reduction in Time: 5.4 seconds = 14.1%
Reduction in Distance: 326 feet = 18.1%

Table 7.5. Time and Distance of Water Run - Flap Change Takeoff.

Float Bottom	Painted		Low Drag Film	
Takeoff	Time,sec.	Distance,ft.	Time,sec.	Distance,ft.
1.	29.5	1270	22.8	958
2.	28.3	1399	26.3	1055
3.	30.0	1450	22.0	930
4.	28.8	1486	24.3	1020
5.	32.3	1587	24.7	1077
Average	29.8	1438	24.0	1008

Reduction in Time: 5.8 seconds = 19.5%
Reduction in Distance: 430 feet = 29.9%

The aircraft was instrumented with a cockpit chart recorder which recorded water pitot pressure and water speed transducer output. The airspeed indicator was calibrated using a narrow beam Doppler traffic radar. Takeoffs were recorded on video tape which showed elapsed time to 1/100 seconds. Indicated airspeeds and other conditions transmitted by the pilot were recorded on the audio portion of the video tape. Each takeoff technique was repeated five times. Water run time and distance was determined by producing time-speed graphs from all data sources. Distance of water run was acquired by determining the area under the time-speed curve.

After the low drag tape was applied to the float bottoms, the experiment was repeated on a day that was environmentally similiar. Density altitude was within 50 feet and the wind was again 4-5 mph. Tables 7.4 and 7.5 show a comparison of takeoff performance, using two takeoff techniques, with and without low drag film. Time and distance to lift off is shown for the test aircraft which was a Cessna 180F (1963) with Edo 2870 floats, at gross weight of 2800 plus or minus 20 pounds. Center of gravity was located mid-range.

Conclusions

It was apparent to the pilot, and confirmed by these tests, that low drag tape decreased drag and improved takeoff performance. Also, it was apparent to the author that the low drag tape improved takeoff performance from glassy water and increased landing run, although no measurements of these effects were made. No adverse handling characteristics were noticed that could be attributed to application of the low drag tape.

Use of low drag materials on floatbottoms aft of the step.

Since the time of the above study, which was done in 1987, low drag tape (14-19 mph) was applied to the heels of the floatbottoms (all of the floatbottom aft of the step). This was an attempt to determine whether it is worth the expense and effort, in terms of additional improvement of performance, to treat this large surface area since it is only in contact with the water during the displacement and hump phase of the takeoff.

Results of testing indicated that, for the Cessna 180 at gross weight and a density altitude of 1250 feet, there was a slight improvement in takeoff performance, but that the differences were not statistically significantly different.

However, when conditions of high density altitude were simulated, the test aircraft was able to accelerate to and get on the step with approximately one quarter of an inch less manifold pressure than the same aircraft with painted floatbottoms.

Therefore, it appears that use of the low drag material on floatbottoms aft of the step is useful only on aircraft that are power limited to the extent that they experience difficulty getting onto the step.

CHAPTER 8

EXTERNAL LOADS

Most seaplane pilots, at some time, wonder and would like to know more about the external loads they sometimes see and more often hear about.

Very little is written about external loads. Possibly this is because there is little common knowlege on the subject. A considerable number of pilots have flown or do fly external loads as a part of their everyday business. They know what they can get away with (aerodynamically) because they have tried it and were successful. Some highly experienced pilots know their limits with respect to external loads because they have approached those limits and gotten away with nothing more than a good scare.

Most pilots, given a choice, would prefer not to fly with external loads, especially ones they have not flown before.

External loads are usually flown because there is a real need to transport the object to a remote location and the object is simply too large to get it into the interior of the aircraft. Building materials, furniture, appliances, working and sporting goods such as canoes and boats have been transported externally.

Hazards

The hazards of flying external loads are many. Anything attached to the outside of an aircraft will have an effect on the airflow over and around the flight surfaces. Lift may be increased or decreased, drag will normally be increased, airflow over the control surfaces will be altered -- sometimes to the extent that the handling characteristics, stability, etc. are drastically changed. This will change the stable, docile old seaplane into a machine whose next move is totally unpredictable. The external load may shift, separate, spread apart or depart the aircraft, taking some of the tailfeathers (or propeller) with it.

How's this for predictability? Let's secure a 16 foot canoe, mostly inverted, onto the left struts and floats on a Cessna 180. See figure 8.1. Wouldn't you predict that the canoe will create extra drag on the left side, thus requiring some right rudder to be held in cruise flight? Also, wouldn't you predict that if the lines securing the canoe loosened up, the canoe would move aft, causing a rearward C.G. problem to become increasingly more severe?

Wrong on both predictions! Left rudder will be required! The reason being that the inverted canoe is an airfoil, creating lift on the left side. Also, spiraling propwash will upwash an external load on the left side (and downwash one on the right side). The differential lift, requiring left aileron (the down aileron on the right side creates more drag) and the forward component of lift generated by the canoe are causing the requirement for left rudder. Also, to the horror of some past pilots, who watched their lashings loosen on the canoe they were carrying, rather than moving rearward, the canoe was inching forward -- toward the propeller arc! And, some have watched their canoe move aft, so the only certainty is the unpredictability!

Figure 8.1. Double-checking the security of a canoe before flight.

If I were to offer some advice to a pilot who wanted to get some experience with external loads, it would probably go something like this:

1. Seek professional help. Find a flight instructor who is experienced with external loads. Have him teach you how to safely carry your specific load.

2. Remember, if you carry an external load without the required FAA permit (more about this later), your insurance most certainly will not be worth the paper it's written on, you are subject to FAA violation action, and probably have increased liability exposure in case of an incident.

3. If you are considering carrying something that you haven't carried before, you are about to enter the realm of test piloting.

Figure 8.2. Destination: Wilderness, with a canoe on each side. Photo by Bill McCarrel.

4. The aerodynamics of objects is sometimes unpredictable.

Open bedsprings are notoriously dangerous. They are very lightweight but they create such a turbulent airflow that they effectively destroy the necessary tail-down force that is created by the horizontal stabilizer-elevator combination, causing a strong pitch-down tendency. Christmas trees, reindeer horns and other yet-unthought-of-items fall into this same category.

5. Individual pieces of lumber should be attached to each other by nailing, strapping, wiring, etc. so that separation and slipping cannot occur. For example, four pieces of plywood will create many times more drag if they can separate, with air passing between each sheet, even if it is only 1/4 inch of space between each sheet.

Figure 8.3. This pilot carries his land transportation with him. Photo by Bill McCarrel.

6. Blunt ends of objects should be faced into the airflow, pointing forward. In other words, a canoe with a transom for mounting a motor must be attached with the transom facing forward.

7. The best advice, I think, is: before you get too committed to having to fly an external load, try hard to find another way to solve the transportation need.

Authorization

FAA permits, which are now granted by the regional FAA office instead of the local office, will allow external loads to be carried legally. While operating under an external load permit, the aircraft will be operating in the 'restricted' category, with named pilot (and possibly, required crew) as the only occupant(s).

The FAA probably will require, as minimums, that the pilot have experience equivalent to that of a commercial pilot and have 50 or more hours of pilot in command in make and model. Further restrictions might be expected to be: boat length 12', canoe 16', lumber 12', maximum one square foot frontal area and 300 pounds in weight. Items exceeding these guidelines would require the pilot to prove need and that the flight can be conducted safely.

Techniques

One hears of and occasionally reads information about techniques for carrying external loads which sometimes fall into the category of cocktail party tales. Others seem to be the result of someone's incomplete thinking about aircraft aerodynamics and performance. A recent article in one popular publication stated that external loads should be carried on the right side of the aircraft because of propeller slipstream. I still haven't figured that one out. Another, more authoritative author indicated that perhaps the right side should be favored to counteract the left-turning tendencies of the aircraft. OK, but what about the example of the canoe?

Besides, left-turning tendencies are significant only at very low airspeeds where airflow over the vertical fin and rudder are minimal. The parasitic drag from the external load won't have much effect at those speeds. The great and competent gentleman that taught me to fly external loads flew his on the left side where he could keep an eye on it, unless docking considerations made the right side a better choice (then he flew from the right seat!).

For further information about external loads, refer to the FAA external load advisory or application form. Also, I recommend that you read Arvid Weflin's excellent article in Water Flying (8.1).

Finally, perhaps there is an old adage that applies here. I am thinking of the one that says, "if in doubt, don't".

CHAPTER 9

Stability on the Water

They actually build trapdoors or hatches in the bottoms of some seagoing (cruising) catamaran and trimaran sailboats so that, if and when one of these vessels reaches its ultimate stability (upside down), the crew can continue to live in the boat, making survival at sea much easier.

Floatplanes are catamarans. Floatplanes are most stable when upside-down. The floatplane that has reached its ultimate stability state is a sad sight to see (reference the sequence of pictures on the two last pages of this chapter, so ably photographed by Bill McCarrel).

When we think about how floatplanes get to this sad state, we find we can categorize the process in different ways such as power-on and power-off accidents, or on the basis of the type of maneuver being attempted, or as takeoff or landing accidents, step turn accidents, etc. Each way of looking at the problem results in a beneficial thought process where learning and understanding can occur.

Since this is a chapter about stability, let's stay with the conventional method of discussing aircraft stability, which is to discuss

a) **stability about the lateral axis** of the aircraft (pitch stability)
b) **stability about the longitudinal axis** (roll stability)
c) **stability about the vertical axis** (yaw stability)

As a review, the **lateral axis** of the aircraft can be imagined as a line scribed to pass through the center of gravity of the aircraft and be parallel to a line drawn from the left wingtip to the right wingtip. Motion about the lateral axis results in the aircraft pitching nose up or nose down.

The **longitudinal axis** is a line passing through the aircraft's center of gravity and parallel to a line drawn from the tip of the nose to the tip of the tail. Motion about the longitudinal axis occurs when the aircraft rolls into a left or right bank.

The **vertical axis** passes through the center of gravity of the aircraft and is perpendicular to both the lateral and longitudinal axes of the aircraft. If the aircraft is flying straight and level, we can imagine the vertical axis being vertical, that is, the end of the vertical axis that extends out of the bottom of the aircraft points toward the center of the earth. Motion about the vertical axis results in yaw.

Any pilot would do well to review the subject of in-flight stability, which is well covered in books such as Kershner (5.1), as this chapter deals only with aircraft stability while on the water, and principally with the stability of floatplanes, as they are the most numerous and least stable because their center of gravity is much farther from their center of buoyancy, as compared to the monohull or boat type seaplane.

Pitch Stability

Nearly all of the upset accidents of floatplanes occur with pitch down motion. That is, the aircraft went "over on its nose". This is misleading, though, because only a few upsets occur because the airplane nosed over directly, without roll or yaw. This usually happens only if there are tremendous drag forces on the bottom of the floats, as in the case of landing an amphibian with the wheels down, or contacting a reef or sand bar while moving forward, or if the floatbottom was severely damaged. Also, most of these upsets occur with power off, at or below landing speed so the pilot has very little airflow over the elevator thus very little elevator authority to work with in any attempt to counteract the strong pitch-down moment.

Nose-over requires one or both of the following conditions to be present:

I. The aircraft's center of gravity is forward of the center of buoyancy, as in figure 9.1. This usually occurs in the final stages of the upset and at low speed.

II. The aircraft's momentum (acting from the center of gravity) and hydrodynamic drag (acting from near the bottom of the floats) oppose each other, creating a pitch-down moment that is too strong to be opposed by the buoyancy of the forward part of the float. See figure 9.2.

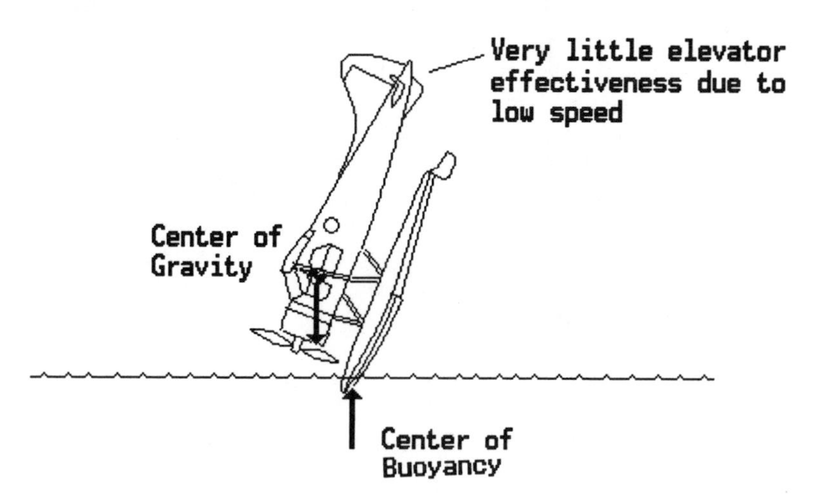

Figure 9.1. Nose-over condition one.

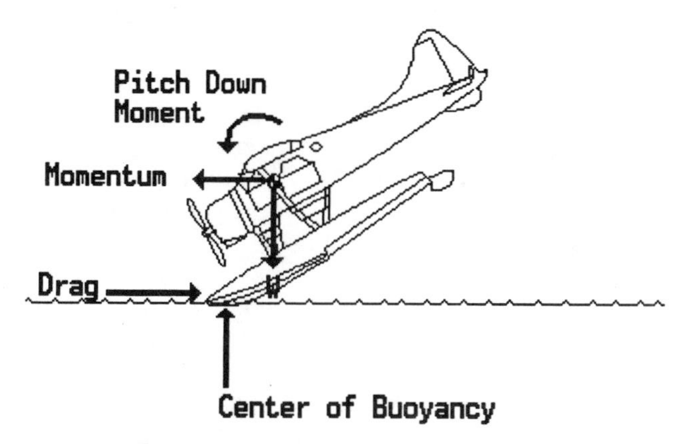

Figure 9.2. Nose-over condition two.

Roll Stability

In many cases, development of the pitch-down momentum occurs after a wing tip contacts the water. For the Beaver, about 30 degrees of bank will cause the wingtip to contact the water.

In order for the wingtip to contact the water (if the aircraft is below flying speed) most of the weight of the aircraft must be supported on the float nearest the wetted wingtip. The rest of the weight is supported by the vertical component of lift and, if power is being developed, by the vertical component of thrust. If the wingtip "digs in", it must have contacted the water with a low angle of attack, or it would have "skipped" off the water like a thrown flat stone skips off the water.

So, if the wingtip digs in, the angle of attack of the wing (relative to the water) was low which means that the center of buoyancy of the wetted float was well forward.

The large drag force on the dug in wingtip is going to yaw the aircraft sharply to the side of the wetted wing. The rest of the story of this upset is told in the discussion of yaw stability. Before going on to that, let's look at causes and prevention of the wetted wingtip.

Dynamic Rollover - the case against high speed step turns.

Dynamic rollover is a term every good helicopter pilot knows about. But, interestingly enough, it is probably more likely to happen to the floatplane pilot, yet is rarely taught. Dynamic rollover of a helicopter may be easier to understand than the same phenomena occurring to a floatplane, so let me try to explain it first.

Dynamic rollover occurs if a helicopter attempts to lift off with one skid more firmly attached to the ground than the other (stuck in the mud, frozen to the ground, impaired by contact with a small tree stump, etc.). Because of the impaired skid, when lift is applied, a roll moment is set up and a sideward momentum of the entire helicopter mass begins. Also, since the helicopter is now tipped sideways, the lift vector of the main rotor is tipped in the direction of the helicopter's momentum. See figure 9.3. As bank angle increases, the horizontal component of lift increases rapidly, as does sideward momentum of the mass. At the same time, the forces needed to tip the helicopter over decrease rapidly toward zero as the helicopter's lateral center of gravity moves toward a position directly over the grounded skid.

The only hope is for the pilot to quickly decrease lift before the C.G. is over the grounded skid. If this is not done, the helicopter will tip over, with major damage occurring.

Much the same occurs to the floatplane during a step turn. Both centrifugal force and lift (if there is any list or bank angle) act together to tip the aircraft toward the outside of the turn. Opposing these tipping forces is the counteracting aileron moment and the moment

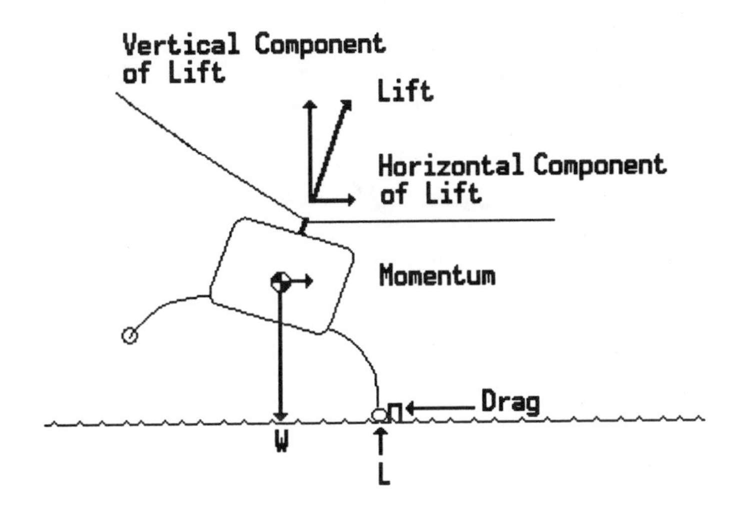

Figure 9.3. Dynamic rollover forces acting on a helicopter.

created by the weight of the aircraft acting on an arm which is the distance from the lateral C.G. to the center of buoyancy of the float that is to the outside of the turn. See figure 9.4.

As the upset forces increase (due to higher speed, shorter radius turn, change in wind direction as the turn is made, or an unexpected wave) the outside float is forced deeper into the water, thus increasing the upsetting moments due to lift and decreasing the arm from the C.G. to the center of buoyancy, which decreases the righting force.

Figure 9.5 shows two charts generated from data taken from De Remer and Winrich (9.1). This paper presents a computer study of estimated righting and upsetting forces on a DHC-2 aircraft during step turns at various speeds and turn rates. From these two graphs, one can get a good idea of the relative contributions to upset of speed and turning radius (the two pilot-controlled variables) and angle-of-bank (an induced variable).

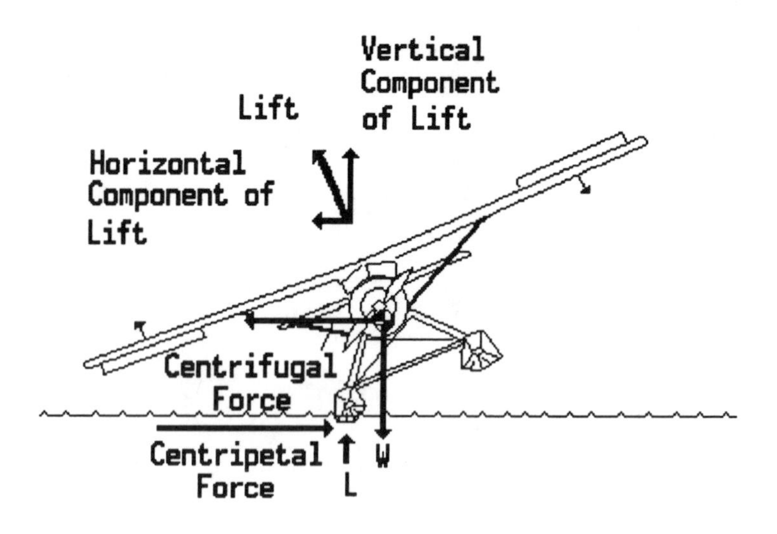

Figure 9.4. Dynamic rollover forces acting on a floatplane.

From the standard rate turn chart, it appears that the Beaver can safely accomplish a standard rate turn at 45 mph if the wings are kept level, but upset will occur, under the same conditions, with a bank angle of less than 5 degrees. All it would take to cause upset in this scenario would be a wave from a small boat or a wind generated wave slightly larger than the rest!

Close comparison of the two charts (Figure 9.5) gives the seaplane pilot some very useful information. That is: slowing down only 2 mph has the same effect on decreasing the chance of upset as does decreasing the rate of turn by 50%! Also, keeping the wings as level as possible helps to keep the upset process from getting started, so *always* use *full* aileron (roll the aircraft toward the center of the turn) while step-turning. Keeping ailerons neutral until needed to prevent upset isn't prudent because once the upset starts, it goes to completion very rapidly -- probably faster than the pilot can recognize and act to input full aileron deflection. The picture is becoming quite clear, that:

First and most important: STEP TURNS SHOULD BE ACCOMPLISHED AT THE SLOWEST POSSIBLE SPEED! Why? Because:

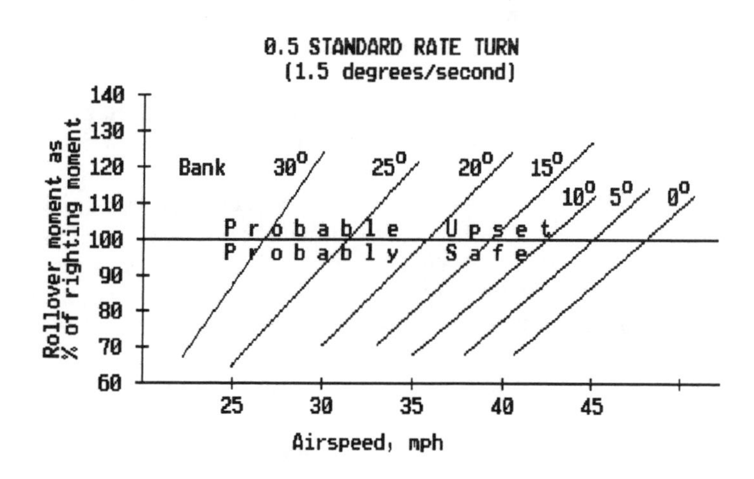

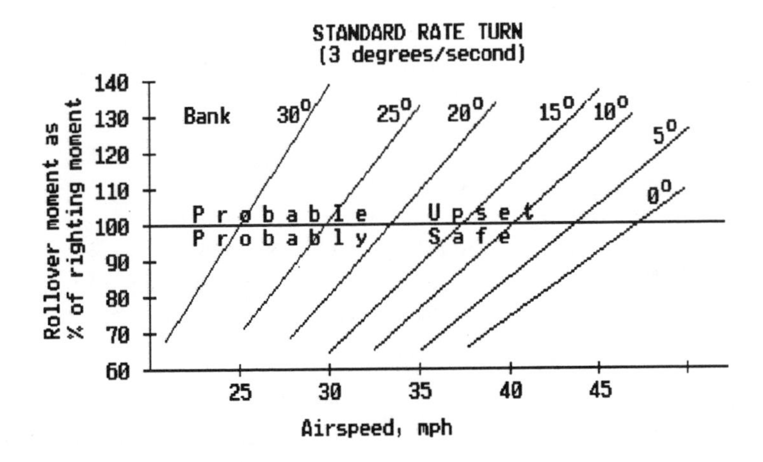

Figure 9.5. Rollover potential as a function of angle-of-bank (list) and airspeed at two rates of turn for the DHC-2 aircraft operating with ailerons neutral, no wind.

1. *Speed* is the most significant contributor to upset moments in a step turn.

2. If the water surface is large enough, there should be NO reason (other than for training purposes) to make a step turn, and if the water

surface is small, then a small diameter turn is needed, which requires the step turn to be accomplished at *slow speed.*

3. For a given water surface size, a step turn made at *slow speed* allows the use of a slower rate of turn which also decreases the upset forces.

Therefore, pilots need to become skilled at making step turns with speed controlled, probably within 5 mph of "falling off the step". Take another look at Figure 3.4. What speed do you think is most appropriate for step turns in this airplane? Isn't it the speed that requires the minimum amount of power?

Second, use full aileron deflection into the turn while step-turning.

Third, it is clear that either a small increase in crosswind from the center of the turn or a small wave, or both, causing angle of bank to increase, may be just enough to increase upset moments to values above righting moments. Once started, the upset forces increase very rapidly. So, once the aircraft starts to tip over, the forces rapidly go in favor of a rollover, and the pilot has no instrument and no prior experience to know how much turn rate and how much speed will start this fast-acting upset process!

For you mathematicians: I assumed the Beaver's vertical center of gravity to be 62" and the center of lift to be 90" above the center of buoyancy of the float and the lateral center of gravity to be 58" horizontally from the center of buoyancy, and that the Beaver is capable of lifting its own weight (5000 pounds) at 50 mph, so you can see if you can get about the same answers I did.

For you physicists: I am aware that, in recent years, physicists would rather talk about centripetal force than centrifugal force, but I went to school more than "recent years" ago, and most aviation texts use centrifugal force. In this book, centrifugal force means the reactive force, directed away from the center of curvature of a mass moving in a curve, equal and opposite to the force which causes the mass to move in a curve (centripetal force).

For those of us who aren't mathematicians or physicists: I hope I have succeeded in my attempt to write this chapter for the many fine, skillful seaplane pilots who aren't much into math and physics. If the above discussion of dynamic rollover is a little fuzzy and you do really want to understand it, I suggest a review of a chapter on circular motion in a high school or beginning college physics text such as Beiser's Modern Technical Physics (9.2).

Remember! In a step turn:

1. With a constant rate of turn, if speed is *doubled*, diameter of the turn is *doubled* (table 9.6). **SO, SLOW DOWN!**

2. With a constant radius of turn, if speed is *doubled*, the centrifugal (upset) force is *quadrupled*. **SO, SLOW DOWN!**

3. If the diameter of the circle is doubled, the centrifugal (upset) force is halved.

4. There is no way to judge whether upset forces are nearing a dangerous level, nor to anticipate the one wave which may tip the aircraft just too much. **SO, SLOW DOWN!**

5. While in a step turn, if engine power or rudder control is lost, the aircraft will track in the direction it was headed at the time of power or directional control loss. So, give yourself plenty of distance from the shore!

Table 9.6 Diameters and centrifugal forces for the DHC-2 Beaver at 5000 pounds in a standard rate (2 minute) turn.

Speed, mph	Centrifugal (upset force)	Turn diameter, ft.	Upset moment, in.-lbs.
25	300 lbs.	1400	91,099
35	420 lbs.	1960	168,138
45	540 lbs.	2520	268,378

Teaching and learning step turns

Therefore, pilots, students and flight instructors, step turns should be learned (and taught) to be accomplished with skill *at the slowest possible speed without falling off the step!*

Speed on the step can be regulated by elevator input (just as elevator controls airspeed when flying) or with throttle, or a combination of the two. A change of speed over the water can be easily detected by the pilot as it results in a change of attitude. Slowing, the nose rises and the accelerating aircraft will nose down. In other words, as speed increases more aft elevator pressure is needed to keep the aircraft from nosing down, so this becomes the method whereby the pilot can gauge speed on the water. The seaplane pilot should understand this, and that more power is needed in the turn to overcome the induced drag of centripetal force. Further, the skillful seaplane pilot is able to demonstrate that s(he) can control speed, rate of turn and diameter of the turn path while keeping the rollover forces to the minimum.

Finally, most wilderness seaplane pilots agree that step turns have no place in wilderness operations because: (1) a good seaplane pilot avoids having any need for this maneuver as the risks are too great, and (2) step operations of any kind, except momentarily for takeoff and landing, in the wilderness increase risk unnecessarily.

Yaw Stability

A yaw on the water produces a turn, which produces upset forces (centrifugal force and horizontal component of lift). The above discussion of step turns indicates the need for absolute control of the yaw, to keep upset forces to a minimum.

One common yaw stability problem that often results in ultimate stability of the seaplane is the **water loop**. The water loop is a very close relative of the ground loop. Ground loops are common to conventional gear (taildragger) aircraft because their point of rotation on the ground (main wheels) is forward of their center of gravity. If the longitudinal axis of the taildragger is not parallel to the aircraft's track down the runway, then the main wheels attempt to lead the aircraft in the direction the aircraft is pointed but the mass wants to keep going in the direction it was going. This results in the tail of the aircraft wanting to lead the parade!

Imagine this: you are pushing a wheelbarrow. The wheel of the barrow represents the mains of the taildragger (the aircraft's point of rotation) and you represent the center of mass of the airplane. While pushing, you continue walking in a perfectly straight line, but the wheel is a 1/2" off to the left of this straight line. If you continue walking straight, the barrow will turn left, jacknife, and soon will be following you. In this condition, it is stable (directionally) as it will fall in line and follow you as you walk, even if it was off to one side earlier.

Therein lies the secret of the docility of the tricycle gear aircraft! All that's needed for directional stability on land *or water* is that the center of gravity be forward of the center of rotation!

The seaplane is very directionally stable as long as it is landed so that its center of gravity is forward of its center of rotation. The seaplane's center of rotation in the air is its center of gravity, and on the water it is its center of wetted side area of the float(s). This is difficult to visualize, as it changes with speed and attitude of the aircraft on the water. It can be considered to be close to the center of buoyancy. The main thing to remember is to keep the center of rotation aft of the center of gravity. Keep the center of rotation aft, period, until the aircraft has slowed and settled off the step.

To make this point, I have occasionally told my students, "the water rudder's main purpose, when in the up position, is to be landed on". Actually, an ideal attitude for landing is to touch the step and the heel of the float simultaneously. When on the water in this attitude, the center of gravity is well forward of the center of rotation so the floatplane,

Figure 9.7. In the early part of a water loop? This one wasn't severe - it had a happy ending. Photo by Bill McCarrel.

like the tricycle gear aircraft, is directionally stable.

If the seaplane is landed in a nose low attitude (airspeed is too high) the water is contacted at a point on the floats which is forward of the center of gravity. The water loop starts with a strong yawing moment which rapidly increases centrifugal force which rolls the aircraft which increases the horizontal component of lift. Centrifugal force, momentum and horizontal component of lift all team up to cause a wingtip to contact the water at a low angle of attack, with ultimate stability the end result after a brief ride during which the pilot, passengers and other contents are subjected to abuse something akin to the abuse a rat gets when shaken by a terrier.

The classic water accident described above is well depicted by the water loop accident filmed in the movie "Mother Lode".

This is why glassy water landings, which are done at higher than normal landing speeds, are done with no or minimum flaps. Full flaps produce a more nose-down attitude for any given airspeed.

Like the helicopter pilot who must recognize a dynamic rollover in process and react very quickly with down collective (decrease lift), the seaplane pilot must recognize the first sign of the water loop and react very quickly. If the pilot is quick enough, the maneuver may be saved with quick, firm backpressure. Fortunately, the needed reaction is a natural one (for the helicopter pilot, it is not).

To stop the water loop, the pilot must shift the center of rotation aft, behind the C.G. This is done with up elevator which will raise the nose, which will shift the center of rotation aft or cause the aircraft to fly again, if the airspeed is sufficient. There isn't time to add power, unless the aircraft becomes airborne in which case power may be needed. Only a nearly instantaneous elevator input will do the job and then only if the water loop conditions are not too severe. The best management of this risk is prevention. Keep your tips up!

Yaw stability on the water at slower speeds is important, too, especially if there is a brisk wind. Taxiing downwind must be done with nothing more than minimum power so that the turn to upwind can be done at the slowest possible speed to avoid burying a float. Keep the water rudders down so that rate of turn can be controlled.

Anders Christenson has some good advice on this subject in chapter 17.

Figure 9.8. Anatomy of an upset I. Photos by Bill McCarrell

Figure 9.9. Anatomy of an upset II. Photos by Bill McCarrell.

CHAPTER 10

Flight Planning and the Decision-Making Process

If it weren't for the infinite variety of weather conditions that are encountered while flying floats, the challenges to the pilot's capabilities would be decreased considerably.

Weather Planning

The key to good weather planning is good weather information, which requires good communications. It is easy to acquire the "big weather picture" if you are near a telephone or can walk into a flight service station. It is quite another thing to be heeled up on the beach of a beautiful lake two hundred miles from the nearest civilization. Out there, weather information may be limited to what you can see of the sky and your ability to interpret what you see.

My weather planning starts in the late winter, before the water turns from white to black to blue and the floats go back on the airplane. During the winter, I sit down for a thorough weather review. It is easy to forget, in a year's time, which way a low rotates and what is that about that old adage about "with your back to the wind, the low is off to your left" -- or is it "right"? And cirrus clouds are precursors to what type of front?

I pay particular attention to those items of weather knowledge that will be useful to me in situations where the sky and my knowledge is the only source of weather information and I am the forcaster, too. I use many sources for this study, but the three standard works are:

1. NOAA Weather books (10.1, 10.2)

2. Weather Flying, by Robert N. Buck, (10.3)

If I am planning an extended trip (anything over two days), I have a few personal rules which I try to observe. They are listed here, in the hope that you can use them, and add to them, to make your flying more enjoyable.

Rule number 1: Never push the weather in a seaplane.

SPA Field Director John Pratt Jr. offered me three pieces of advice before my first float trip to Alaska. They were: one - Don't push weather; two - Do not push weather; and three - Don't push the weather. We didn't, and had a superb 30 day 62 flight hour trip through the Northwest Territories, Yukon, Alaska and British Columbia. On that trip we had only three weather days, during which we did some great sightseeing from the ground. Because of weather, we changed our routing only once.

In order to "not push weather", extra time must be allowed for the trip, so the weather windows (see rule # 2) can be properly played. A trip requiring five days of flying that MUST be completed in a week is a plan that may be headed for trouble.

Rule number 2: Work the weather windows.

For each pilot's and airplane's capabilities, there will be limits to the type of weather that can be flown. Most floatplanes are limited to VFR flight. Some are capable of "limited IFR". For each, weather windows move through, opening as the weather improves, then closing as the weather goes bad again.

It helps me to plan a flight if I think in terms of periods of time when the weather will be good enough to fly (this is the definition of an open weather window). I try to plan my departures at the beginning of a weather window, and sit out the bad weather period in an interesting place with an interesting companion. At the very least, I try for a safe wait in a comfortable place.

Rule number 3: Flight into improving weather is far superior to flight into deteriorating weather.

If you can plan your departure so that you are departing into improving weather, some nice things seem to happen. Anxiety levels are lower, the amount of time until again encountering bad weather is lengthened, and, it has been my experience, the flight will usually be smoother.

Rule number 4: "Slow Lows" are the summertime float flier's nemesis.

Slow or stalled low pressure systems or troughs provide extended periods of treetop ceilings, cold, drizzle, rain and low visibilities. They also seem to cause the same feelings that I remember having as a little boy, nose pressed against the glass, watching the rain come down for the third day in a row, wishing hard that it would stop so I could go outside to play. That feeling, added to being 200 miles from a hot shower, steak and frivolous laughter, plus everything in camp being wet from the drizzle and extreme humidity, and the fish aren't biting, is strong motivation to make a bad decision to GO. It is well to have developed a good plan to counteract the effects of the "slow low".

Rule number 5: Flying from low pressure (altimeter setting) to high pressure will always require a WCA (wind correction angle) to the right.

Navigating long distances over areas with few or no distinguishing features presents the pilot with exposure to off-course possibilities. If the flight must be made at low altitudes and/or in poor visibility, the problem is compounded. Just knowing my destination's altimeter setting tells me something about how to guess at my wind correction angle for a trip from nowhere, back to civilization, under these circumstances.

Rule Number 6: Intensity of weather associated with a front usually depends on how far from the low pressure center one is, and how deep the low is.

Rule Number 7: If the upwind side of an upslope area is clear, the downwind side will also be clear. But if you first observe the downwind side to be clear, the upslope side will not necessarily be clear (orographics).

Rule Number 8: (The Seaplane Pilot's Rule of the Wind, or Murphy's law No. 387): If the wind is strong, the water will be too rough and if the wind is light, there will be fog.

Seriously, it is necessary to consider the surface wind at the destination and its effect on your arrival. If the body of water is small, wind speed and direction is of little consequence because fetch (the distance across the water that is affected by wind) is insufficient to work up waves. If, however, the destination lake is large, flight planning calls for an alternate. For example, seaplane pilots planning to fly to OSHKOSH know that their destination is Lake Winnebago, which is a large body of water. The seaplane base is in a protected lagoon on the west side of the lake but the lagoon is too small for landings and takeoffs, so landings must take place in the lake. If the wind is strong from the southeast, it may be too rough to land. I try to plan an alternate as near as possible, with a small body of water or with the SPB on a south shore (if the concern at the destination is a south wind). Shawano works well in this case. Its seaplane base is on a south shore and there is a motel within walking distance.

Rule number 9: The beautiful sandy beach can be a trap.

Weather and Mother Nature, in the form of wind and waves made that beautiful sandy beach, unless it was glacially deposited. It may look inviting now, but will it still be so when the wind shifts? Before I heel up and tie down on one of these delightful beaches, I consider my options and have an alternate plan. This interesting decision making problem is discussed in considerable detail in the "site selection" discussion in chapter 15 and some suggestions for heavy weather mooring on a beach in chapter 13 are pertinent.

Rule Number 10: In weather decision-making, the quality of a GO, NO-GO decision can, and should be, evaluated.

In the following scenario, which we will call scenario "A", imagine that for three days you have been heeled up on a nice beach, 200 miles from the nearest civilization, while the clouds topped the trees and a slow drizzle soaked everything. BOY! How you would like a hot shower, some dry clothes and a steak! Agonizingly slow improvement has been taking place today. The rain stopped at 9 a.m. and you could see the tops of the trees by 11 a.m. At 2 p.m., you asked your companions to strike camp while you lit the fire and went around the pattern once to measure the ceiling and check the visibility. You found that the clouds were 200 feet above the treetops and the visibility was 2-3 miles. The terrain is flat and the chart shows no higher terrain between you and civilization. It consists entirely of trees and scattered lakes. Calls on the radio brought no answers and no weather reports at your destination to the south. You have put off making a decision but it is 3 p.m. now, with only 5 hours of daylight left. Should you go for it?

Making a Go, No-Go Decision

There are many, many aspects to making a decision like this. It provides the pilot with an extremely complex problem. In fact, I believe that the most complex Go, No-Go decisions I have ever had to make have come while flying floats - often because there is inadequate information on which to base a sound decision.

Perhaps some clues can be found in the following: In 1986, an invitational symposium was held at the University of North Dakota on the subject of Go, No-Go decision-making. Fourteen very high time pilots were invited to participate in a day of brainstorming about this decision-making process. Over 175,000 flight hours were represented by these fourteen pilots, who were from all phases of aviation in the U.S. and Canada. As you can imagine, many subjects were discussed. A condensed version of what I learned from participating in that symposium was this:

We make decisions in two ways: intuitively and logically. Intuitive decisions are made subconsiously, with feeling or "gut reaction". Most pilots have, at some time in their flying careers, had butterflies doing loops and snaprolls in their stomach and screaming "Please, Mr. Custer, I don't want to go!". That would have been a very strong example of an intuitive feeling for a No-Go decision.

Probably, the shirt, blouse or tie you selected from your closet this morning was chosen because, this morning, you (or your wife) "liked" it, or it "just seemed" to fit your mood. This is another example of an intuitive decision. We use intuitive decision-making for the vast majority of the decisions we make in our lives so we are pretty good at it, and comfortable with it.

The more complex the decision-making process is, the less suitable is the intuitive process, as compared to the logical process. Decision-making which requires consious thought to apply principles we (are supposed to) know becomes more appropriate as the problem becomes more complex.

Perhaps you have already made an arm-chair decision as to whether or not you would go, in scenario "A", above. If you did, you probably made it quickly and used the intuitive process. You just about had to, because I didn't give you enough information to make a good decision using logic. I won't go through the entire logic process needed to deal with this scenario - it would take at least a couple of chapters. Let's just look at a few of the thought processes needed.

What about navigation? I can't get high enough to use VHF (VOR) navigation - to do so would require IFR flight which is not a good idea because my destination is 200 miles away and I don't know if the weather there will be good enough for circling minimums on the non-precision NDB approach. Since I would be in uncontrolled airspace, I could start toward my destination at an altitude of my choice, but, once there, I might not be able to get down and I am unable to identify an alternate. So, if I go, I must stay underneath where I can find a place to land if the visibility and ceiling aren't to my liking. This means pilotage navigation at very low altitudes, which is difficult and demanding, especially with limited visibility.

What about Dead Reckoning? Who ever came up with that term, anyway? I never have liked it. My dictionary defines a 'reckoner' as one who guesses. The first word is one of a group of words of little suitability to Aviation. Words that should not be uttered in a cockpit, lest a passenger should hear include words like "crash", "burn", "lost", "low oil pressure". We could call it "time-distance navigation", "rhumb-line navigation", or just "DR" for short.

DR is an effective method of navigation by itself, and should be an integral part of the process called Pilotage. It requires the ability to hold a constant, precise heading even when other duties abound in the single-pilot cockpit.

The use of DR by itself (without pilotage) requires a long and easily identifiable landmark that crosses the course being held, and passes through the destination or waypoint. For example, there is about 180 nautical miles of virtually unidentifiable terrain between Uranium City, in northern Saskatchewan and the little indian village of Snowdrift, NWT. But, Snowdrift is on the shore of the Great Slave Lake, which presents 350 miles of shoreline running perpendicular to the DR course. Railroad tracks, highways in sparsely settled areas and waterways all make good cross track indicators. The problem of which way to turn to get to the destination, once the cross track indicator is found, is solved by pilotage or by using the ancient mariner's trick of being sure to be on one side of the correct course by the time you arrive at the indicator. In this case, DR only is an acceptable system of navigation.

In scenario "A" above, a check of the chart shows a railroad track and a highway approaching our destination from the west- northwest and a highway heading northeast. Perfect! When we get to the highway, if there is a railroad track, we are west of our destination, so perhaps DR is an acceptable mode of navigation, especially if supplemented by pilotage when identifiable landmarks appear.

If we decide to go, it will have to be underneath, and we will be using a combination of DR and pilotage to find the destination. Our passengers will wonder for the rest of their lives how the heck we found our way! This is an example of how the human mind is able to analyze a miriad of complex aspects of the decision making process, using logic, until one of the aspects analyzed becomes a limiting factor, resulting in a No-Go decision. If no limiting factor appears, a Go decision results.

The problem with this system is that the pilot may not be experienced enough to make a proper logical evaluation of the situation (the waves are two feet high - the worst wave condition that the pilot has successfully handled is 8-10 inches - can the pilot safely accomplish a takeoff?). For this pilot, there may not be a logical answer, especially if the pilot is off in the bush somewhere, where expertise is not available.

There are many other aspects to the decision about our scenario "A", above. As long as each and every aspect is being dealt with individually, the pilot is probably thinking logically. Some aspects (factors which affect the decision) won't have sufficient data with which to make a logical decision. This is when we slip back into the intuitive process, often by using value judgements. Example: How bad do I not want to spend another night in a wet sleeping bag? Answer: BAD! How bad do I want a hot shower, dry clothes and a steak? Answer: BAD! How is this subjective data applied to the decision-making process? It is not done logically because quantification of the data and the answer is not possible or not well defined. It is difficult to redefine how bad the shower, dry clothes and steak are wanted in terms of RISK. So, one can only go so far with logic in decision-making a complex situation.

With respect to the decision-making process, most of the high- time pilots at the symposium did agree on the following:

(a) the "logical" process should be used first and to the greatest extent possible in making the Go, No-Go decision, and (b) the decision to "Go", if made, should be evaluated.

This can be done in two ways: Exploring options and/or evaluating risks.

Evaluating the Quality of a "GO" decision by the OPTION TEST.

There's an old aviation saying that is typically passed along from flight instructor to student which says: "when flying, always leave yourself an out". It means many things, such as: "always have a place to land picked out in case the engine quits" or "don't fly into a box canyon" or "always fly a canyon from top to bottom" or "always approach a mountain ridge at a 45 degree angle so you only have to turn 90 instead of 180 degrees in order to fly away from it". What is really meant is "don't let the options available to you decrease to zero".

If the options decrease to zero, you are no longer in control of the airplane, your life or your destiny. Conversely, the more options you have left, the more you are in control. Therefore, an evaluation of options remaining available to you after you have made a GO decision will be a good indicator of the quality of the GO decision. A GO decision that increases one's options is a good decision, whereas one that decreases the number of options is not as good and a decision that has the potential of decreasing the number of available options to one or less is a very poor quality decision.

For example, if a decision is made, for scenario "A", to GO and fly the 200 miles to civilization at 200 feet, and the engine should quit en-route, the options would be reduced to one or two. If there is a lake within gliding distance when the engine quits, we would have two options: land in the lake or land in the trees. As long as I have the option of landing in the water, I am comfortable. I am not very comfortable with only the one option of landing in the trees. If making the decision to GO decreases my options in any respect, I must judge the decision to be of questionable quality, indicating the necessity of risk assessment.

MANAGING RISK

Many good textbooks are available on the subject of risk management. Pilots could do well to steal some of the ideas that have been developed in other fields such as business, medicine and law and apply them to managing risk in the operation of airplanes. The basic steps in risk management are:

1. **IDENTIFY the risk.** Define it as sharply as possible. As an example, we have identified the risk of having to land in the trees with our seaplane if the engine quits.

2. **AVOID the risk.** The only sure way to do this is the NO-GO decision, but perhaps the pilot can identify and choose a route with a higher occurrence of lakes, thereby avoiding the risk. Probably, doing so would improve the quality of the decision and the pilot's comfort level.

3. **MINIMIZE the risk.** The route choice with more lakes might not avoid the risks totally but would surely minimize the risk. The pilot will also minimize this risk by any action which improves engine dependability.

4. **EVALUATE the risk** against the expected gains. This may be an intuituve process, at least partially. But remember, you are good at it - you do it every day.

The pilot's "Seventh Sense"

One more thing that a good flight instructor strives to instill is the development, in the student pilot, of a seventh sense which identifies those times or conditions when the pilot is, or will be, "AT RISK". In other words, the pilot should automatically and continuously search for and identify risk as part of the process of in-flight management.

The pilot who is accomplished in this risk identification process does this BEFORE the aircraft actually arrives at the AT RISK condition. Let me give you a very common seaplane example. Each time we take off from a lake, we may expose the aircraft to a serious AT RISK condition when departing over the far shoreline. For a period of time the airplane is at a low altitude over trees or some other form of hostile landing surface. The pilot should recognize this potential high risk condition BEFORE the takeoff and take steps to avoid and/or minimize the risk:

1. Minimize the risk by choice of takeoff path and climbout route. Once the pilot has an awareness of the risk, a better way may be found, such as routing or a different takeoff technique. See figure 10.1, which shows a significant decrease in the amount of time the aircraft is at risk because the pilot chose a better takeoff path and climbout route in (A) than did the pilot in (B).

2. Minimize the chance of engine failure.

a. Tanks sumped? See discussion of this topic in chapter 12.

b. Takeoff power management. Statistics show that, for all piston aircraft, a very high percentage of engine failures occur at first power reduction. Knowing this, the pilot can manage risk by delaying first power reduction until a safe altitude is reached or make the first reduction just after liftoff when there is still enough water to land on if it gets quiet up front.

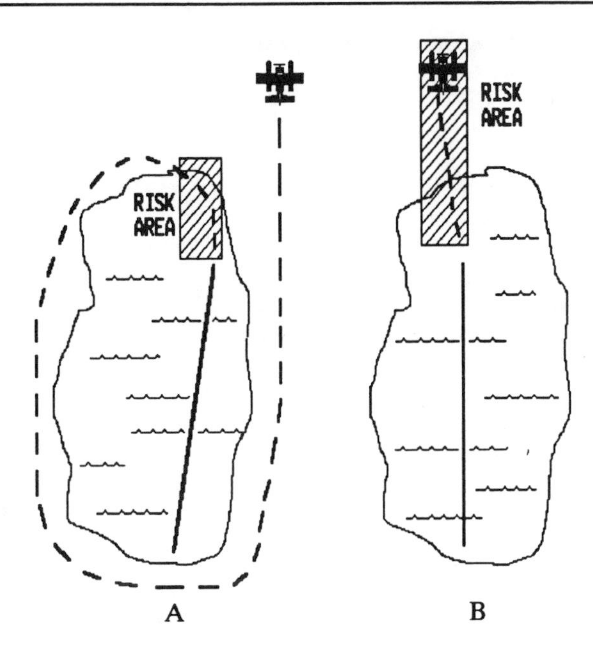

Figure 10.1. Minimizing risk by takeoff path selection.

To review the decision-making process:

1. Gather data from which logical conclusions can be made about each aspect of the decision.

2. Use logic to deal with as many aspects of the decision as possible.

3. Apply risk management techniques to those aspects that you are not comfortable with. Avoid and minimize risk as much as possible.

4. Does a Go decision decrease options uncomfortably? If so, re-evaluate the decision.

You have made complex Go - No Go decisions before. Can you think of one now? Did you make that decision logically or intuitively? Could you have tested that Go decision by evaluating its effect on your options? Did you identify the risk(s)? Could you have done anything else to avoid or minimize the risk? Did you consiously take note of what point in the flight the risk occurs, judge the amount of risk, and weigh that against the benefits of the Go decision? Now you can, should you care to.

CHAPTER 11

Flight Planning for the Wilderness

There are two important parts to flying cross country in the wilderness: Planning and Execution. A successful flight requires both to be accomplished with thoroughness and skill. This chapter addresses some of the planning aspects. Execution is discussed in chapter 14.

Here are some helpful concepts for planning flights into wilderness (sparsely settled) areas:

Concept 1: Plan as if no radio navigation aids will be available. A skillful pilot doesn't need such aids when going VFR, but will use them, when available, to confirm his pilotage techniques.

Concept 2: It is difficult to navigate a track across a chart unless there is one, so decide on the track you will follow and draw an easily seen line on the chart, but be careful not to obscure details on the chart.

Route selection

Many factors may influence the route you select to fly. I start out with a direct route on a sectional chart, as it is nearly the shortest (the shortest is a great circle route which curves somewhat towards the nearest pole on a sectional chart except routes that are true north or south), but before marking the chart, I look the chart over very carefully to see if a slightly different route will provide more water under the aircraft for emergency landing purposes.

Other aspects should be considered. Can I avoid high ground (often obscured by low ceilings and probably rougher terrain) and low ground (sometimes fog shrouded)? Do I need to avoid prohibited areas? Will a dogleg course give me better (more easily identified) checkpoints? Any of these factors may cause me to alter the track I draw on the chart, and the course I fly.

Risk Management starts in the planning stage

Just as flying over solid trees makes me nervous, so does flying across very large bodies of water as they are often very rough or, just as bad, glassy smooth. Planning a route over these types of terrain places the aircraft in a greater risk category. A power-off landing out in the middle, in either case, will likely have an unwanted result. Perhaps a few degrees change in routing will keep us near the windward shore or within gliding distance of some islands where we can land in calmer water and drop an anchor.

Large swamps aren't my favorite either. They are usually full of mosquitos and other things that think me delicious, things that go bump in the night and things that do both. One thing is for sure - it only takes a few moments in the planning stage to avoid exposing ourselves to the risks of a night (or several) in a swamp, or a landing in the heavy seas of a large lake (even if we pull it off, we are in for a terror-filled ride and a sure case of sea-sickness).

Ready to draw the line on the chart? Do it. Now that we have a line, there are several things we can do to make our job in the cockpit easier.

Concept 3: In order to do a good job of flying a track, we need a good sense of time and distance, so I like to start at the destination of each flight segment and mark each 10 mile segment along the line indicating the desired track, working back toward the departure point. See figure 11.1.

Now it is easier to visualize:

a. the distance remaining to the next waypoint or destination.

b. at 120 knots, each tic is 5 minutes, so a sense of time and distance traveled is developed.

c. using the tics on figure 11.1 as a distance reference, Lake Meanbear is about 5 miles across and it is about 10 miles from the east end of it to Lake Tufluck, which is only about a mile across. This provides a good perspective of terrain feature size and distance apart, making it easier to relate what is seen on the chart to what is seen out the window.

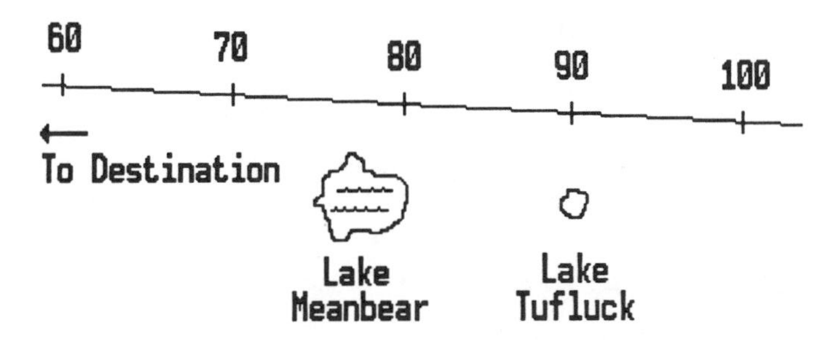

Figure 11.1. Marking and scaling the route assists greatly with pilotage in the busy, single-pilot cockpit.

Concept 4: During the flight planning stage is the time to answer many of the questions you will have while you are busy flying the route, such as:

a. destination and enroute communications radio frequencies.

b. destination and enroute navigation radio frequencies and identifiers.

c. navigation frequencies along the way from which we can get cross bearings.

d. notation of the most prominent terrain features.

e. note points of interest (many are overflown and never seen).

f. note alternate destinations in case of weather, emergencies.

Concept 5: Distance between checkpoints should be less when checkpoints are less prominent or visibility is low. When more than 50% of the area is covered with water in the form of many small lakes, it becomes difficult to find recognizable checkpoints (which must now be VERY close together). One must literally read nearly every terrain feature while moving across it, in order to remain oriented. As soon as the next terrain feature doesn't fit (agree totally with the chart), you are lost and need to do something about it.

Selection and marking of what appear on the chart to be prominent, easily recognizable checkpoints will really help when flying a difficult leg.

Concept 6: A wily old bush pilot told me once: "Look for the bacon-savers, lad." Translation: "lad": I was 50 years old at the time. He was ageless, as near as I could tell and so was his experience. Everything

Figure 11.2. An experienced co-pilot is a big help at preflight time

is relative, isn't it? Bacon-saver: (noun) often used by experienced or lucky pilots to come up with a miracle when sorely needed; object, device or system used to CYA (standard aviation term: Cover Your Ass).

Prominent checkpoints can be bacon-savers. There is almost always a bacon-saver at every destination. Example: on the leg from Uranium City (59.34N/108.36W) to Snowdrift (62.25N/110.40W), a flight of 181 nautical miles, there is a lot of bush, small lakes and exposed

Canadian shield rock and virtually no prominent checkpoints. The little indian village of Snowdrift has no navaids, no communications radio, but it has a classic "bacon- saver" called the Great Slave Lake. This lake is more than 350 miles long and lies across the route of flight. Snowdrift is on its shoreline, which is hard to miss, for sure.

I believe this is the second time I have mentioned this difficult leg. You haven't gotten the impression that I once got (a little bit) lost up there, have you?

It is a good idea to identify what the bacon-savers are, for each destination and enroute. Learn to identify them on the chart. Radio navaids are good, but are subject to outage, especially in remote areas. There should be a bacon-saver as a backup to a single radio navaid in remote areas. In fact, it is best that a single radio navaid be given back-up status only, for planning purposes.

Other bacon-savers would include such things as highways, railroads or major hydro (electric power) lines which run across your route of flight. Lumber and pulp mills produce smoke that can be seen for many miles but don't confuse them with small bush fires (which should be reported). The Giant gold mine shaft tower at Yellowknife, NWT, can easily be seen from 45 miles out and pilots use the nickel mineshaft tower to pinpoint Flin Flon, Manitoba, from 60 miles out on a clear day. You must be at the right altitude to place these towers on the horizon, however.

IFR (I follow the road) and iron compass (railroad tracks) offer considerable peace-of-mind when properly followed, but don't relax too much. Publications which offer advice about flying the Alaska highway warn about pilots who followed some of the many roads which branch from the main highway and lead the unwary pilot into a blind canyon.

Concept 7: When the chart doesn't match the ground any more, you are lost and it is decision making time. If you can climb without losing forward and side visibility, do so. Pilotage navigation at 4-500 feet is much more difficult than at higher altitudes, provided you can still see well.

If you are not recognizing ground features, it is likely that you are either (1) ahead or behind, or (2) left or right of track. If you have been holding a good heading (and no one has set a zinc coated steel juice can on the panel near the compass), it is probably due to a change in the winds aloft. The winds aloft can change a great deal on a 50-350 mile leg, causing a 20-30 mile, or more, difference in where you are and where your DR position shows you should be. So, consider the possibility that we are right, left, ahead or behind where we think we should be, on the chart. Attempt to find a prominent ground feature and scan the chart for it at greater and greater distances from where your DR position is. Returning to the last known fix may not be a good idea. If the winds aloft have changed and are not allowed for, we will be twice as far off course at the time we should be back to the last known fix. If there is a large, well-defined landmark ahead on your proposed track, and visibility is good, you may wish to continue until such time as your DR calculations show you should be near the prominent fix. If none of this works, it is time to use your "bacon-saver".

Concept 8: If the weather is not good - you are scud running with the clouds nearly down on the trees, navigation by pilotage becomes very difficult, even for the old pros. Checkpoints should be closer together, headings must be held precisely using a compass you trust because you have recently proven it to be correct (see "Compasses", this chapter). Under these conditions, I NEVER fly past a missed checkpoint unless I have a great bacon- saver a short distance ahead. The reason for this becomes apparent when we consider that if checkpoints are only 10 miles apart, you must fly 20 miles from the last proven checkpoint to the vicinity of the missed checkpoint and back to the last proven one, and we managed to get lost in only 10 miles!

Concept 9: If you think you are pretty good at TOM (thumb-on-map) pilotage, the next time you have a cross country to do across unfamiliar territory, fly it at 500 feet AGL, with all navigation radios off. You will not find it an easy task, but it will be easier if you pre-plan, with checkpoints close together, track drawn on the chart with 10 mile tics and baconsavers identified. Cockpit workload becomes very heavy for this type of single-pilot flight. Accurate headings must be flown, with time/distance updating of the chart position, towers must be watched for, farmsteads and towns must be flown around, not over.

This simulation of flying the bush at low altitudes is tough but actually easier than doing it in the bush because checkpoints are usually closer together and directional information (section lines) are probably available to the pilot. It is mentally easier, too, because you know that you can climb up for a better view, turn on your VOR and LORAN and relax when (notice I didn't say "if") you declare yourself lost at 500 AGL.

Figure 11.3. Pre-planning fuel stops is important. The landing area assessment at Regina Beach, Sask. revealed that access to the fuel pump was not possible. We tied up at the launching ramp and carried fuel from the pump with our Jerry-jugs. Good exercise after a long ride from Calgary!

It is possible to become proficient at pilotage navigation at low altitudes. Practice, and you will find that you are picking up the skills necessary to be quite good at it, and that you understand much better what you will be up against if you decide to push weather by scudrunning.

THE COMPASS, FRIEND OR (WORD FOR SOMEONE WHO BETRAYS YOU)

The compass is a magnificent instrument. It is simple, with few moving parts. Only one moving part, in the case of the "whisky compass" or standard aircraft compass. Older models utilized alcohol as the internal fluid. Now, odorless (don't you believe it) kerosene is used. The fluid dampens the oscillations of the compass card, lubricates the bearing that the card rotates on and decreases the loading on this bearing by floating the compass card somewhat. Therefore, it is important that sufficient fluid is in the compass. If you can see a bubble of air in the compass window, the compass should be serviced and the rubber diaphragm (which allows for expansion and contraction due to temperature and pressure) replaced before heading for the bush.

You should also "swing" your compass and make up a new deviation card. I try to do this once a year. A check of deviation cards in aircraft on any given airport usually shows that most cards are very old. There is no reason for this, when it is so easy to swing an aircraft compass. Here is how I do it.

An aircraft compass should not be swung on the ground, except as a first approximation, as many errors will exist there. The greatest error is produced by the fact that the magnetic field produced by the generator or alternator is not present unless the engine is running up to speed. Try this, next time you do a runup: with the aircraft on a constant heading and with engine idling, note the compass reading. Then increase rpm until the alternator or generator is showing an output. Note the compass reading. The compass is actually a pretty good alternator/generator output indicator, isn't it? Pilots should know how much effect on the compass there will be if the alternator quits (and in which direction), in case such a failure should occur on a critical leg, going cross country. Other errors may be present with a "ground swing" but you won't be aware of them. They include variations in the earth's magnetic field due to ferrous (iron) metals in the ground such as rebar in the concrete, metal hangars nearby, etc.

So, swing your compass while airborne. Besides, its a great excuse to go flying. Getting bored on a long, smooth cross country? Swing your compass - it will only add a few minutes to your trip time.

If you are in an agricultural area, section lines work very well. First you must determine the magnetic direction the section lines are running. If you have forgotten how to apply the old "East is least and West is best" rule, look at a VOR rose on your chart. The chart is laid out on the basis of true direction. The VOR north arrow is pointing to magnetic north. If you are in an area of easterly variation, the VOR north indicator will be pointing east of true north. A straight edge, placed over the VOR station on the chart and aligned North-South (parallel with a meridian) will tell the magnetic direction of the North-South section line and make it clear to you how the magnetic variation must be applied..

Line the centerline of the aircraft up with the section line and set your directional gyro to the MAGNETIC direction of the section line. Example: if the magnetic variation is 7 degrees East, the north section line is pointing 353 degrees magnetic, if variation is 7 degrees West, the section line is pointing 007 degrees magnetic.

If there are no section lines in your area, use the runway centerline of the nearest paved airport. The tower will be happy to give you the runway magnetic heading to the nearest degree. If the field is not controlled, ask the airport manager for the precise runway heading before you go flying. Then, fly down the runway in a low pass, align the aircraft centerline with the runway centerline and set your gyrocompass.

With the gyrocompass set, it's readings become the FOR numbers in your deviation card and the magnetic compass readings are the FLY values. While holding a 360 degree heading on the gyro, read the magnetic compass. If it reads 003 degrees, the first entry on your deviation card should read: FOR 360 (degrees), FLY 003 (degrees). Repeat this process every 30 degrees then check the gyrocompass against the section line. Your deviation card can now be made up. Be sure to include the date and conditions (radios on, etc.) on the card. It might be well to repeat the flight process in the opposite direction to be sure you get the same numbers. If you don't, then you had an error in your process or the compass is "hanging up" a little bit.

There should not be deviations greater than 10 degrees on any noted heading. If there is, then the compass should be adjusted. Refer to an instruction book on how this should be done, make the corrections and repeat the swinging process as described above.

Vertical card compasses

Vertical card compasses have come on the scene recently and are enjoying quite a bit of success. They have a stronger sensing magnet and therefore work quite well in the north country. I have used mine to 65 degrees North latitude, and it was going strong while the whisky compasses I have flown in the North are useless in light turbulence north of 50 degrees North and become totally useless "North of sixty".

They just turn slowly around and around. With respect to vertical card compasses: Do not panel mount - they are sensitive to vibration, so they need to be mounted quite loosely. If you have to mount one near the panel support bars that are found on many seaplanes (I did), you will need the external magnets as the internal adjusting magnets will not be sufficient to produce good results. Some people have not had good luck adjusting out large deviations in their vertical card compasses. It is absolutely imperative that the manufacturer's instructions be followed exactly, during the adjustment process, as it is easy to get the adjusting magnets aligned so they are fighting each other, producing more errors than are being corrected.

A quick check of the compass before a critical leg is a good idea. There are good directional indicators everywhere. If there are no section lines or paved runways, use the direction of a line drawn between two prominent points on your chart, such as two islands 10-15 miles apart in a lake. While flying over one island, align the aircraft's centerline with the distant island and set your gyrocompass. Now check the compass' indication against the gyro reading when headed in the general direction of the critical leg that is yet to be flown.

As mentioned before, the standard aircraft compass isn't much good in the far north or south. There, the lines of magnetic force point down into the earth, so the horizontal component of that force is small, making for poor direction sensing capability of the parallel magnet compass.

In the north country, many pilots don't rely on the magnetic compass at all. They use the flux gate compass or they set their gyrocompass to the runway heading at the beginning of the flight and compensate for its known errors enroute, by utilizing an astrocompass (see figure 11.4), or a shadow-pin pelorus and computer (discussed in more detail below), or simply by applying corrections for the gyrocompass' known errors and hoping that precession errors, which are not totally predictable, remain small.

Perhaps a discussion of each of the above items is in order.

Gyrocompass errors

Drift, sometimes called apparent precession, is caused by the fact that the earth is turning but the gyro wheel remains rigid in space. This error increases as one goes from the equator (zero drift error) to the true north or south pole where the error is slightly more than 15 degrees per hour.

Figure 11.4. The astrocompass, when aligned with the sun, indicates true heading.

To help understand this, let's park an airplane on the ice at the true north pole, facing an igloo we built there. The engine is running, so we have suction to drive the gyros. The brakes are set and the airplane is tied down. We would be correct in setting the gyrocompass to 180 degrees because no matter what direction we are headed, we are headed south, right?

As every hour passes, the gyrocompass will show that we have turned left about 15 degrees, even though we are still tied down and pointed at the igloo. The gyrocompass is correct. The earth has turned under us. Had we been airborne over the north pole, flying a south heading, we would be pointed at the same point in space that we were an hour ago but we would be flying a path over the ground in a southwesterly direction. If we flew for 24 hours by the gyrocompass' south heading, we would cross every line of longitude!

If you are having a little problem with this discussion, it is time to find a globe of the earth. Start the globe turning (counterclockwise as viewed from the north pole, right?). Now launch your flight from the north pole, headed south (in any direction!). Note that the path over the ground is a spiral which crosses every meridian of longitude as the globe completes one revolution.

Note: *if you want to get something started, bring this up at the next cocktail party where there are some pilots in attendance!*

Please keep in mind that this is a theoretical discussion, aimed only at understanding gyro drift, and that I said "flying over the north pole". Keep the airplane at or very near the north pole for the 24 hour flight mentioned above.

Now let's get practical for awhile. It is obvious that flying in the *extreme* north requires some special techniques and applications, which won't be dealt with any more here because so few readers will have the opportunity to use them. The following discussion of gyrocompass errors has application for all pilots.

Gyro drift is a predictable error which the pilot can compensate for. Here is how its value is calculated.

Gyro drift <H> of a stationary airplane can be found with the use of the formula:

15.04 x Sine of the latitude = <H>, degrees per hour

For example, at 30 and 60 degrees north latitude, the drift of a stationary gyro would be:

15.04 x Sin 30° = 7.52 degrees per hour

15.04 x Sin 60° = 13.02 degrees per hour

Gyro drift in flight

In order to have zero drift, the gyro would have to remain stationary with respect to space rather than move with the surface of the earth. At the equator, a point on the surface of the earth is moving at a speed of 900 knots (as viewed from space), so the speed of a point on the earth at any latitude can be found by:

900 x Cosine of the latitude = knots

For example, at 30 degrees north, the surface of the earth is moving at a speed of:

900 x Cos 30 = 780 knots

If we departed a point on the earth at 30 degrees north latitude and flew west at 780 knots, from space it would appear that we were remaining stationary and the earth was turning under us at a speed of 780 knots. Since the aircraft would be stationary with respect to space, the gyrocompass would have zero drift error.

At 60 degrees north, the aircraft would only have to fly west at a speed of:

900 x Cos 60° = 450 knots

in order to remain stationary with respect to space, and have zero gyro drift error. Now we know that a flight to the west will reduce gyro drift error and a flight to the east will increase it, over the stationary value. We can now compute the amount of drift of our gyrocompass while moving in flight in any direction.

On a flight to the north or south, drift <H> will be:

15.04 x Sin of the average latitude = <H>

For example, if we fly from 49 degrees north to 51 degrees north, the average latitude is 50 degrees north so drift will be:

15.04 x Sin 50° = 11.52 degrees (decrease)

To correct the gyro drift on this trip, the pilot will need to add about 11.52/4 = 3 degrees every 15 minutes.

If the flight is to the east or west, gyro drift will be <H> (the stationary drift rate) minus (westerly) or plus (easterly) the drift rate due to aircraft speed.

The drift value for aircraft speed easterly or westerly can be determined by reasoning that, since the earth's speed <J> at 50 degrees north is 450 knots, and the stationary (zero speed) drift rate <H> is 11.52 degrees per hour, the drift rate will be zero if the aircraft flew west at <J>, it would be <H> if the aircraft was parked and twice <H> if the aircraft flew east at <J>.

Our trusty steed, the floatplane, is a plodder compared to these speeds, but still a great improvement over walking through the bush. At 100 knots, drift due to east or west movement would be:

[east or west movement per hour(knots)/<J>] x <H> = <K>

and total drift <D> for flight in any direction is:

westerly: <H> minus <K> = <D>, and

easterly: <H> plus <K> = <D>

Our gyrocompass should be corrected by adding the amount of the drift <D> each hour or, better yet, add one-fourth of <D> every 15 minutes.

To help the reader-pilot get a feel for the values of drift, table 11.5 shows values of drift for various latitudes for flights to the north, south, east and west.

Flights to other points of the compass are easy to estimate. Just use the average latitude (actually, at our speeds, latitude of any point on the flight is close enough). For the east-west speed component, use the number of nautical miles you will go to the east or west in one hour as the entry value.

Remember, as we fly north, gyro drift error increases to a maximum of 15 degrees per hour at the pole. Flying east increases and flying west decreases the error. Drift is a predictable gyro error and can be corrected by adding (in the northern hemisphere) the proper correction to the gyrocompass every 15 minutes.

If you didn't understand all of this discussion of drift correction the first time through, pat yourself on the back -- you are normal and of above average intelligence! If you really want to understand it (and you can!), here is how:

1. Read and understand Kershner(5.1), pages 52-67.

2. Re-read the gyro drift discussion in this chapter.

3. Calculate drift for six trips you have taken or will take (check the results with table 11.5).

Table 11.5. Gyrocompass Drift values, degrees per hour.

Latitude,	Flight Direction, at 100 knots		
degrees	N. or S.	West	East
30	7.52	6.5	8.5
40	9.67	8.3	11.1
50	11.52	9.5	13.5
60	13.02	10.1	15.9
70	14.1	9.5	18.7
80	14.8	5.3	24.3

4. Prepare and give a lecture on the subject of drift to your local pilot's group.

If you do the above, congratulations! You have graduated. For a graduate course, you can come try to explain it to my students!

The other predictable gyrocompass error

When flying by gyrocompass, the pilot should understand all of the errors inherent in the instrument that lead him or her to the destination (or astray, as the case may be). The three major errors of the gyrocompass are drift, or apparent precession, changes in magnetic variation and precession. The first two are predictable. Precession is not.

Changes in magnetic variation encountered enroute will affect the magnetic compass reading but not the gyrocompass. Therefore, the magnetic compass and the gyrocompass will disagree by the amount of change in magnetic variation. If the gyrocompass is not corrected, it will show an error with respect to the magnetic compass.

In the north, large changes in magnetic variation occur in relatively short distances. This is one reason why, in the far north, all navigation is done with respect to true north. Magnetic north and the magnetic compass are not used. Even the VOR's up there have their 360 degree radials aligned with true north instead of the customary magnetic north.

If the pilot is using magnetic headings, (s)he should remember that the gyrocompass and magnetic compass will disagree by the amount of any change in magnetic variation. For example, on a trip from Grand Forks, ND (7°E.) to Duluth, MN (2°E.), magnetic variation changes by 5 degrees. For this example flight, let's assume the gyrocompass has no other errors. Departing GFK, we establish a heading of 112° magnetic. Both magnetic and gyro compasses are reading 112°. The gyro is not reset during the trip. If we steer by the magnetic compass, the gyrocompass will be reading 107° when we get near Duluth. So, it can be said that the gyrocompass has developed, over whatever period of time the flight took, an error of -5 degrees. To be correct, the gyrocompass must have 5 degrees added. This is another "apparent" error (the gyro wasn't really wrong, it was reading correctly with respect to space, but we wanted direction with respect to magnetic north).

The unpredictable gyrocompass error

Precession, it is called. It is caused by forces applied to the axis of the gyro wheel. These forces are due to small amounts of friction in the gimbal bearings that support the gyro wheel. While the gyro wheel attempts to remain rigid in its orientation in space, the aircraft is rolling, pitching and yawing. This causes the gimbal bearings to move with every aircraft movement. Since the bearings are not perfectly frictionless, the aircraft's movements apply small forces to the axis of the gyro wheel, causing it to precess from its original orientation. This translates to changes in the aircraft's indicated heading - an error.

Precession error increases if:

1. There is an increase in the aircraft's movements (turbulence, pilot induced attitude changes).

2. Gimbal bearings are worn or contaminated with oil, tars, nicotine, etc.(including body and machine oils and other residues from smoking).

Precession error (not total error) should be less than 3 degrees in 15 minutes. Pilots should be alert for indications of poor gyro health, such as increasing precession error, short spin-down time, vibration and noise from the gyro after engine shutdown.

Using the gyrocompass in the north

In the far north, where there are no section lines and the magnetic compass is unreliable, other means are used to periodically reset the gyrocompass.

Occasionally, terrain features of known alignment (from plotting on a sectional chart) can be used. Another old standby for this purpose is the astrocompass (figure 11.4). With inputs of time (Local Hour Angle), approximate latitude and declination, and alignment of the instrument so that sunlight casts a shadow in the sighting tray, true heading can be read from the instrument and the gyrocompass corrected.

The astrocompass is somewhat cumbersome to use in a small seaplane but is ideal for use in larger aircraft, especially those fitted with a sighting dome, where the astrocompass can be properly mounted.

With the advent of the small, programmable microcomputer, the shadow-pin pelorus has become a useful instrument to keep the gyrocompass set properly. It is far simpler than the astrocompass to use, and takes up far less space in the aircraft. It consists of a compass rose of 3-5 inches in diameter with an upright pin in the center of the rose. It is mounted level on the sun shield on top of the instrument panel in front of the pilot. Sunlight, falling on the pin, casts a shadow on the compass rose. If the sun's azimuth from the aircraft is known, the reciprocal of that number is the true direction from the sun to the aircraft. In the example of figure 11.6, the sun's azimuth is 261 degrees, so the direction from the sun (the direction the sun's shadow falls) is 081 degrees true. Knowing this, the pilot rotates the compass rose of the pelorus until the shadow falls on 81 degrees. The compass rose now indicates true direction. The pilot can read the true heading of the aircraft at the lubber-line (line indicating alignment with the longitudinal axis of the aircraft), and re-set the gyrocompass accordingly.

The difficult task of computing the sun's azimuth is made easy by the use of a small microcomputer such as the Sharp PC1500 series or its equivalent Radio Shack model. A software program, such as the one written by Thurman Smithey(11.1), will provide the sun's azimuth given date, time, latitude and longitude. Smithey's program is convenient because it allows the pilot to input the latitude and longitude of the point of origin of the flight, aircraft speed, direction and starting time. The program DR's, with updates every few seconds, so at any time during the flight the pilot has access to the DR position, sun's azimuth and reciprocal (pelorus input). As long as the sun is shining, gyrocompass error is a thing of the past!

Preflight planning

This is one of the most enjoyable parts of a trip. It is done in a non-threatening environment and the pilot is always in complete control. No decisions have yet been made that decrease options.

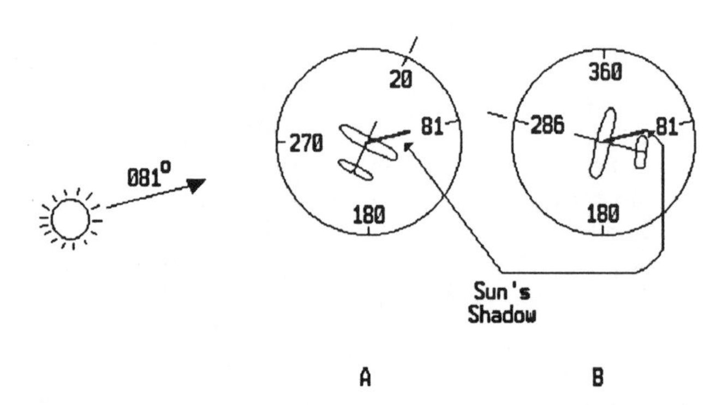

Figure 11.6. Use of the pelorus. In this example, sun's azimuth is 261 degrees true, so the sun's shadow will be 081 degrees. The pilot rotates the compass rose until the shadow falls on 81 degrees and reads the aircraft's true heading of 020 degrees for airplane A and 286 degrees for B.

To do a thorough job of preflight planning, there is much to do. A tentative route must be selected to the chosen destination. Fuel stops must be identified and then verified (by phone unless it is a major facility listed in a current publication). Even then it is well to call ahead. We arrived at The Pas one day to find that the aviation fuel pump had been inoperative for several days! We Jerry-jugged fuel from town three miles away.

Some places have nearly no overnight transient parking available. Yellowknife, NWT is a good example of this, as is Whitehorse in the Yukon (see figure 11.8). Some facilities, Whitehorse for example, charge an extra fee to come out to fuel your airplane making an already high price per gallon really exorbitant. Check it out before you go and keep the fuel tanks as full as possible all the time.

Figure 11.7. Preflight planning is important. Landing here without prior permission (easy to get) will net the pilot a $300 fine. Patterson Lake, Dickinson, ND.

Information Sources for flight planning

In the United States, the airport/facility directory is useful for lat/lon of navaids and airports. It lists some seaplane bases but is not as up-to-date as the SPA Water Landing Directory. The AOPA Airports Directory assists with phone numbers for local airport offices and FBO's when local knowledge is needed. Often, the SPA Field Director for the area is a good, current source of information on all aspects of seaplane flight planning. Their names and phone numbers are listed on the table of contents page of every issue of Water Flying(2.5). If you aren't a member of this fine organization or its Canadian affiliate, you should be, for many reasons - especially the subscription to Water Flying.

Figure 11.8. No room at the "Inn". Whitehorse, Yukon Territory.

Canada

In Canada, flight planning requires a current copy of the Canada Flight Supplement, Water Supplement and Northern Supplement (if you are going that far north - into Canada's Northern Domestic Airspace). Canada has recently converted to the US sectional chart style, which is a great improvement over the old quadrangle style chart. Charts and the supplements are available from Lake & Air (11.2), Sporty's or several locations of the Canadian Provincial Government (11.3).

The Canadian VFR Navigation Chart (same scale as the US sectional chart) is significantly better in detail than the sectional chart, so is far easier to use for pilotage navigation.

Canada's flight rules differ somewhat. See chapter 14.

Alaska

There are some informative publications available if you are flying to Alaska. You should write to the FAA FSDO in Fairbanks(11.4) for copies of anything they have that is current.

There are many good articles about flying to Alaska in past issues of Water Flying. I suggest you contact the SPA office (2.5) for copies.

Maintenance Flight Planning

If the planned flight is a long one, regular maintenance should be pre-planned. It is not too difficult to plan where oil changes will be needed. If possible, I carry enough oil with me for the trip, carrying it in the float chamber nearest the aircraft's C.G. Not only does it save money but it is the only way to be sure that your engine will have the same oil. Oils should not be mixed.

We needed an oil change in Whitehorse one day. The weather was beautiful (85°F.) so I could wear my most easily washed mechanic's uniform (bare skin). But, it was discovered that the special hose I use to drain the oil was not in the airplane. We searched all over town for a plastic hose of the correct dimensions. Finally, a bright, florescent-green hula hoop of the correct diameter was located, trimmed and put

Figure 11.9. Oil changes enroute are made easier by warm temperatures, scarcity of insects and a decent ramp - a rare combination!

to use. The need for a checklist covering items needed for a trip became obvious that day.

See chapter 14 for checklists and operation in Canada.

A seaplane driver named Dummy
was probably a little bit rummy.

Didn't check fuel during preflight
but took off at first light

He crashed before it was sunny.

CHAPTER 12

Fuels and Fueling

The two main hazards of the fueling process are (a) fuel contamination of the aircraft's fuel system and (b) static sparks. Both of these hazards can and have been lethal, so the processes involved should be understood by the pilot.

Fuel Contamination

Contaminants can be classified into three categories:

1. Solid contaminants, including dust, dirt, leaves, bugs, lint off the sweater of the fueler, etc. In other words, anything solid that will not dissolve in gasoline but remains a solid in the tank. Over the years, these solids accumulate and build up in the tank. Depending on their density, they may remain forever on the bottom of the tank (until cleaned out) or, if lighter, these particles may be disturbed by turbulent sloshing and be taken up by the outflow of fuel into the fuel lines.

Figure 12.1. Fueling on the Missouri R. near Bismarck, N.D.

If the particle is large enough, it will be stopped by the screen in the gascolator (see figure 12.2). Also, some aircraft fuel tanks have a coarse finger screen in the tank outlet. It will prevent large objects from blocking fuel flow from the tank outlet. If the contamination is small enough to pass the screens, it may pass through the carburetor without notice. The fuel injection system, however, is less tolerant of small particle contamination. This, then, becomes one of the advantages of the carburetor for a bush plane.

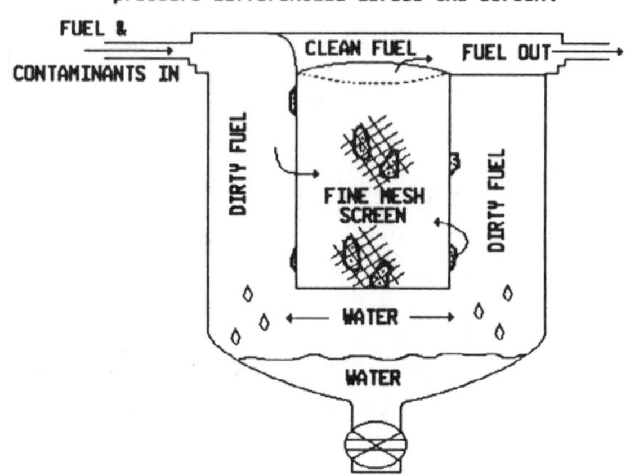

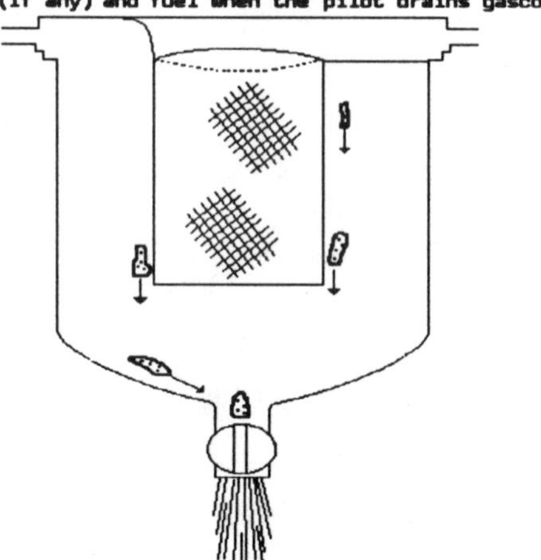

Figure 12.2. The gascolator in operation.

If solid particle contamination in the fuel tank builds up over the years, it may become great enough to cause a power loss, especially if the flight is very turbulent, stirring up the trash in the bottom of the tank so that enough of the solid contaminants pass through the fuel lines to the gascolator to plug up the screen to the extent that fuel flow becomes limited. Then the pilot will experience power loss due to excessive leaning of the mixture and finally, fuel starvation.

Have you taken a flashlight and looked down in the depths of your fuel tanks recently? Note to some bush pilots: it is recommended that you do not use a match for this purpose!

2. Liquid contaminants not soluble in gasoline. The principal culprit here is water, and water is a real killer! In the past two years there have been six lethal seaplane accidents that I know of in which "fuel contamination-water" was found to be a major cause. Water found its way into the fuel tanks and was not detected because the pilot did not sump the tanks. When the engine was started and the airplane taxied, water, instead of fuel, was sucked up from the tank. Fuel in the carburetor bowl, gascolator and fuel lines kept the engine running for taxi and takeoff but all this time, water was filling the fuel line, and the gascolator bowl. When the bowl was full of water, it overflowed into the short line to the carburetor or injector fuel pump. Shortly after that, the engine stopped. In each accident, the aircraft was airborne and no longer in a position to make a proper landing. In my personal opinion, those weren't accidents. By the simple act of neglecting to sump their tanks, each pilot committed something akin to negligent manslaughter.

Fuel tank sumps should ALWAYS be sumped before every flight. Especially if the aircraft has been fueled since the last flight, remained overnight since the last flight, or if it is raining or has been raining. No matter if you have sumped tanks 11,387 times and never found any water! Actually, it has been my experience that I have found water very often in seaplane operations. Probably, I find water somewhere in the region of one hundred times in seaplanes for each time I find it in landplane operations. This alone is a pretty good indication that being around water, in water and doing bush type fueling operations is conducive to getting water contamination.

Some Other Thoughts on Water Contamination of Fuel

Water is slightly soluble in gasoline, and even more soluble in some other organic compounds that are completely soluble in gasoline (alcohol, for example). Therefore, since we don't have much control over what is in the fuel we buy, it is possible that there may be more water in our fuel than we think. This is especially true in warm weather because fuel will hold more water in solution if it is warm than it will if it is cold.

The above is a potentially dangerous situation because airplanes very often fly into a colder environment after departure. As the fuel in the tank cools off, water droplets form because the fuel can no longer hold that much water in solution. Fortunately, quantities of liquid water formed are not great. Usually the only way we know for sure that this is happening is because a few drops more of water can now be sumped from the tank sump and perhaps, once in awhile, an alert pilot who takes the trouble to catch the discharge from the gascolator will find a few drops of water in that sample, even though the aircraft has not been refueled.

More evidence of this readily shows up in a fleet of landplanes that are stored in a heated hangar in the winter in the north country. When the pilot sumps the tanks before the first flight of the day, no water is found. After a flight of an hour or so, the fuel cools and releases some water which sinks to the sump area, then cools more and freezes. The tank fuel sump valve is found to be frozen, when checked before the next flight!

Please keep this in perspective, though. In the last example, a temperature change from plus 50 degrees F. to minus 20 degrees F. is occuring, so larger amounts of water are coming out of solution due to the large temperature change of the fuel, and even those amounts of water are very small. Small enough so the water remains in the sump of the fuel tank. Even if all of the water from this source found its way to the gascolator, it would be contained there and probably never reach the engine.

There are two other, more dangerous side effects of this phenomena of soluble water in fuel. They are power loss due to ice crystals blocking the fuel strainer and fuel dye transferance.

Is it snowing in your tanks?

If you should take off from the water somewhere and fly into an air mass of a temperature below freezing, you might experience this phenomonon. Here is what can happen: As the fuel cools off, it can hold less water in solution, so tiny water droplets form. Since they are small, the water droplets remain suspended in the fuel, then freeze as the temperature of the fuel descends below freezing. As it crystalizes, the droplet transforms into a beautiful snowflake!

These snowflakes are large enough to be stopped on the gascolator screen. When and if enough of them accumulate there, fuel flow is impeded and the engine fuel mixture is effectively leaned. Eventually, this leaning very likely will cause a power loss.

What can be done to prevent this? Prevention can be accomplished by adding the recommended amount of the recommended type of alcohol or Prist, which lowers the freezing point of the water that comes out of solution so that it is unlikely to freeze. The tiny water droplets simply pass through the engine with little effect.

If alcohol is not used, the pilot should be alert for symptoms of leaning that are unexplained. The "first alert" will come from the EGT gauge, with a rise in temperature. The pilot can richen the mixture, for awhile, by use of the mixture control. When that is no longer effective in keeping the EGT at the correct value, the carburetor heat will effectively richen the mixture because (a) less dense air decreases the amount of oxygen getting into the cylinder, thus increasing the fuel:air ratio, and (b) higher air temperature will do a better job of vaporizing the fuel, thus increasing the fuel:air ratio. When the application of carb heat no longer gets the job done, the pilot must decrease the throttle setting in order to keep the engine running. By good knowledge of what is happening, the pilot has kept full power (or nearly full power when carb heat is in use) much longer than the unaware pilot, and was forwarned sufficiently that, when the power loss comes, the aircraft is on the water somewhere, or nearly so.

A more common problem, unless you operate a lot in trans-freezing temperatures, is the one of dye transferrence. When we acquire a sample of fuel in the little cup, we look for a meniscus or line showing separation of fuel and water. The water is on the bottom because it is heavier. If there is no meniscus, there is no water, right? Wrong! What if it is ALL WATER? How do we tell if the liquid in the cup is fuel or water?

Figure 12.3. At the marina, North Sterling Reservoir, Colorado.

Smell it? It will smell like fuel anyway. The cup smells like fuel. The back of my pickup smells like fuel because I have spilled fuel there in the past. Our nose is not a very useful test instrument in this case.

By the color of the fuel in the cup? No good. If you are using 100 or 100LL exclusively, the green or blue color may be present in the cup in either the fuel or the water because the dye may be soluble in water or in some of the compounds in the fuel that are soluble in water. If you are using autogas or Mexican 100 octane avgas, both are colorless or at least without dye. With any combination of the above, the dye will be diluted to the extent that identification of dye color may be iffy.

Fortunately, water flyers have the perfect test kit very close at hand. Just put a drop or two of water off a finger dipped in the water under your feet in the cup. If the drops are visible at the bottom of the cup, the rest of the liquid in the cup is gasoline (or kerosene or jet fuel, in which case your nose is the ideal test kit).

3. That brings us to the third classification of fuel contaminants: contaminants that are soluble in gasoline. These can be many different types of organic compounds that are liquids at normal ambient temperatures.

The most common one seems to be jet fuel, as it is readily available at most airports and some seaplane bases. The best defense against this sort of contamination is a vigilant pilot or crewmember standing by or helping with the fueling process. As mentioned above, sumping tanks is a must, with a sniff test included, not to determine if the solution in the cup is gasoline or water, but to determine if the solution is contaminated with kerosene or jet fuel.

Fuels

Aviation gasoline today seems to be limited to three grades, which are:

80 Octane, or 80/87. This fuel is dyed red for identification. It contains 2 grams of lead per gallon as tetraethyl lead, and must meet specific ASTM standards. Many models of aircraft engines still in use today were designed for use with this fuel. "Rare" is another word describing this grade of avgas. It is manufactured by only a few refineries now, and sold at very few airports. It is more readily available in Canada and Mexico.

100 Octane is dyed green and contains 8 grams of lead. In the United States, this fuel has also become very rare. It contains more lead than most engines need. The extra lead contributes to fouling of plugs and adds more than necessary amounts of lead to the other pollutants of the atmosphere. This is the fuel most often found at airports in Canada and Mexico, although Mexico's isn't colored.

100LL (100 octane, low lead) is dyed blue and contains 4 grams of lead. This is the standard aviation fuel in the United States today. It is a fine product but contains too much lead for older engines that were designed for 80/87. Those engines require judicious leaning to prevent lead fouling when operating entirely on this product.

Other fuels available for use in engines designed for 80/87 fuel, as long as the aircraft is STC'd properly include:

Unleaded autogas. This fuel is of the correct octane but contains no lead. Most engine manufacturers and mechanics agree that a fuel with adequate lead must be used during the engine's break-in period, so that deposits of lead oxide, which acts as a lubricant, especially for valve guides and valve stems, can build up in the new engine. Many people have used this fuel successfully for many, many hours but there are those who promote it's disadvantages which include (a) not knowing exactly what the quality of the product is that you are buying to put in your airplane, (b) possibility of contamination with alcohol (there is a simple test for this), and (c) possibility of increased potential for vaporlock (there is a simple test for volatility, too). Depending on the aircraft and the fuel, some rubber, plastic and other components in the carb, fuel lines, floats, etc., may be damaged by some of the volatile components of autogas (and agvas, for that matter). In my opinion, item (a) is the most legitimate argument against the use of autogas.

I try to be as careful as I can be, when buying autogas, that I buy from a proven source, but buy it I do. Mainly I use it because of the economics and availability. I have a 50 gallon tank in the back of my pickup with an electric pump, water and particulates filter. I have to have the tank anyway, to service the aircraft as it is moored where fuel is not available. Also, the economics are such that, in 1200 hours I will have saved enough on fuel costs that I can overhaul the engine with the savings. As always, economics is a very strong force.

Regular autogas. Although still readily available, this fuel grade will become extinct soon. It differs very little from unleaded autogas now, as it contains not more than one tenth of a gram of lead per gallon.

Those operators who are operating many large engines, particularly the round engines, for many hours each year, such as some crop sprayers, are mixing autogas (for the economics) and 100 octane (for the lead content). This is done in large storage tanks at the time of delivery. Since autogas reputedly has a short storage life compared to avgas, use should be in large volumes to keep the tank storage time to a minimum.

I have found that if I use autogas when operating from the home base and whenever I can find it enroute, I still buy enough 100LL and 100 octane (in Canada and Mexico) to give my engine good exposure to lead. Please note that, although I do use autogas, I only have about 600 hours of experience with it. I am not trying to convince anyone that they should or should not use it. I believe that each owner should research the subject thoroughly, evaluating the value of each source's arguments, and decide accordingly about the use of autogas as an aviation fuel.

Use of autogas in Canada, even in U.S. registered aircraft with proper

STCs is not approved by Canadian authorities. Their reason is that Canadian autofuel does not necessarily meet the U.S. ASTM standards called for in the STC. Fortunately, much of Canada has ready access to avgas with many more seaplane bases than found when flying cross country in the U.S.

Fueling

There are two main hazards for the operator/pilot when fueling. They are (a) static electricity generated spark ignition of the fuel while it is being transferred to the aircraft, and (b) contamination of the aircraft's fuel system.

Assuming the pilot has located a fuel source by some method such as those suggested in chapters 10 or 11, the following steps seem prudent to me, for the fueling process:

1. Investigate the vendor's filtration. If the filtration is aircraft quality, and the source is used by several aircraft each day, probably purchaser filtration is not necessary and will only slow the fueling process. If the vendor's filtration is an unknown or at all suspect, use of filtration provided by the purchaser is appropriate. Filtration systems available for use by the pilot are many and varied. The old standbys of the metal funnel and either a chamois or felt hat worked for years but have some disadvantages which include the fact that an already wet chamois will pass water and both the chamois and felt hat do dispense particles or fibers of chamois and felt into the tanks. Another objection to the chamois system is that the chamois will smell of gasoline in the aircraft cabin for hours after departing the fuel dock. I have, in recent years, developed confidence in the Filter Funnel marketed through the Lake and Air catalog (12.1). It stops free water, flows 8 gpm and is made of a conductive plastic. It dries quickly while I am paying the fuel bill and weighs only 9 oz. Stamped in the plastic of the funnel appear the words "not approved for aviation fuels", apparently the manufacturer's attempted defense against this country's incredible liability history.

2. Before fueling the aircraft, my next step is to turn the aircraft's fuel selector valve to the 'off' position. Two reasons for this:

(a) fuel cannot transfer from the filled tank to the empty one while I am relocating to and filling the second tank. That way, I know the first tank filled is completely full.

(b) if one or both of the tanks are contaminated with water, etc., the contaminant is confined to the tank(s). The rest of the ship's fuel system remains clean. This makes decontamination much easier and quicker. The selector valve must be left in the 'off' position until the pilot has determined that no contamination has occurred (by sumping the tanks after fueling).

3. If the fueling is to be done with the dispensing hose reaching the aircraft, I prefer to do the job myself unless there is an experienced, well trained, caring individual who wishes to do the job. Care must be taken not to drag the fuel hose over the windshield as it will surely be scratched.

Figure 12.4. Some boat fuel docks present interesting problems, such as this roof overhang. Long Lake, N..Y

4. Touch the metal fuel hose nozzle against metal of the airplane before opening the fuel filler port to discharge any developed static

electrical charge. A static charge can develop on a hose anytime the hose is moved, especially if it is dragged across or over something, or if something is moved over or dragged across the outside of the hose, or if there is flow inside the hose. This static electrical charge on the hose establishes a different electrical voltage on the hose than is on the airplane. When the hose and the airplane come in close enough proximity to each other,a spark will jump across the small space, moving electrons to equalize the voltage on both sides. Just like a spark from a spark plug, it is capable of igniting fuel-air vapors if they are present in the right mixture. The results are immediate and not pleasant. After such an occurence, when the fueler comletes the apex of his trajectory, he should try to set up a glide to land in the water rather than the hard dock or sharp metal of the floats or other airplane parts!

5. Keep the nozzle in contact with the metal parts of the filler hole or the conductive plastic or metal of the filter funnel all during the fuel transfer. If there is not a low resistance (metal to metal or metal to conductive material to metal) electrical connection between the hose nozzle and the aircraft, an electrical charge may build up on the hose, ready to discharge (arc) just before the next metal to metal contact.

6. After fueling is complete and filler caps are firmly back in place, wait 15 minutes (time enough to settle your bill with the supplier and let the filter funnel air out), sump each fuel tank to check for the three types of contamination listed above.

If water is found, continue sumping until no more water appears in the cup. Then rock the wings and lift the tail up and down several times and sump again. Repeat this procedure until no more water is found. Now open the fuel selector valve. Next, sump the gascolator and inspect this sample for water. Continue sumping until the fuel is clear (cloudy fuel is an indication of microscopic water droplets dispersed in the fuel). To be very sure that all the water is out of the system, taxi around the lake for 5-10 minutes, stop the engine and sample the gascolator again. Being of a suspicious nature, I would probably sample the gascolator and tank sumps again after the completion of the flight, to see if flight movements and turbulence caused any more water to settle out.

There are several things the fueler can do to prevent the spark jump of an electrical discharge, including:

1. When possible, use of grounding cables from nozzle or refueler to aircraft should be used. If not available, the following suggestions can help.

2. Don't let the static charge build up. Discharge it often, or better yet, continuously, by touching hose and or nozzle or jerry jug to the metal of the aircraft at a point far enough away from the filler hole, and upwind, so that no fuel vapors exist where the spark might jump. Allow the filler hose to lay up next to the metal skin of the aircraft somewhere along the length of the hose. Be sure to touch the nozzle of the hose to the metal of the aircraft before opening the filler port.

3. Keep the spark gap wide. When using a plastic funnel/filter, the hose nozzle is separated from the metal of the aircraft by a considerable distance. If the plastic funnel is capable of conducting an electrical or static charge, the funnel is constantly touching the metal filler cap so the charge can dissipate. If the plastic funnel does not conduct, then the spark gap between nozzle and aircraft is kept too wide for a spark to jump. Therefore, the nozzle should be touching the plastic funnel during the fueling process, even if the funnel is not conductive or if you aren't sure about the funnel's conductivity. It is preferable not to use a non-conductive funnel as large voltage differentials can build up, making the non conductivity of the funnel questionable. It may be non-conductive at low voltages but at high voltages, unpredictability reigns.

The fact that there is rarely an incident of fuel ignition during fueling is a good indication that it is a pretty safe process. It is very safe if the pilot is aware of the two hazards of fueling. So, keep these hazards and recommended processes in mind each time you fuel up.

Improper fueling procedures can lead to an out-of-this-world experience!

A flier by the name of McDull
moored out his new mono hull

He woke up from a nap
and 'bout took a rap
when he found his new bird was now missing

All over he looked,
he did no effort forsake
'til he found it, well moored
down, under the lake.

CHAPTER 13

Mooring

Part of "comfort" on a trip anywhere is knowing that your aircraft is safe and free from any harm. For those that don't carry "not in motion" hull insurance, there is an even greater urgency. We all like to know that our aircraft is secure.

I watched a seaplane arrive and its operator go off with the aircraft heeled up on a beach and tied with a 10 foot length of heavy twine to a spindly bush which was the only thing close enough to the shore for the length of cord available.

"Good grief!", I must have muttered. Another observer said, "Maybe he wants the insurance company to own it, it is pretty ratty looking". When away from home base, our mental comfort requires a good job of mooring. Some would say that I have used the word 'mooring' improperly here. Chapman (13.1) defines 'mooring' as "a semi-permanent anchorage installation, consisting of a heavy anchor, chain, buoy and pennant".

I am using the word as a verb, meaning the act of making a boat or aircraft secure and safe from harm in the water.

Since the seaplane spends much of its time in a marine environment (on the water), much marine terminology comes into play. There are many excellent books covering marine operations, including marine rules of the road, handling, anchoring, docking and seamanship, some of which should be available at your local library. I mention Chapman's book, "Piloting, Seamanship and Boat Handling" (13.1) as it is a classic and is readily available.

You may wish to refer to the Glossary of terms after chapter 17 to refresh your memory of some of the marine terms used herein. On the dock, for example, use of the word "rope" will immediately label the user as a landlubber to an experienced mariner - the user has become a person not to be trusted.

Line

Generally, the word rope is not used in the marine environment, except in reference to wire cable, or as part of a name to describe its use, i.e.: toerope. The correct term is **line.** Lines that are used for a specific special purpose are referred to by specific names which indicate their purpose, such as rode, painter, pennant, sheet, halyard, mooring line, dockline, bow line, stern line, spring line, hawser.

One **heaves** a line, which means to throw it or pull on it. In the opposite direction, it is **cast off** to release it, **paid out** to lessen the strain or **eased**, to lessen the strain slowly. A line is **belayed** when made fast without knotting. **Belay**, as a command means "stop" or "cease". Please see the glossary for these and other terms.

The seaplane pilot is faced with decisions about what type, size and amount of line should be carried on board. Line is available made from nylon, polypropylene and polyester in synthetics and manila and sisal in natural materials. Table 13.1 is a rating of each material's general characteristics.

A look at table 13.1 indicates that each material has its strong and weak points. Generally, nylon is the line of choice for docklines, shorelines and anchor rode because of good elasticity and good handling characteristics. Polypropylene is less desirable for the above purposes because it is less elastic and it floats (more subject to being cut by passing propellers) and is very slippery so does not hold a knot well. Poly makes a good lifesaving line for use in a throwing bag or attached to a life ring because it floats.

I use stranded (twisted) nylon line of 3/8" diameter exclusively for all purposes on board. I carry 3 or 4 lines of 40 foot length and 2 lines of 100'. The 3/8" is a good compromise because it is strong enough (see table 13.2) yet is light weight. A 100 foot length, properly coiled up, can be carried in one hand without effort.

Table 13.1. Characteristics of line. Rating 1 = best, 4 = poorest

	Nylon	Polypropylene	Polyester	Manila	Sisal
Shock Load	1	2	3	3	4
Rot Resistance	1	1	1	4	4
Mildew Resistance	1	1	1	4	4
Sunlight Resistance	3	4	1	1	1
Handling	1	2	1	3	4
Heat: Weakens at, F.°	350	150	350	>600	>600
Can Store	wet	wet	wet	dry	dry
Oil and Gas Resistance	1	1	1	3	3
Acid Resistance	2	1	1	4	4
Abrasion Resistance	1	3	1	2	4
Floats	No	Yes	No	No	No

Table 13.2. Strength of new line, pounds.

Size	Nylon		Polypropylene	
	Working	Breaking	Working	Breaking
1/4"	124	1125	113	1025
3/8"	278	2500	244	2200
1/2"	525	4750	420	3800

Note 1. Nylon line ages, loosing strength and elasticity. It should be replaced when it is abraded or has lost its form, or "life".

Note 2. Working strength computed at 11% of breaking strength - a very conservative approach.

I find that the 100 foot lengths are needed, more often than not, for wingstrut shorelines (see figure 13.4). I prefer not to splice loops into one end of my shorelines. With spliceless lengths of line I can start the task of securing with either end - I don't have to hunt for the correct end. Also, using a splice requires the entire 100 feet be run through the splice to secure the spliced end. Although it is true that the splice removes less strength from the line than a knot will, a knot must be used at the other end of the line, so the line is only as strong as the weakest point.

Knots

The purpose of a knot is to secure a line. A good knot will secure with a minimum of strength loss and will be easy to untie, even if it has been under great strain. Table 13.3 shows the effect of a knot on line strength.

There are many good knots. Each is probably slightly better than another for a specific purpose. I spent many years on sailboats, where one is never more than arm's length away from one or many working lines, so I learned the proper uses of many knots. I have not, however, had good luck convincing my seaplane students that they should learn anything of the craft of knot tying. I am always amazed when a young man who is doing such a good job of mastering the complexities of flying, stands on the dock with a line in each hand and a look of total dismay on his face regarding what to do with those lines, even though I showed him how to do it last week.

Table 13.3. Effect on line strength by knots and splices.

Knot or splice	% Efficiency
Normal line	100
Anchor bend	76
Rolling hitch (airport knot)	65-70
Double half hitch	65-70
Bowline	60
Square knot	45
Eye splice on thimble	90-95
Long Splice	87
Short splice	85

There are probably just 3 or 4 knots that a competent seaplane pilot really needs to know. Every pilot should know the **rolling hitch** or **airport knot**, just to be able to tie down the airplane. This knot is a variation of the **double half hitch**. The **anchor bend** is a must for securing the rode to the anchor, and it is easy to tie. The **bowline** is handy for many things, especially when the loop formed by the knot must not slip. It is a very dependable knot and always easy to untie after being under a heavy strain. The **fisherman's knot** is especially handy for joining two lines to make one longer line, and is also easy to untie. These knots, and how to do splices, should be looked up in a book of knots (13.2) or in Chapman (13.1), and practiced.

Useful points to remember about knots and line

- A knot joining two lines reduces the total strength to little more than half that of the weaker line.

- It is not always true that a stronger line is best, because elasticity also has to be considered.

- A line that has twice the diameter of another has four times the strength.

- Repair fraying ends immediately. They look terrible and quickly consume many inches of useful line.

- Keep line neatly coiled and hung up if possible so it will quickly dry.

- Don't buy rope that is too stiff and don't believe the clerk that tells you it will soften with time. Also, don't buy twisted rope (in the store it is probably called rope) that is too soft as it may give very unsatisfactory performance. 3/8" twisted nylon can be purchased most reasonably as 500 or 600 foot reels. I find that a 600 foot reel lasts me about 5 years.

Heeling up

A float plane is heeled up by bringing it to the beach tail first, then bringing the heels of the floats up onto the beach as far as possible. This may be done on a rocky shore, provided the rocks slope down into the water steeply enough so that there is no chance for the forward parts of the floats to contact those underwater rocks when the airplane is pitching up and down from wave action. Where rocks or gravel exist, it is necessary to place a log or old tires under the heels of the floats. This becomes the fulcrum point for the aircraft's pitching motions. The process of approaching any rocky beach must be done with great caution, engine off and with the paddle or wading in with the airplane if it is shallow.

The process of approaching a normal heeling up site is not difficult. If it is a location strange to the pilot, the approach should be done with considerable caution. The pilot has looked the situation over from the air, noting shallow spots, rocks, etc. A more thorough job of looking can be done while taxiing by circling, getting closer with each circle.

For a rocky or uncertain shore, or one encumbered with brush, tree branches or rapidly rising ground and if the wind is calm near the beach, stop the engine so the airplane looses way and stops just short of the beach. Use your paddle to turn the airplane tail to the beach, then move into the beach, watching for rocks and snags in the process.

If there is a wind, ALWAYS approach heading into the wind. If the wind is blowing from the land directly offshore, contact the beach with the left float (if you are flying from that side) so the left wing will extend over the beach. Grab that wingtip before the aircraft weathercocks and/or moves back offshore. Walk the wingtip along the beach, turning the airplane until you can reach the stabilizer, then grab the stinger and beach the airplane, caring for the water rudders, which you remembered to put up before you left the cockpit, didn't you?

If the wind is blowing offshore from any angle, keep in mind that when you step ashore, the weight of your aircraft is decreased by 5-15% in most cases, and the bird just might sail away, leaving you alone on the shore. This maneuver is usually followed by the pilot getting quite wet.

Now, unload the aircraft, then pull it up on the beach as far as you can, thus decreasing the angle of attack of the wing. Keep a close eye on the aircraft while unloading, as it is getting lighter with each item removed!

If the wind is blowing along the shore, contact the shore at a 45° angle (into the wind) with the downwind float. If the wind is blowing from your left, the left float will be the offshore float so you will need to use the crossover wire to get to the right float, to get ashore with dry feet, or ask your right seat passenger to get out on the float (which is a good idea, and should be done before coming ashore so you can slide over to the right seat for a better view of obstructions as well as having a quick route ashore).

If the wind is blowing onshore, less effort is needed on the pilot's part. Many different approach angles can be used. The idea is to arrive at a point just offshore and upwind from your selected landing site at zero speed. Now put the water rudders up. The wind will turn the bird tail to the beach and she will sail back onto the beach so you can step ashore with dry feet, tip you hat to the crowd, grab the stinger and pull her up on the beach a bit, so she will stay firmly aground while unloading. Often the easiest approach is parallel to the beach and out far enough to avoid going aground.

Regardless of the direction of the wind, the most important part of going ashore is planning. Take time to plan and get ready, including instructions to your passengers. Even if you have to circle a few times, a smooth, damage free landing with dry feet is worth it.

Securing the heeled up floatplane

Figure 13.4 shows a preferred method of securing the floatplane that is heeled up on the beach for an overnight stay. The tail shorelines should form an angle with each other as close to 90° as possible. The wing strut shorelines should be as close as possible to parallel to the shoreline.

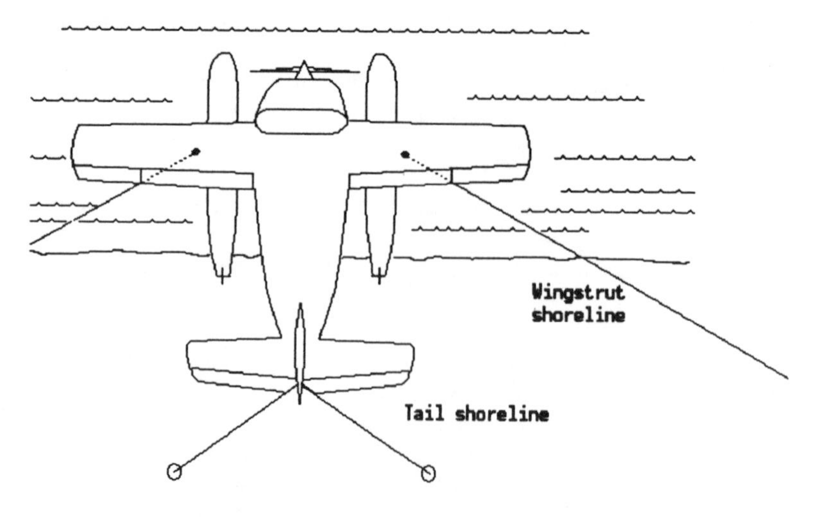

Figure 13.4. Securing the heeled up floatplane overnight.

A "next best" alternate to the above would differ only in that only one tail shoreline is used, tied to the tree most directly behind the airplane.

If you are just stopping for awhile and not going to leave the vicinity of the airplane, a single tail shoreline is adequate. If there is not a handy tree, use your anchor (see Figure 13.5)

If heavy weather is expected

For heavy weather, some prefer their aircraft to be at anchor or on a buoy. Others prefer to heel up on a beach.

I fall into the latter category, provided I can find a sheltered place to heel up, because the aircraft is where I can get to it, during the storm, to add lines, add ballast (water) to the floats, pull it farther up on shore or even move it. Also, if the aircraft is damaged by the storm, I would rather it was ashore where I could fix it rather than upside down in the water or at the bottom of the lake.

The two main disadvantages of heeling up include the damage that may be caused to the floats by the up and down pounding of the aircraft responding to wave action, and the inability of the heeled up aircraft to respond to a wind direction change. A change in wind direction may result in large waves coming onshore to what earlier was a sheltered beach.

Figure 13.5. The Bruce anchor works ashore, too. A strong pull on the line would cause the anchor to bury itself ever deeper.

Often, after frontal passage, the wind will settle down to a steady breeze lasting a day or more. One option to allowing the aircraft to pound for hours while heeled up is to move the aircraft a few feet off the beach, anchoring it there (figure 13.7). Yes, you will get wet wading or swimming back to shore but the aircraft can lie there, bobbing up and down, a few feet from shore, without damage.

To move the aircraft in such a breeze takes some planning and preparation. Get out your ground tackle (anchor and rode). Flake the rode down in a figure 8 just behind the pilot's seat so it will run out smoothly after you drop the anchor. Have the bridle fashioned and tied (for the propeller or bow cleats), clear of tangles and handy. I like to use a 100 foot long line for the rode in this case as it gives me more margin for error in placing the anchor yet still allows me to select how far from shore the aircraft is tied. I like to lay the bitter end of the rode along the top of the left float and tie it off to the bow cleat, just in case things don't go exactly as planned and the rode slips from cold, wet fingers. The pilot's door won't close completely with the rode tied outside but that's OK.

Figure 13.6. An ideal spot to heel up - a wooden ramp constructed with the correct slope. Note tires under heels of the floats and fore and aft wing strut shorelines - a very secure tiedown.

Now take your other 100 foot line, tie one end to a tree or bush near the beach and the other end to the tail stinger tiedown point. Flake the rest of the line on the beach, so it cannot tangle as you taxi away from the beach. This line serves at least two purposes: (a) to tell you when you are 80-90 feet from the beach by the tug on the tail when you taxi out, and (b) later, when the wind abates, it will keep the anchored airplane from swinging or drifting away from shore, thus preventing a long swim to the airplane.

Now, the game plan is to taxi out 75-90 feet from shore, kill the engine, drop the anchor and drift back, snubbing the rearward drift before you reach shore. Tie the rode off temporarily to the left bow cleat and attach the bridle to the prop. Note: check magneto switches off before rotating the prop, then slip the bridle on the prop blade closest to you, rotate the prop downward (counterclockwise as seen from the pilot's seat) while holding the bridle tight so it won't slip off while the blade is down, until you can get the other loop of the bridle over the other prop blade.

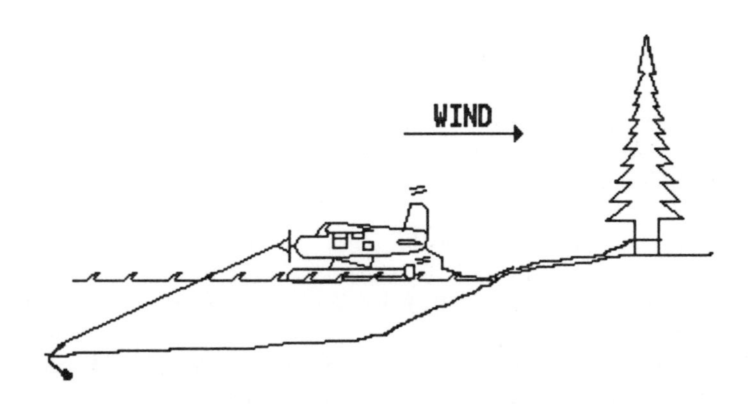

Figure 13.7. Anchored just off the beach.

Ah, you have discovered an advantage of attaching the bridle to the prop instead of to the bow cleats! The whole process can be accomplished from the left float. Now remove the rode from the left bow cleat where you temporarily secured it, and attach it to the center of the anchor bridle.

The last steps are: (1) move the fuel selector valve to the "off" position to prevent fuel transfer from wing to wing. (I prefer not to use Cessna's "left" or "right" positions because if I forget the fuel selector valve on the departure checklist, the engine will quit after a few feet of taxi - the perfect reminder. If it is "left" or "right" and I forget, I might take off with it that way, which is a no-no.) (2) insert the control lock to keep the elevator from thumping the stops if the aircraft gets to pitching up and down from wave action. (3) close the door, double check all lines and knots and practice your "walking-on-water" back to shore. Now is when you will appreciate that roaring campfire and dry clothes hung out as part of your earlier preparation.

The line tied to the tail of the airplane and the tree on the beach should be left slack, but you can mark it and check it once in awhile to see if your anchor is dragging. If the anchor drags, the worse case scenario is that the aircraft is back on the beach again. If the holding ground is good, a good anchor will dig in and the aircraft will bob up and down with some pitching but happy not to be bumping the beach.

Should the water rudders be up or down? That depends on who you ask! There are those who feel that the rudders should be up because there will be less wear and tear on the rudder hinges. Others will point out that the airplane will swing or sail at anchor much less with the rudders down, putting less strain on the ground tackle, which is true. Mine will be down unless I have reason to distrust my anchor set or the quality of the holding ground. If the aircraft drifts back onto the shore, and I'm not there to catch it, it would be best if the water rudders were up.

Let me pause here to make the point that anchoring off the beach would not be a good maneuver if the wind were to get very strong. I would consider anchoring off if the wind was expected to stay below 30 knots. If it gets a lot stronger than that, there is the possibility the aircraft would fly at anchor because the wing's angle of attack will get large every time the nose pitches up to accomodate a wave. If really serious wind is anticipated, pull the aircraft up on the beach as far as possible and scuttle the floats (fill one or more chambers with water). Keep in mind while ambitiously putting water into the floats that, when the wind abates, that water must come back out. This may take hours or even days with one small seaplane float pump. Properly scuttled, the floats will rest on the bottom with waves breaking over them but (hopefully) under the fuselage.

Also, anchoring off is not advised unless the leeward shoreline is friendly. In other words, the shoreline that the aircraft would sail to if the anchor dragged should be free of rocks and snags.

If you have an aversion to getting wet, and you are going to stay for a few days, you may want to rig up a "clothesline" mooring for your airplane, as shown in figure 13.8. This requires at least one but preferably two blocks. Use two lines of 100 feet each, tied into the blocks with knots located as shown. A 50 foot rode on the anchor will do, provided the scope is adequate (at least 7:1 or more). In this case, the anchor will need to be placed about 130 feet from shore. Rigging this system is greatly facilitated by the use of a boat, and is much easier to rig if done before the onset of onshore winds.

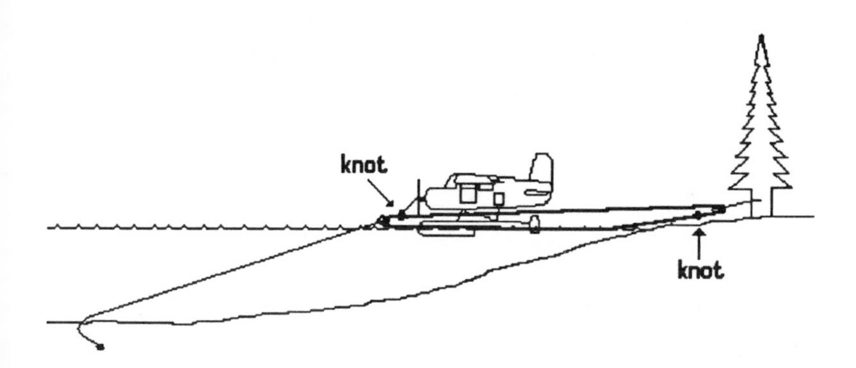

Figure 13.8. The "clothesline" mooring.

The clothesline mooring greatly facilitates bringing the aircraft out to anchor and back again to shore but has the disadvantage in that there is always a chance that a line will chafe in two on a float keel. If this occurs, the system would be disabled but the aircraft would not be lost, if knots were properly placed and tied.

Anchoring

Although our ship's logs show that I have been at anchor more than 1000 nights in all kinds of weather in many strange, beautiful or unusual places on our globe, I still don't feel completely comfortable at anchor. There's something about relying on a piece of metal you can't see and some nylon line to combat the forces of mother nature that makes a skeptic of me. Yet, every statistic available indicates that anchoring, if done properly, is a secure process. In all the times that I have anchored, I have only drug anchor once and have never broken any ground tackle.

There are some excellent anchor designs on the market today. One of the most recent successful designs is the Bruce anchor from the

United Kingdom. It was originally developed to meet the rigorous requirements of the offshore oil and gas drilling rigs in the North Sea. It did seem to outperform other types of more conventional anchors in those very difficult conditions, so it was manufactured in smaller sizes for pleasure boating. The Bruce is claimed to have the holding power of other designs 3 to 4 times its size and weight.

To describe the Bruce anchor verbally is difficult, but basically it has an L shaped shank developed at its toe into a radiused triple palm. It is designed so that no matter how it lands on the bottom, it will turn over and dig in, usually within its own length. Most of a Bruce anchor can be seen in figure 13.5, where it is being used to secure a tail shoreline.

The two main disadvantages of the Bruce are that it does not fold up so it is more difficult to store and it is more expensive than most conventional designs. Storage is not that much of a problem, I have found, because the anchor is so small in dimensions. The additional expense is justified because the anchor is made of very high tensile steel.

I carry two of them, one of 2 Kg. (4.4 pounds) and the other 5 Kg. (11 pounds). They nest together for storage. With two anchors, the options for anchoring increase considerably. Anchoring in a gale is a much surer process, or the anchors can be set in such a way that the radius of swing of the aircraft at anchor is greatly reduced - this is

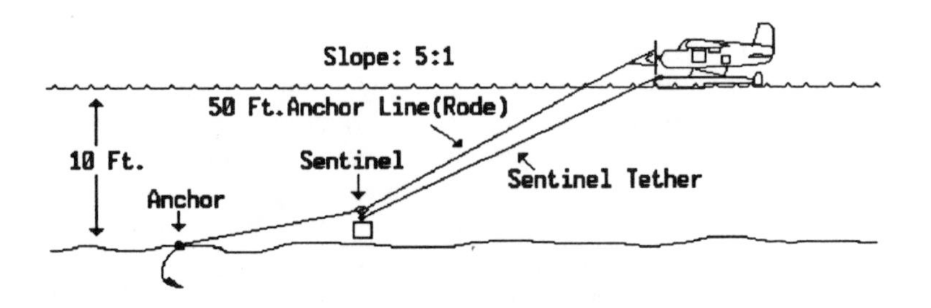

Figure 13.9. The Sentinel in use on an anchor rode.

very helpful when anchoring in small places. Two anchors are also very effective when used ashore while heeled up where there are no trees to tie to.

Anchors will dig in well if the pull on them is horizontal, or at least much more horizontal than vertical. Vessels that use line for anchor rode generally use chain for the first 10-20 feet, in order to weight the rode so it pulls more horizontally on the anchor and because chain is more abrasion resistant when dragged across rocks and sharp objects on the bottom.

Because of the extra weight and storage problems of chain, the seaplane typically will use 3/8" nylon line tied directly to the anchor (with an anchor bend knot, please). Therefore, to get a proper horizontal pull, sufficient scope must be used. The **scope** (ratio of rode length to water depth) should never be less than 5:1 and 10:1 will usually be better, unless the rode is abrading on rocks on the bottom.

A method to improve the holding ability of a small anchor in severe conditions is with the use of a sentinel. The sentinel is a weight which is passed down the anchor rode by means of a block, to a point 2/3 of the way down the rode (see figure 13.9). There, it acts as a weight to cause the rode to pull more horizontally on the anchor. It also absorbs shocks of the airplane tugging on the rode by being lifted off the bottom. I have not yet encountered the need for this but I know I can easily fashion a sentinel using the plastic milk storage box (in which I keep my ground tackle and other assorted but necessary junk neatly stored in the airplane) filled with rocks.

Alongside a dock

When tied to a dock in heavier weather, the seaplane is only as secure as the dock itself. How secure is the dock? Not being able to answer this question is one of several great reasons not to use a dock for mooring when the wind is expected to blow.

Another reason is that, tied to a dock, the aircraft may be in quite deep water which means that the aircraft will go under if the floats are damaged in very many places. Also, the dock is hard and durable and the floats are thin!

Figure 13.10. Moored on the edge of a bed of reeds.

The comfort of a dock is alluring. It is a great place to load and unload the aircraft but it may be best to relocate the aircraft if staying long.

Sometimes mother nature provides some good places to moor that are a bit unusual. It is a good idea to be alert for these. Figure 13.10 shows a floatplane pulled in against a bed of reeds. The reeds grow out into the water that's deep enough to float the aircraft, yet they provide a "bumper" that is soft enough to tie up to.

When tied to a dock, it is a good idea to rig some sort of a standoff. The aircraft in figure 13.11 is getting some help in staying away from the dock by a bungee cord attached to the wing strut tiedown point and the dock.

To provide a better angle for a standoff, some aircraft have another tiepoint installed farther out on the wing.

Figure 13.11. Lying off a dock with a standoff rigged.

An easy to build seasonal or short term dock.

If long logs are available, one can easily fashion a seasonal dock on a lake or in fast water like one I used on the Yukon River in Alaska. See figure 13.12. The pivot log is lashed firmly ashore. One or two more logs are lashed to the pivot log for adequate footing. A long, thin log is cross-lashed at the seaward end so that the dock can be brought into or away from the shore to accomodate changing water levels. The aircraft is moored facing upstream in fast water or toward the lake, possibly with lines ashore.

On a permanent mooring

A permanent mooring is only as good as you know its weakest fitting or line to be, or as heavy or well set as you know its anchor to be. Excellent permanent moorings can be made in the wilderness using three anchors as in figure 13.13. The advantage of this system is that the necessary components, 3 anchors, some chain, a pennant and buoy, are lightweight and don't require much space in the airplane to get them out to the wilderness site. They will work as well or better than trying to fly in an old motor block or barrel full of cement.

Placing the anchors will require some thought and effort. They should be placed 120 degrees apart so that no matter what the wind

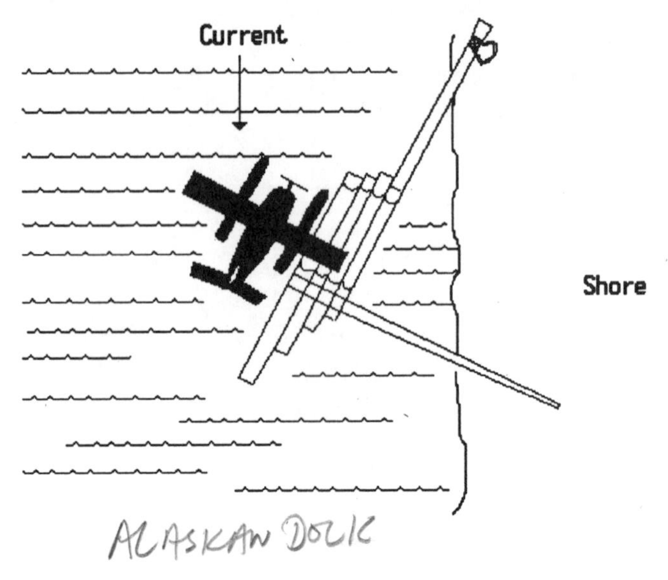

Figure 13.12. An easy-to-build seasonal dock.

direction, one or two anchors will be upwind. Set each anchor as well as you can before linking the three together to the rode line or chain with a shackle.

The permanent mooring is properly marked with a buoy, white in color with a horizontal blue stripe. If a buoy is used, it should be of the type that transmits load directly through the buoy using chain or rod.

When anchoring a vessel, the buoy performs a useful function in that the pull on the vessel is more horizontal, allowing the vessel's bow to rise more easily to waves. This may not be a useful function for seaplane anchoring in that it is not desirable for the seaplane's bow to rise to a wave or gust as that will increase the wing's angle of attack and, consequently, its lift. Tethered flight is not the desired result! Therefore, it may be best to have a small float to mark the mooring's location and to hold the pennant end at the surface, rather than a proper buoy.

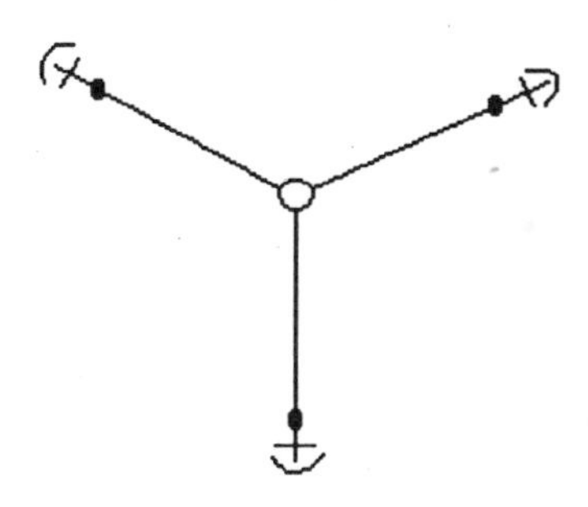

Figure 13.13. A lightweight permanent mooring

Suggested mooring equipment, 2500-3500 lb. seaplane.

The knowledge needed to properly use the following, and
2 anchors of choice of two sizes.
3-4 lines, 3/8" diameter, 40-50 feet long.
2 lines, 3/8" diameter, 100 feet long
2 blocks, for 3/8" line
1 thimble, for 3/8" line (to fashion a prop bridle, etc.)
2 chafe guards
1 box or bag to contain and restrain anchors and blocks,
useful as a sentinel when filled with rocks.

A float pilot, name of R. Potter
chased after the farmer's daughter

when he didn't, he fished
and flew around as he wished.

Loved the wild bushes, he did
'til he found her with kid

then his seaplane went to the slaughter.

CHAPTER 14

Wilderness Operations

If one word could be selected to describe successful wilderness operations, it would be "CAUTION". If two words were permitted, they would be "EXTRA CAUTION". Because an incident, accident or just plain bad luck that causes us inconvenience or expense when near civilization, may be life-threatening in the wilderness. All wilderness operations should be thought up, thought through and accomplished with EXTRA CAUTION foremost.

Many seaplane operations have been discussed, in detail, in other chapters. Most discussions have centered around how knowledge of basic principles can be used to promote safety in seaplane operations. They need not be repeated here, except to again mention the concept of the pilot's "seventh sense" (chapter 10). Basically, that seventh sense is nothing more than a habit of constant awareness of risk. "If I do this or that, how much risk will I expose myself or my passengers to?" This question needs to be asked, and the risk management principles applied if there is risk. This concept is valid whether one is picking up an axe to cut firewood or thinking out the consequences of step taxiing instead of displacement taxiing the rest of the way from the landing place to camp.

Preparation for the Wilderness

Time spent in remote areas can be enjoyed more, with more comfort and less stress if the participants are prepared and have the right equipment.

Tom Hron and St. Cloud Aviation, an individual and organization skilled in wilderness operations, have suggested the following as the <u>minimum</u> recommended qualifications for arctic flying:

Pilot Skill

1. Competent pilot skills in 25-35 knot winds.
2. Ability to navigate by maps at low altitudes.
3. Ability to hold heading within 2 to 3 degrees for long periods of time.
4. Good skills in inbound and outbound tracking with ADF.
5. Sound knowledge of actual fuel consumption of the aircraft.

Aircraft equipment

1. Radio equipment for communications.
2. ELT (2), one personal or portable type, waterproofed.
3. Accurate compass.
4. Accurate D.G.
5. Accurate ADF.

Clothing (in addition to other common clothing normally used).

1. Lightweight winter underwear.
2. Wool socks.
3. Warm trousers and shirts.
4. Goosedown vest and jacket.
5. Waterproof leather boots.
6. Gloves.
7. Lightweight hip boots.
8. Rain gear.
9. Warm cap or hat.
10. Mosquito head net.
11. Repellant jacket.
12. Life vests.

Outdoor Equipment

1. Cooking gear and stove with fuel.
2. Tent and sleeping bags.
3. First-aid Kit.
4. Sterno and waterproof matches
5. Rope
6. Tool kit suitable for seaplane.
7. Mosquito coils and repellants.
8. Fuel cans
9. Siphon hose (doubles as oil drain hose)
10. Filter funnel

Optional Items

1. Firearm (required in sparsely settled areas of Alaska, Canada).
2. Honing stone or file.
3. Flashlight with spares.
4. Sewing kit
5. Candles.
6. Pump for fuel.
7. Battery or battery charger.
8. Inflatable raft with floor and air pump.
9. Outboard motor with extra shearpins.

As you read the chapters in this book, it becomes apparent that many skills are important or valuable for wilderness flying. Perhaps one of the real challenges in water flying is that no one person ever reaches the ultimate level of knowledge and experience. We are all learning and having fun while doing it.

Operations in Canada

One area of interest to the pilot flying into a foreign country is the rules of flight that are different in that country. Most seaplane flying outside of US airspace is done in Canada, so here is a brief summary, valid at time of publishing, of differences from US rules, to keep in mind when flying Canada.

Some major differences in Canada-US procedures:

1. "1000" on top (VFR on top) is not permitted under VFR rules.

2. Only IFR and "controlled VFR" flights are permitted in the Block Airspace (see the Supplements or A.I.P.)

3. Magnetic tracks are used in the Southern Domestic airspace and True tracks are used in Northern Domestic airspace. (see Supplements)

4. Positive Control Zones (PCZ) surround all large Canadian airports. A pilot must obtain clearance from ATC to enter a PCZ, even if VFR. While within a PCZ, the pilot must maintain a listening watch

on the appropriate ATC frequency and comply with ATC instructions.

5. Altimeter setting procedures are detailed in the supplements.

6. When enroute in uncontrolled airspace listen on 126.7 MHz. Always broadcast, on the same frequency, position reports, cruising level, and immediately prior to doing so, any altitude changes, and other flight manoeuvers, in order to alert and inform other pilots in the vicinity of your position and intentions. When it is the intention to land at, or when operating in the vicinity of, uncontrolled airports with no air/ground communications pilots should broadcast position reports on 123.2 MHz. Many uncontrolled airports in Canada have Mandatory Frequencies (MF) which must be used to transmit intentions. Pilots are urged to consult the VFR, Water and/or Northern Supplements for MF information.

7. There are special requirements for flight in designated sparsely settled areas. These are detailed in the Supplements (and discussed in this chapter).

8. The procedures to be followed with regard to the use of an Emergency Locator Transmitter (ELT) are detailed in the Supplements.

9. Compliance with rules pertaining to Air Defense Identification Zones is required. Procedures are detailed in the Supplements.

10. Pilots are required to file a flight plan or flight notification for every cross-country flight when more than 25 nautical miles from the aerodrome of departure. Specific requirements are detailed in the Supplements. A flight itinerary may be filed in lieu of a flight plan or flight notification on an extended itinerary.

11. Special procedures are in effect at some Land and Water aerodromes with which all operators of aircraft using these aerodromes must comply. These procedures are published in the appropriate Supplement.

12. As in the US, there are several classifications of airspace, with different VFR minimums. These are listed in the A.I.P.

Sparsely settled areas are defined by a special line on Canadian VFR Navigation charts (equivalent of the US Sectional chart) and in the

RAC section of the A.I.P. For flight into sparsely settled areas in single engine aircraft flying more than 25 nautical miles from an airport or SPB, the following must be on board the aircraft (RAC 2.12.5):

1. Emergency food supply of 10,000 calories per person, sealed in a waterproof container and of a type not subject to deterioration by heat or cold.
2. Cooking utensils.
3. Matches in waterproof container.
4. Stove and fuel (if operating north of the tree line).
5. Portable compass.
6. Axe - weight not less than 2.5 pounds, handle not less than 28 inches.
7. Flexible saw blade or equivalent cutting tool.
8. 30 ft. of snare wire plus instructions for use.*
9. Fishing equipment appropriate to the area.
10. Gill net, not more than 2" mesh.*
11. Mosquito netting and insect repellant.
12. Tent or other means of shelter.
13. Signal mirror.
14. Flares.*
15. Knife.
16. Conspicuity panel.

*(Author's note) Gill netting is very difficult to find. I have found that asking for it in stores in Canada or the US usually results in frowns and a lecture as it is illegal to use in most areas. Many survival experts agree that gill nets and snare wire are not useful applications of survival energy unless one is skilled at setting these devices. I have always been nervous about carrying pyrotechnics (flares) aboard my aircraft. They are considered hazardous materials if transported in interstate commerce.

More lists

The checklist of equipment I carry in the aircraft is divided into two categories:

Equipment that stays in the airplane while it is on floats:

ground tackle (see chapter 13)
2.5-3 pound axe with 28" handle

bow saw, collapsible
aircraft survival kit (see listing, this chapter)
duct tape (100 mph tape)
aluminum foil tape (250 mph tape)
paper towels and windshield cleaner
oil drain (and siphon) hose
flashlight, extra batteries
tool kit
fuel funnel/filter
toilet paper
aircraft documents
cargo net and bungee cords
fishing kit, micro (rod, reel, lures)
life vests, inflatable
waterproof matches
insect repellant
float repair kit, containing:
    030 aluminum patches
    self-tapping metal screws
    Goop
    water activated fiberglass repair kit
my personal life vest, containing:
    matches in waterproof container
    plastic bags, 1 gal. ziplock
    space blanket
    compass
    wire saw
    insect repellant
water filter and thermos

Equipment added to the aircraft for wilderness trips:

aircraft oil sufficient for trip
jerry jug, 5 gal. (1 or 2)
appropriate charts, facilities directories, supplements, IFR kit
rifle, ammunition

See chapter 15 for camping equipment.

Survival kit

Mine weighs 10 pounds, is 4" in diameter, 20" long and fits under the rear seat, if installed. It contains the following items:

4 solar blankets
1 6'x 8' plastic tarp
4 plastic ponchos
2 fire starter/flare sticks
1 liquid filled compass
1 ring saw
1 whistle
1 chemical light stick
50' nylon rope, 100 lb. test
50 matches, waterproof
2 candles
1 signal mirror
2 safety pins
1 razor blade
3' wire
1 knife, multi purpose
10' duct tape
4 aluminum foil, 18"x 3'
2 ziplock bags
1 metal match
1 sewing kit
1 sun screen stick
1 fish hook, line, sinker
4 limb insulators
1 tool kit
1 strobe light

Medical supplies

1 roll surgical tape
16 bandaids
8 2x2 gauze pads
8 3x3 gauze pads
8 4x4 compress bandages
1 roll gauze bandage
1 triangle bandage
3 antiseptic towelettes
3 alcohol wipes
3 soap
6 buffered aspirin
21 salt tablets
1 ammonia inhalant
1 decongestant tablets
1 antibacterial ointment

1 tweezer
1 pkg. insect first-aid pads
1 tourniquet
2 burn dressings
10 water purifier tablets
1 vial
1 finger splint

Food Supplies **Note:** Only * items have a shelf life of 5 years and are packed in the 10 pound survival kit.

20,000 calories, consisisting of
granola bars
peanut bars
raisins *
instant soup mix*
sugar*
boullion cubes*
hot cocoa mix
survival rations*

Kit packaging

1 4"x20" PVC cylinder
2 4" rubber caps
1 survival and first-aid manual
1 contents and weight label
1 plastic handle & strap

Shelf life of survival kit contents is a difficult problem. After five years, I dissasembled the original kit and found that some things just do not store for that length of time. Normal batteries will not store that long. Food with oil such as nuts will not store well and should be replaced at a maximum of 2 years. Raisins store very well if you don't mind the sugar in them having crystallized. Some medicines probably lose their effectiveness in that time, especially at extreme temperature.

The above kit, which was made up from individually purchased items, should give you a base list for comparison purposes, when making up or purchasing a survival kit. When making up a list, keep in mind what you normally carry in the airplane and personal toilet kit. Probably, some of those items do not need to be duplicated in the survival kit.

The difference between remote area and civilized area navigation

I have always considered myself at least an adequate navigator. As skipper and navigator on voyages up to 2800 miles of open ocean, and many hours of cross country flight, I have always ended up where I wanted to go. The most frustrating navigation I have had to do was my early experiences at low level or low visibility "bush" navigation. This type of navigation requires some special skills to be developed, along with some 'tricks-of-the-trade'.

Most pilots are 'part-time' navigators. Their cockpit workload distracts from the continuous terrain recognition needed to accomplish pilotage navigation in the bush, which offers the multi-headed problem of low visibility, short distance to the horizon due to low altitude and often featureless terrain. Flight in 'civilized' areas doesn't require continuous attention to terrain recognition because features are usually well-defined, flight is at higher altitudes so the pilot can see farther, and navaids, including Loran reception, remove the guesswork. In short, the pilot becomes a lazy navigator.

After watching me try with little success to apply "civilized" navigation procedures to low level or low visibility wilderness navigation, an "old-timer" said, "look, I know what you are trying to do. It doesn't work very well up here. You are trying to identify a point on-course up ahead, and fly to it. That works fine when you are a few thousand feet above the ground and the visibility is fifteen plus. Up here, forget that! Use your compass. Once you have reached cruising altitude, maintain your chosen heading, even though you can see it is taking you somewhat off course. Fly that chosen heading for 6, 12, or 15 miles. Then determine how far off course you are. Use the **rule-of-sixty** to determine how many degrees you are off course and Bingo!, you know your wind correction angle (WCA)."

Using The-Rule-of-Sixty

This rule says that a right-angle triangle with the adjacent side [a] being 60 units long will have an opposite side [b] of length in units equal to the number of degrees of the angle. For example, if side [a] = 60 units and side [b] = 2 units, the angle will be 2 degrees (see figure 14.1A). Or, according to figure 14.1B, if you fly for 60 miles and are 10 miles off course, you are 10 degrees off course.

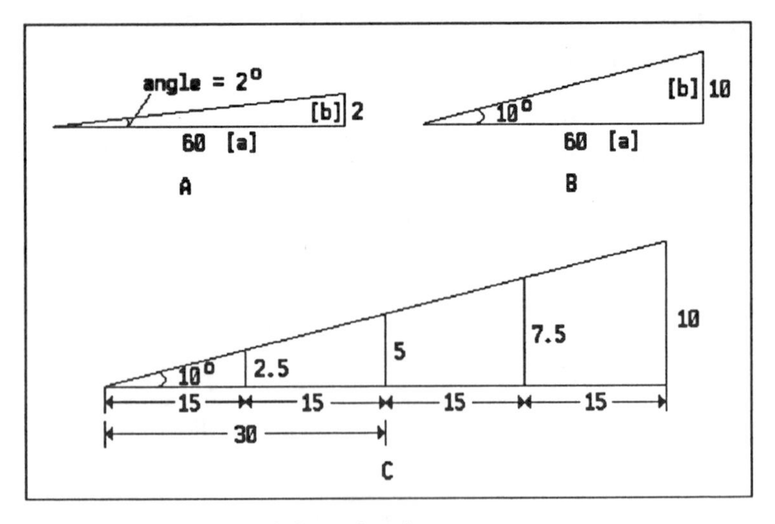

Figure 14.1. The rule-of-sixty triangle.

The triangle is proportional. If you are 10 degrees off course, you are 10 miles off course in 60 miles or 5 miles off course in 30 miles, or 2.5 miles off course in 15 miles, etc., as depicted in figure 14.1C. If a distance of 15 miles is used, 60 is divided by 15 an even 4 times, so multiply the off course distance by 4 to get the angle. With very little practice, this sort of mental problem will be easier and quicker to do than spelling your own name!

Let's try one. We fly for six miles (3 minutes at 120 knots or 4 minutes at 90 knots) and find, by reference to the chart, that we are one mile to the left of the course line drawn on the chart. Six is one tenth of sixty, so 10 x 1 mile off course = 10 (the length of side [B]), which is equal to the angle. We are 10 degrees left of course (see figure 14.2). A correction of 10 degrees to the right will cause us to parallel the intended course, one mile to the left of it. Ten degrees is the WCA. If we were on our intended course, adding 10 degrees to our old heading should keep us on course.

The rule-of-sixty will also tell us how much more we should turn right in order to get back on course. First, we must decide how many miles we are willing to proceed before returning to the original course. For this example (figure 14.2), we wish to be back on the original course line 15 miles after making the correction. So, for the rule-of-sixty triangle, side [a] is 15 miles, side [b] is one mile, so the angle is __? Look at figure 14.2 and figure it out.

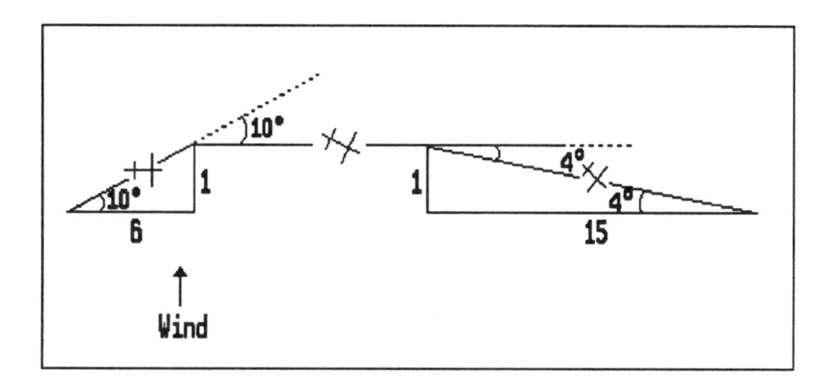

Figure 14.2. The rule-of-sixty will find the course correction.

You are right if you came up with 4 degrees. If we are paralleling the course, one mile left of course then turn right 4 degrees, we should be back on course in 15 miles. Once back on course, correct 4 degrees left and we will be on a heading that will carry us along the desired track unless the wind changes.

The "old-timer" was right. It is easier to hold a precise heading, determine the WCA and correct the heading, then identify terrain features while flying a precise heading, as compared to trying to identify a feature ahead, on the desired track and fly to it. This is because, when the visibility is 3 miles, there is rarely a ready-made feature just 3 miles ahead when you need it.

Some <u>WARNINGS</u> and notes:

<u>WARNING</u>: The rule-of-sixty becomes inaccurate for angles of 30 degrees and more.

Note: If you would like to test the "old-timer's" concept and develop your low level or low visibility navigation skills, find at least 100 miles of featureless terrain to fly over that is unfamiliar to you. Fly over it at minimum safe altitude. You will probably find yourself trying to navigate by what the "old-timer" called "civilized navigation". See how long it is before you cry "MAIL!" (<u>My</u> <u>A</u>__ <u>I</u>s <u>L</u>ost!). Now try the "old-timer's bush navigation" seriously for several trips, until you are skilled at it. Then decide for yourself if he was right. For me, it really works.....most of the time. When it doesn't, always have a "bacon-saver" (chapter 11).

To summarize the "Old-timer's" point, bush navigation at low levels or in poor visibility requires a change in technique and philosophy. Instead of using pilotage (selecting direction based on identified landmarks, which is the way we navigate when all conditions are good, and the way we drive a car and walk across the street, so we are used to doing it this way) as the primary direction reference, we must use precise heading control from our gyrocompass (which is why this instrument was dealt with in detail in chapter 11).

The gyrocompass becomes primary for direction control, the rule-of-sixty makes easy the task of determining the WCA, and pilotage is the backup system. This requires we break an old habit. The more this new skill is practiced, the better the results will be and the more the pilot becomes a confident bush navigator.

The Automatic Direction Finder (ADF)

We all know how to calibrate or determine the accuracy of our VOR navigation system but little is written about ADF accuracy. To many pilots, the ADF is a navigation system that is of little use. Occasionally, it is turned on to listen to a ball game (come to think of it, the last time I turned mine on was to listen to the presidential debates), or to watch the needle swing. Most of the time, the ADF just gathers dust.

On a trip into the wilderness, however, it is likely you will use it. So, part of your preparation to go should be a calibration flight. It is as easy to calibrate the ADF as it is to do the magnetic compass.

Let's start with a brief discussion of ADF errors.

Night error - at night, radio waves at ADF frequencies propagate differently. During the day these waves travel by what is called groundwave propagation. In this mode, the waves travel in a tunnel between the earth and the ionosphere in a reliable (or predictable) manner. At night, skywave propagation becomes common. In this mode, the waves are bent and reflected from the ionosphere, making the waves travel farther and creating justifiable doubt about the direction of the origin of the signal. This is evidenced by a wandering and nervous ADF needle.

Shoreline error - radio waves travel at slightly different speeds over water, ice masses and land. So, when crossing a boundary between two of these landforms, the radio wave changes direction somewhat. If the wave crosses the boundary (shoreline) at a 90 degree angle, little bending takes place but as the angle changes from 90°, bending increases (see figure 14.3). If the aircraft is homing on the station, a slight turn at the shoreline would be required but if the aircraft in figure 14.3 is taking a fix on the station, using a line of position from the station, an error in position would result.

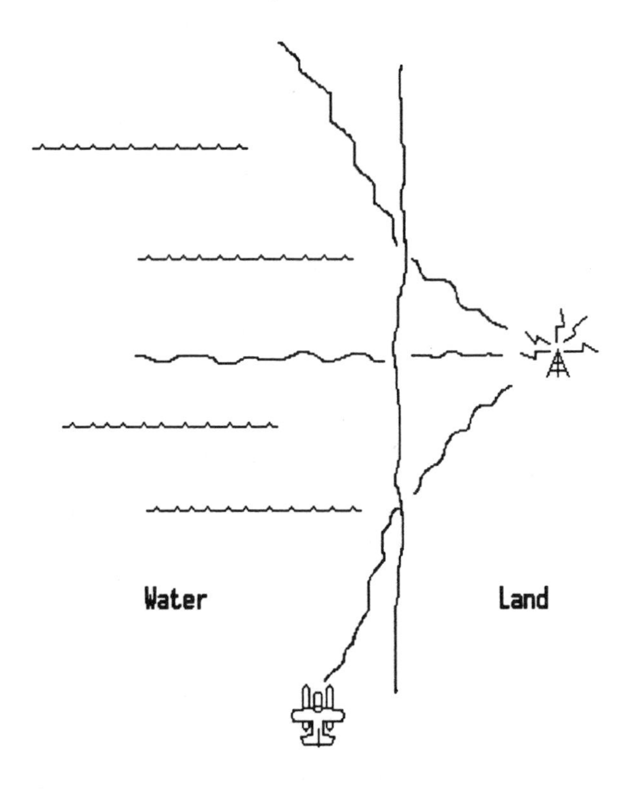

Figure 14.3. Shoreline error.

Quadrantal error is an error induced by the structure of the aircraft itself. Because of the geometry of the aircraft structure, relative bearings (relative to the nose of the aircraft) are typically more accurate at 0, 90, 180, and 270 degrees, and less accurate at 45, 135, 225, and 315 degrees relative bearing. This error can be virtually eliminated by calibrating your installation as outlined below.

Instrument error is error in the instrument (radio and antenna). This error also is eliminated by the calibration described below.

ADF Calibration

From the discussion of errors above, it should be apparent that ADF error may differ depending on where (relative to the aircraft) the signal is coming from. Therefore, we need a "deviation card" for the ADF just like the one for the magnetic compass (see figure 14.4).

Here is the procedure:

(1) Select a nearby station in the aeronautical radio beacon frequency range. Preferably, it should be one whose location is visible from a considerable distance (5-15 miles).

(2) Locate the station, and another prominent point 15-30 miles from the station, on the chart and draw a line on the chart between the two points and determine magnetic direction (bearing) of the line. Let's assume we find it is 086 degrees magnetic to the station for the following example.

(3) On a day with good visibility, light low-level winds and little turbulence, depart the airport and fly as far away from the transmitting station as you can yet still be able to see where the station is. Point the aircraft at the station, carefully aligning the longitudinal axis with the visible location of the station. Note the ADF relative bearing.

Figure 14.4. An ADF bearing deviation card.

ADF Indicated Relative Bearing											
360	030	060	090	120	150	180	210	240	270	300	330
ADF Actual Relative Bearing											
002	034	063	089	117	148	180	214	245	272	304	336

Figure 14.5 and 14.6. Wilderness navigation is certainly not all featureless terrain. The above picture was taken at 6800 feet in the Yukon. The picture below was taken at 11,000 feet (yes, from a floatplane!), looking north from just southwest of Mt. McKinley, Alaska.

(4) If the RB is not within 10 degrees of 360, an avionics technician can correct this error if the error is known. This should be done before proceeding.

(5) Now fly to the vicinity of the point you selected on your chart that is 15-30 miles from the transmitting station. Roll out on a heading of 086 magnetic and set your gyrocompass to zero degrees (correct the indicated magnetic compass reading to actual MH using your recently-done magnetic deviation correction card (chapter 11) so that the aircraft is flying the actual magnetic heading of 086 degrees).

(6) After setting the gyrocompass (which is now reading magnetic heading relative to the transmitter site), arrive over the chosen point on the magnetic heading of the line on your chart (086 degrees in this example, which is the actual magnetic bearing to the station and will provide a zero degrees relative bearing as shown on the gyrocompass). Note the ADF indicated relative bearing.

Since the aircraft is pointed at the station, this RB should agree with the one you found in procedure (3). This RB should be noted for later entry underneath "360" on your ADF deviation card (figure 14.4).

(7) Now, just as you did to calibrate your magnetic compass, staying close to the selected ground point, roll out on relative bearings (gyrocompass readings) of 30, 60, 90, etc. (or, if you wish, 015, 030, 045, 060, etc.), read and record the ADF indicated relative bearings. It would be a good idea to do this procedure at least once, circling in both directions. If the values from both directions disagree by a little, average them. If they disagree by a lot, repeat the procedure. If they still disagree by a lot, it's time to visit the ADF hospital or maybe the store that sells new ADF's!

(8) Back at home base, make up an ADF deviation card for installation on the panel near the ADF indicator, and enjoy ADF navigation on your wilderness trip, confident that you really do know how much "truth" is coming from your ADF indicator!

An inconvenient or expensive mistake near civilization can be life-threatening in the wilderness!

There once was a great seaplane pilot
whose name, you'd agree, was a riot.

He ate as he flew
'til one day he grew

in serious need of a diet.

CHAPTER 15

Seaplane Camping

Going Light.....In Comfort

As far as I'm concerned, comfort camping is the name of my game. I've been cold, wet, thirsty, and hurt but only to the point of being uncomfortable.

Those experiences were learning ones. I learned that I could be even better prepared to go into the bush, and, if I was, I could be comfortable and better able to enjoy the bush and all its beauty.

The Plan

In planning for an excursion into the bush, I like to look at the worst case scenario and the best case, and plan for both. This requires some imagination because each trip is different.

An example of a worst case scenario might be planning a trip 400 miles north of the U.S.-Canadian border into Canada's "sparsely settled area", including an engine failure, coming down in trees or into a lake but ending up inverted, with some swimming to do.

The "most comfortable" outcome of this situation depends on preparedness, at least in the following areas:

I. Personal Knowledge
a. First Aid, including knowledge of hypothermia and its effects
b. CPR training
c. Survival training (see chapter 16)
d. Some knowledge of submerged aircraft recovery
e. Knowlege of the ELT/EPIRB/SARSAT system, how it works best and what its limitations are.
f. Some knowledge of aircraft mechanics and emergency repair
g. Knowledge of wilderness seaplane operations

II. Personal Resources (pilot and passengers)
a. Able bodied
b. Bush experience
c. Areas of expertise
d. Special equipment

e. Personal equipment

You may wish to look over the above list of personal knowledge and resources to see if there are some areas in which you are deficient. If there are, rejoice! You can have a wonderful experience, taking a course or doing a personal study project in preparation for future floatplane camping trips. For example, the Wilderness Pilot's Association, a large organization of aviation students at the University of North Dakota, each year sponsors a wilderness survival activity of at least 3 days duration. To prepare for this experience, the participants must first become first aid and CPR qualified and attend a one day survival lecture given by the same expert who conducts the excursion. During the excursion, advanced wilderness first aid is taught. A great deal of learning occurs and a lot of confidence is built during this sort of activity.

It is amazing how attendance at this sort of "hands-on" training activity improves one's confidence and even changes one's mind about such things as what needs to be aboard the aircraft and what one's flight clothing should be. We each can become our own authority about what needs to accompany us into the bush in our airplane, rather than reading it in a book and taking someone else's word for it.

For example, I find my thinking has evolved considerably, over the years, about such things as life jackets. At first, I didn't carry life jackets in the floatplane. Then one year, I listened to a presentation on life jackets at a seaplane safety seminar, and, since life jackets were for sale there, I bought three. I threw them back on the hat rack shelf and felt like I had made a great stride forward in water safety. A year later I saw a video on getting out of an inverted seaplane and watched a demonstration in the water. Two of the life jackets came off the hat rack and took the place of some other junk in the pocket in the back of the co-pilot's seat. More recently, I have found that I am most comfortable WEARING an inflatable fisherman's life jacket. It looks good and has lots of pockets, which are filled with other "personal assets" that are worth more than gold in a survival situation where one must get out of and away from the aircraft quickly. Those items include the first two items on my personal survival equipment list: waterproof matches and "bug dope" (regional Canadian slang for insect repellant). Other items in the floatation jacket include a space blanket, 2 one gallon ziplock bags, a portable compass and other assorted items that vary, depending on the nature of the flight.

About the only other item in this category that is always aboard my seaplane, and located where I can grab it in a hurry when going out the door, is a second ELT with it's own antenna, stored in a waterproof container (two ziplock bags). The fixed ELT in any floatplane is worthless if the floatplane goes inverted in the water, isn't it? Even if it activates and works under water, the antenna is now on the bottom of the airplane, 5-10 feet under water!

Self preparation to be confident in the wilderness is an enjoyable activity in itself. If you looked at the list above and felt like you didn't know where to start, don't give up - have fun! It will take some time to accomplish but preparation is an enjoyable activity in and of itself. Some interesting reading on the above subjects can be found in (15.1, 15.3, 15.4, 15.5, 15.6, 15.16).

A major factor in the success of any camping excursion into real wilderness is the companion you select to accompany you. It seems safe to say that the more knowledgeable your companion(s), the more confidence they will have, the more they can contribute and the more they, and you, will enjoy the trip. So, perhaps an inventory of personal knowledge and resources applies to your passengers as well as yourself.

Equipment

Comfort while camping is also affected by the equipment available. Fortunately, we live in a period of time where great strides have been made in the development of lightweight camping and trail equipment. There are many mail order companies offering these goods in their catalogs, so one of the pleasures of outfitting is learning about these products and shopping for the comfort level that suits you at the allowable weight for your aircraft. Some examples of these companies are listed in the resources section for this chapter. (15.9, 15.10, 15.11, 15.12, 15.15)

Unless you are flying the Beaver category of seaplane or larger, it is probably not possible to carry all the gear necessary for a 7-10 day outing for 3 to 4 people, but there is a way to do it using the shuttle method. Carry the essentials for survival, some camp gear and one experienced person on the first trip into the area, select the campsite from an aerial survey of the area, land and discharge your cargo and passenger who can start setting up camp.

Figure 15.1. You want me to put it where?

Remember, in the wilderness each person should never be separated from their own survival necessities! So, unload your passenger's sleeping bag, medications and other essential survival equipment, but not your own!

Then, return to the nearest predetermined point where you can meet the rest of your group who have arrived there by landplane or auto, and shuttle them out to camp.

That method worked great for 3 of us last summer when we decided we needed 7-10 days in the Black Lake area of Saskatchewan, near the Northwest Territories border. We met at Red's Place in La-Ronge. We flew together to Stony Rapids where they landed their Cessna 172 at the airport and hitched a ride for themselves and all their gear down to the river. On the way in, I detoured to survey for a good campsite on Black Lake, so I could tell someone in Stony Rapids where we were going. One person and an airplane full of gear was then flown out to camp. By the time I arrived with our third person and the rest of the equipment, camp was set up and the coffee was on!

Equipment selection is a personal matter. For me, I have found that I am almost always sorry if I don't buy the best. Some items that I have been very pleased with include:

Tent- My tent selection was predicated on a rule I have established over the years which says: "if I am going for more than 2 days, I would like to have a large, comfortable tent and if I am going for less than that, I can afford to stay at a lodge". Therefore, I only need a large, comfortable tent. My most recent selection was a modern, 10' x 10' Eureka! Space II tent which features large, screened windows on all sides that can be opened with a zipper from inside and has an additional 10' x 10' covered and screened front porch which is a great place to sit and enjoy the great outdoors, or to cook if it is raining and the outdoors is not so great. This home-away-from-home weighs 32 pounds and is stored in a bag that is 14" in diameter and 34" long. It got nicknamed the "Hussy Hilton" by a couple of sturdy Canadian lads on its first journey into the north country as we set up camp on Hussy Lake.

Figure 15.2. The Hussy Hilton on Sand Lake, Ontario.

As I said, equipment selection is a personal matter. The "Hussy Hilton" is probably not the tent for the pilot of a J-3 Cub on floats. Eureka! has a very nice catalog with many model tents illustrated. See (15.10).

Air Mattress - I probably wouldn't even mention air mattresses except that I found one that is really remarkable. The "Therm-a-rest" mattress by Cascade Designs, Inc. (15.7) is self-inflating and the most comfortable and best insulating mattress I have ever used. While friends I have camped with struggle through the night with their mattresses, I am oblivious to their problems and getting a good night's sleep. This mattress, although only about an inch thick when inflated, even allows me to sleep comfortably in my Cessna 180, oblivious to the seat rails and tiedown rings. (see Camping in the airplane, this chapter.)

Chairs - Humans, especially pilots, spend a lot of time sitting down. I have two favorite places to sit when camping. In the heat of a sunny day, the boarding step on my Edo floats is a great seat. The fuselage is the backrest and the floatdeck is the footrest. I am in the shade of the wing and there is good airflow all around and there's cool water nearby. Later, when it cools off and the bugs are getting too thick to breathe, a nice chair on the screened front porch of the tent becomes preferable. The Gadabout folding chair, at 3 1/2 pounds, with armrests and backrest is my favorite (15.8). This British invention is not easy to find, and a little expensive but I wish I'd had 100 of them at OSHKOSH this summer. They would have sold quickly and I would have made more than my trip expenses.

Stove - I have a favorite stove, too. In fact, I have two of them. One is very simple, light weight and has no working parts. It is an old stovegrate which I use for cooking over an open fire. This is my favorite way to cook. Somehow, everything just tastes better that way. For me, a cookfire should be small. All the fuel is less than 1" in diameter. That way, it burns quickly and I can regulate the heat by how I add more wood. If I am staying long, I will elevate the cookfire so I can cook standing up or sitting instead of squatting which, at my age, may be nearly a terminal position. Comfort, remember? There are some good stand-alone grills available but they tend to be heavy and bulky.

The other stove is a MSR, which weighs less than a pound and will burn any fuel. My MSR runs on whatever is in the Cessna's fuel tanks at the time. Get the maintenance kit with it. It is available from REI (15.11) and many good sporting goods stores (15.14). This stove is a backup to open fire cooking during hard rains or dry periods when an open fire is not permitted or not a good idea. It also makes a cup of coffee in a hurry in the morning. With an aluminum foil shield, it works quite well in high winds. See figure 15.3.

Water Purifier- Even though you may be flying to some of the beautiful, undisturbed lakes in the far north, and perhaps have been drinking that water, unfiltered, for years, it is far safer to treat the water before drinking it. I take a jug of water with me and refill it, using the filter system described below.

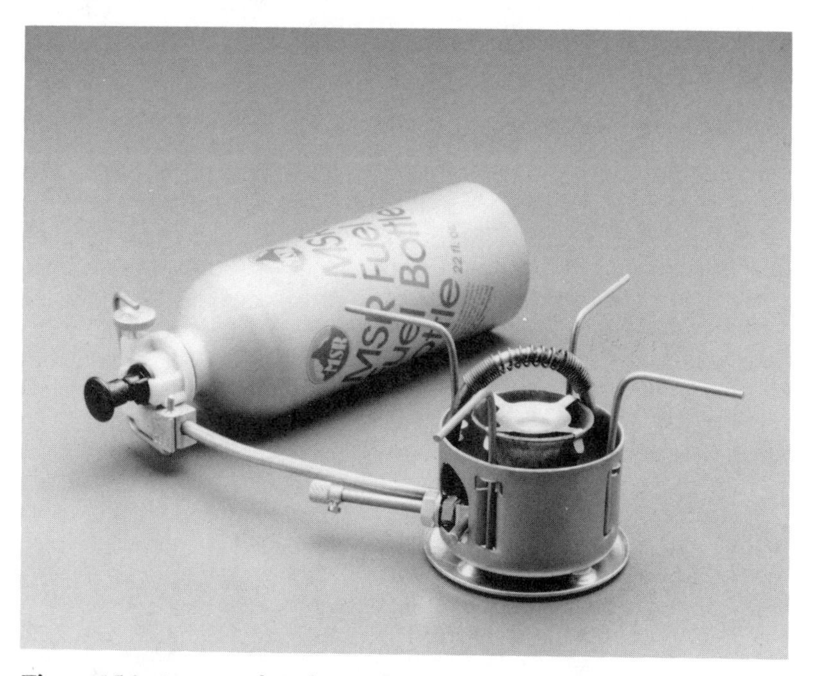

Figure 15.3. An avgas burning stove.

Boiling the water works, as does chemical treatment. The latter is unsuitable to many people because of the strong chemicals that are taken into the body with the water. In recent years, filtration systems have become available that take out of the water most of the "bad guys".

I use the "First Need" filter (15.13) which consists of a hand pump and replaceable filter cartridge. It is effective against Girardia, a particularly nasty small protozoan that produces gastric system distress in humans. Our little dam building friend, the beaver, is reputed to be a Girardia carrier, so filtration or other treatment is a must when water is taken from swampy areas or beaver dams.

I have added four feet of surgical tubing with a small weight at the free end. The other end is attached to the suction end of the pump. A cartridge seems to last me about two seasons. My only complaint is that it is hard to use, as pumping requires both hands, leaving the filter cartridge/discharge spout unmanaged. Overall, I have found this to be a satisfactory system. The water jug and filter remain on board the airplane all of the months of the year that the floats are on the airplane.

Figure 15.4. Wilderness Pilot's Assn. members making filtered water.

Firearms- Another very personal matter. Only rifles and shotguns with barrels of 18" or more may be taken into Canada. I traverse the border regularly with my rifle on board with no problems. I happen to be one of those who is most comfortable with an adequate firearm within reach. Like the lifejackets, I keep it handy, in good condition and I know how to use it, but it is one of the least used "required" items on the equipment list.

My choice for a floatplane firearm is a 10 shot, lever action carbine (Browning model 92) that weighs only 5 1/4 pounds. Calibre is .44 Magnum. With handloads, it will deliver a 240 grain bullet with more energy than a 12 gauge shotgun slug. It is also capable of operating, with handloaded shot shells, as an effective shotgun equivalent to a .410 guage. Commercial shotshells are available but field tests show they are not as effective because the shot tends to ball or stick together in one glob.

I know of no other way to have an effective rifle and shotgun in one firearm of such small dimensions and weight.

USE A CHECKLIST

For camping, a checklist is a must. It is a long way back if you forget something, so forgetting something means doing without. Each of us have different needs, so no one else's checklist is going to totally work for you. One good way to develop your own checklist is to start with one or more checklists from other sources. Sit down and compose your own. Then do an overnight or weekend campout to somewhere near your home, by car or plane. Pick somewhere nearby or at least near a store in case you forget something vital (matches?, toilet paper?). Here is a list to help get you started. Add to this list or subtract from it, to fit your needs. Remember, non consumable items already in the airplane, as part of the airplane's required equipment, aren't on this list. Those items will be found in chapter 14.

Camp

tent	chairs	flashlight
towels	insect repellent	hand soap
first-aid kit	matches	mosquito coils
sleeping bag	cord	tarp
candle lanterns	toilet paper	saw
fishing equipment		

Kitchen equipment

free standing grill	gas stove	hot mitt
deep saucepan	large frypan	long tongs
long spatula	paper towels	liquid detergent
handiwipes	fillet knife	sharpener
plates	cups	glasses

can opener
heavy aluminum foil
sos pads
flatware
water purifier cartridge
empty pop bottle, plastic, 2 quart
plastic bags

Condiments

salt
cinnamon
pepper
instant coffee
equal
Mrs. Dash

Figure 15.5. A good campsite on a glacial esker near 60 north.

Campsite selection

Probably the most difficult task of seaplane camping is selection of a proper campsite. I have probably made more mistakes at this task than any other seaplane operation.

Selecting a campsite is a commitment, just as dropping below treetop height when landing on a small lake is a commitment. Once you have done it, often you don't have the luxury of changing your mind.

Every time I've made a mistake selecting a campsite, it was because I gave more priority to my comfort than to the well being of the aircraft. More than once, an onshore wind has come up while camped in such a spot and the aircraft took a beating from the large, wind generated waves coming ashore where the airplane was heeled up.

Now, my site selection process includes imagining the site with wind coming from each point of the compass, especially directions that would bring waves onto the beach. Usually, prevailing winds come from only two or three directions in any given season of the year. Those directions can be learned from a local pilot or other qualified person. Prevailing winds are longer lasting but from specific directions. Thunderstorm and squall generated winds may come from any point of the compass (blowing directly out of the storm) but are of short duration.

When a beautiful sandy beach looks inviting, remember what made that sandy beach. Usually, sandy beaches are made by wind and wave action and therefore, should be chosen for campsites with some skepticism. The exception to this is the glacially formed esker of sand found sticking out into the lake in some areas of Canada (figure 15.5).

Once I rate a site as 'likely', I develop an alternate location for the aircraft. One where the aircraft will be secure when a wind develops that is unfavorable to the selected site. An additional requirement is that I be able to get safely back to the campsite after securing the aircraft in the alternate mooring.

If a site will meet the requirements for main and alternate mooring sites (most sites do not), then I can relax and concentrate on the campsite itself. Further requirements of a good site are:

1. Good water drainage: not a low area subject to flash flooding, nor swampy, nor low and mossy. Sandy ridges are ideal, with minimum slope where the tent is to be pitched. Figure 15.5 shows such a site, on a glacial esker.

2. The campsite should be near where the aircraft is moored, but a safe distance between the aircraft and the campfire is a must so that windblown sparks from the fire never reach the airplane.

3. There should be good air drainage of the campsite so flying insect populations are minimized and cold air won't accumulate, as it does in low places.

Bears and beasts and feathered flying things

They are all fun to watch and listen to but when they decide your camp is a new grocery store in their neighborhood, what a mess!

Bears are a special problem because of their intelligence and because they are bigger than we are. When camping, I make special efforts not to encourage bears to come into camp. Fish, fish entrails and food scraps are not allowed to remain in or near camp, not even if buried. Food is kept in plastic bags inside sturdy containers, but not in the tent or near the airplane.

Most of the bears encountered when floatplane camping are not as sophisticated as those described by Cliff Jacobson (15.1), so it is unlikely they have learned to check the trees that humans string food up in, but I'm too lazy to keep my food tied 12 feet up in a tree anyway. I just keep a clean camp. But, I haven't had a bear reduce my camp to shambles yet, looking for food. Perhaps my viewpoint is alterable on this subject.

Some Canadians classify bears into two categories: the southern friendly, shy bear that usually has enough to eat and therefore isn't much of a problem, and the northern, hungry, aggressive bear who rarely has enough to eat and is therefore very unpredictable and often aggressive. The imaginary, east-west, wandering line that separates these two bear populations lies well north of the "sparsely settled area" boundary.

One thing is for sure: bears are unpredictable. A clean camp, everyone agrees, is a positive step in dealing with them. Beyond that, my forty-four is never far from hand, but would be used only as an absolute last resort because bears are probably my favorite animal to watch. Some additional reading about bears can be found in (15.1, 15.2).

One other thing I learned about bears while camping and fishing near Yellowstone: they are great swimmers and think nothing of crossing large lakes. They do so in a fairly straight line and are capable of a top speed that is 3 or 4 times their cruising speed. It is not a good idea to get in front of them with a boat or floatplane as they may not alter course!

Probably the most regular night visitor to camp is the mouse. You moved in to his neighborhood, so he checks you out and when he does, he will surely find the cookies or pet food or anything else you didn't seal up well before retiring for the night. In its place, he leaves his neatly formed calling cards so you know he paid you a visit, even if you slept too soundly to hear his nocturnal rustling. If he does wake you, sometimes its hard to distinguish between his rustling near your ear from that of a LARGE! animal a little farther away!

The most ingenious mousetrap I've ever seen is simple to build in camp and very effective. I call it the multimouse trap because, unlike the one-shot, spring loaded mousetrap, this one continues to be effective on all comers, and can reduce the mouse population at a campsite to a tolerable level in one night.

Figure 15.6. The multimouse trap after a hard night, catching mice.

Figure 15.6 shows the multimousetrap, which is just a bucket with three inches of water in the bottom (doesn't work as well below 32° F.), with a soda pop or beer can impaled longitudinally on a stout piece of wire which is laid across the top of the bucket. Smear a little peanut butter on the outside of the can and place the whole contraption with the bucket's top edge within an inch or two of a nearby tree trunk, so the mice can climb up something to reach the rim of the bucket. The mouse then walks the bucket rim to the wire and jumps to the can which rotates and dumps him in the water. It is all over after a little swimming, water treading and splashing about. I have seen as many as 19 dead mice in the bucket in the morning! Don't put the bucket too near your tent, though, the plopping and splashing about might keep you awake.

Bugs

In some places in the bush, particularly after a big hatch of mosquitos or black flies, it can be very dangerous to be out and about unless protected by proper clothing and insect repellant. DEET is presently the best repellant ingredient. Recent studies have shown that there may be some disagreeable side effects from getting too much of this material absorbed into the human system through the skin, especially for children. For that reason, and because of the demonstrated effectiveness, and because it is not necessary to cover up so completely, I am sold on the bug jacket which is a large jacket made of absorbant, open mesh material. It zips up and has a hood.

The jacket is stored in a plastic ziplock bag after it has been treated with a considerable dose of liquid DEET type repellant. During storage the repellant soaks evenly through the jacket material. The bug jacket can be put on, when needed, over a long sleeved shirt or jacket. It never or rarely touches your skin, yet seems to emit enough repellant odor to keep bugs away, even when present in large swarms. With the jacket on, I've never had to wear my bug hat, which I dislike and would wear only if greatly distressed by bugs. The bug jackets are available in most sporting goods stores in Canada (generally less expensive). In the U.S. they are harder to find. One major U.S. source is Campmor (15.15), with their "neverbite" jacket.

Another product that I have found useful in camp is the mosquito coil. They are lightweight and long lasting if used the way I have

In camp, pets bring their problems to you!

found them to be most effective. Thirty minutes to an hour before retiring for the night, I light one in the tent, then go sit on the front porch of the Hussy Hilton so I don't have to breathe the smoke from the coil. Just before bedding down, the coil is extinguished, the tent door zipped closed as the mosquitos have departed the premesis. Used in this fashion, a coil will last several days, a box of two coils is good for a week or more and I am exposed to breathing very little of the stuff.

A word about black flies. This voracious insect is particularly stressful as it carves out a chunk of tasty flesh, even through clothing and flies off to digest it, leaving an open, itching wound that will be slow to heal. If this little surgeon hits a nerve while carving you up, causing you to be painfully aware of its presence, it is difficult to stop your instinctive reaction to smack it - hard! But resist retaliation you should, because if you smash him, it will cause this nasty bug to literally throw up in the wound, leaving you with an infected mess that won't heal for weeks. Still want to go camping? Go prepared!

Pets

In camp, whether large or small, pets bring their problems to you, both large and small! Those who love to take their pets with them must keep in mind that the wilderness is not the domain of the domesticated animal. Our pets are at a disadvantage in this strange environment, and will require special treatment which ranges from rescue from a large, irate animal to removal of porcupine quills to fending off a cold, damp pet intent on sharing your warm, dry sleeping bag.

Mosquitos and black flies will feast on your pet, too, so some protection is needed. If your stay is going to be short, some DEET applied lightly to the outer portions of the fur works well, but I hesitate to use this on a regular basis for more than a very few days for fear of side effects mentioned above. When we lived in the tropics, Shorty (our West Highland White Terrier) was given liquid garlic juice on his food each day. It seemed to give him good protection from the swarms of mosquitos there, but he never could figure out why the pretty girls didn't like his kisses any more.

Camping in the airplane

Usually, when my 180 goes on floats in the spring, the rear seat comes out. Yes, I can carry three or even four aboard and be legal, but not with gear for the wilderness or with adequate range for serious cross countrying. Removing the rear seat is easy (only four bolts) and doing so adds 27 pounds to my payload and seems to double the cargo space. There is a third benefit to rear seat removal, I learned on one trip up north.

Figure 15.8. Fringe benefits of good campsite selection?

My companion was a long-time float plane pilot. For a living, he flew for a major Canadian airline. For fun, he instructed and vacationed in floatplanes. He had supplied the tent for this excursion. It was an older canvas model which, we found out the first night, kept out only the light of day. Faced with the prospect of a second wet night, he decided to share with me a well kept secret: if one removes the front seats and most of the junk from a four place floatplane that is heeled up on shore and stores it under the horizontal stabilizer with a tarp over it (no food in this cache, please), there is more than enough room (about 7 1/2 feet in the older model Cessna 180) for two big fellows to sleep in comfort. After that, on rainy nights we went to sleep to the sound of rain falling gently on aluminum, dry, at least.

Note: be sure to threaten the life of your mechanic when he replaces your windshield or cabin speaker, if your airplane leaks water after the work is done - it may insure a dry night's sleep, heeled up on a shoreline somewhere. Second note: an air mattress is recommended, as seat rails were not originally intended for sleeping on, even with carpet.

Camping in Canada

Most of the Canadian provinces now require a camping permit if you are overnighting and not at a lodge. This is not particularly stressful except the permits are not easy to get (not available by mail) and are issued only for specific dates which sometimes presents problems because of weather. This summer, some really stressful news arrived: Ontario has now closed hundreds of lakes to overnight camping for non-residents.

The discriminatory nature of this action, which appears to have been done for one special interest group, makes this a sad occurence for Canadian and American alike, in my personal opinion. It also makes more attractive camping trips to U.S. destinations such as Voyageur's National Park (right next to the Boundary Waters Canoe Area in northern Minnesota). For information, write to Voyageurs National Park, P.O. Box 50, International Falls, MN, 56649, (218) 283-9821.

If you would like to try Canada, consider the Central Canada Seaplane Fly-in and Safety Seminar next summer. It is held in some real wilderness. You can camp or stay at a lodge or an outpost camp and there will be lots of friendly seaplaners around. Someone is sure to have some extra matches or toilet paper!

For information on areas closed to camping in Ontario, write the Minister of Natural Resources, Whitney Block, Queens Park, Toronto, Ontario, M7A 1W3. Or call 416-965-1301.

CHAPTER 16

Survival!

by Paul Johnston

A DEFINITION AND PHILOSOPHY

No book about flying floats would be complete without addressing one of the inherent risks in this kind of activity; what to do when you run out of airspeed, altitude and ideas all at the same time, and find yourself down in the bush, perhaps hundreds of miles from civilization.

Float flying affords a great deal of choice with respect to when and where the pilot can safely land, and as a result, the likelihood of the crew and passengers surviving a forced landing is quite high when compared with conventional airplanes operating in the same environment. The irony is, that despite this advantage, relatively fewer people survive the ensuing wait for help and rescue from the outside.

Understanding how this could happen is simple enough when we examine the priorities, skills, and attitudes required in the actual event to protect ourselves from the environment, and even use it to our advantage.

Add to this the factors of time, injury, weather, and limited resources, and it becomes clear that to expect any success at all, one will be required to anticipate needs, and plan and practice some basic skills; and like any other emergency drill, the time to learn and practice it is before you need to use it.

Survival versus Woodsmanship

A note of explanation is warranted at this point. There is a difference between "woodsmanship" skills and "survival" skills. Frequently, the two terms are confused.

Woodsmanship has its roots in the technology and traditional skills used by hunter-gatherer societies, which aimed not to survive in the true meaning of the word, but to live comfortably and permanently in their environment.

Two factors are different in a survival situation; first, that we are concerned with relatively short term needs, and second, that as a society, we tend to be heavily dependant on modern technological solutions to these needs.

Reactions to the stress of survival often make it difficult to recognize and use even familiar resources, so that it will be more effective to practice with and use a finite number of familiar tools as a first line defense and to count on your personal woodsmanship skills only as enhancements.

As well, we are faced with the uncomfortable fact that we are in the situation by chance, rather than by choice, and therefore what might be fun to experiment with on a canoe trip, might make the difference between life or death in a forced landing.

STRESS FACTORS, REAL AND IMAGINED

Survival stressors are applied in two forms, psychological stress, and physiological stress.

Psychological stress stems from reactions to fear, loneliness, depression, boredom, anger and frustration, amongst others. Even our suppressed primordial fears of darkness, wild animals, and things that go bump in the night can hurtle to the forefront.

Physiological stress is a result of pain, cold, injury, thirst and hunger, as well as environmental stresses such as weather and geography; while "real", as compared to psychological stressors, physiological stress should be considered both a cause and a function of psychological factors.

Every survival activity has as its main goal, the purpose of reducing or eliminating these stresses. Directed action is beneficial in terms of results and for its own sake.

The operative phrase is "directed action"; the real survival tool is the human brain, and with only minimal preparation it can deal with almost any set of conditions.

Many personality factors come into play, and it is not always, for example, the physically strong who are more effective or handle fear better than the timid and anxious person. Success, in fact, depends entirely on individual ability and willingness to accept the situation, analyze the options available and ability to execute a strategy.

Two very significant emotions that work to increase fear and decrease the chances of success are helplessness and hopelessness. There is no advantage in trying to avoid fear by denying the existence of the situation; there is most always something that can be done to improve the situation once it is accepted. Accept the fact that fear is a natural reaction to a danger and make the best of it.

As was mentioned earlier, survivors frequently have difficulty recognizing the options available to them, even in terms of familiar resources. This is primarily due to a psychological phenomenon known as perceptual narrowing.

Perceptual narrowing, simply stated, is a shift of focus from proactive thought and action to inward preoccupation with failure. An extreme example of this is "panic", where the victim is utterly convinced that death is inevitable and cannot recognize any other outcome.

Fear is a natural reaction, and in fact plays a positive role. It prepares us for the classical "fight or flight" response to a threatening situation. Panic is by definition irrational thought and to that extent is the enemy to be fought.

A few actions that will help to combat inhibiting emotions are:

(1) **Admit** that a forced landing can really happen to you and plan ahead for the possibility; a failure to anticipate will lead to a situation where one is ill-prepared for the event, even when one has a great deal of experience in the wilderness. Proper planning together with knowledge and rehearsal of survival techniques affords a freedom of action that certainly would not be available without the confidence derived from practice.

(2) **Positive thinking** is a good tool for combating fear and panic. Never let the thought of complete disaster enter your mind.

(3) **Minimize physical discomforts** as a way to control negative emotions. Remember that survival stressors occur in two ways, psychological stress, and physiological stress; to a large extent both

are interdependent.

(4) **Have complete confidence in your technical ability** to cope with the situation. This can be best accomplished by pre-planning, and by learning and practicing survival skills, before they are needed in the actual event.

(5) **Have complete confidence in your equipment;** know what resources are in the survival kit, and how they can be used.

(6) **Focus on the goal**; this will result in directed action.

In addition, you must know and understand your enemies: Pain, cold, fatigue, thirst, hunger, loneliness, boredom, and panic. All of us have likely experienced at least some of these, but few have had to combat them all at one time, or to the degree imposed by a survival incident.

However, if you can identify these conditions and emotions, recognize them for what they are, and know how to deal with them, you will be able to control them, rather than allowing them to control your actions.

The Stressors Up Close

Pain:

Pain is, of course, nature's way of telling us that something is wrong with our bodies; mild pain is usually considered a nuisance and ignored when in familiar surroundings. In the wilderness, that same pain seems to be perceived to a much higher degree.

Arguments about perceptions aside, one message is clear; what may in fact be a minor injury or condition at home, may be significantly more serious in the wilderness, because of the remoteness of medical treatment and potential for complication, as well as the potential effect on mobility.

Therefore, first aid treatment will be a constant high priority activity; even apparently insignificant injuries should be attended to.

Actual first aid practices are beyond the scope of this book, but there are many excellent courses and publications available on the topic, and the reader is advised to avail himself of them.

Following first aid treatment, and within the patient's physical ability, directed activity will tend to reduce the perception of pain and reinforces the patient's ability to deal with the situation. In short, activity provides something else to think about.

Cold:

Cold is considered the number one outdoor killer because being cold not only numbs the body; it also numbs thought and willpower. Mountain climbers frequently refer to this condition as "dumb-brain", and are especially wary of its insidious effect on judgement and behavior.

It is technically known as hypothermia, and it can occur at any temperature - even in the tropics.

This is because, in simple terms, the body begins losing warmth faster than it can produce warming energy. In other words, the body lacks the critical elements needed to produce heat, or heat is being leached away too rapidly, or a combination of both conditions.

The body loses heat in five ways: by radiation, conduction, respiration, evaporation, and convection. It produces heat in three ways: by metabolizing food and converting energy to minor muscle movement, by exercise, and by shivering.

Generally our bodies are quite efficient at balancing heat loss against production to maintain body temperature within the normal range, but there are conditions that can inhibit this ability. These conditions range from air temperature and wind chill to injury.

Each heat loss mechanism must be addressed; prevention of hypothermia basically involves assisting the body in temperature regulation; this will involve external heat (fire), shelter from wind and rain, adequate dry clothing, as well as appropriate water and food intake. Each of these aspects will be discussed in more depth later.

The basic message is that hypothermia is an insidious killer and it profoundly affects the basic survival tool - the brain. Its prevention will be a constant activity.

Fatigue:

Fatigue and energy expenditure are not, as many people believe, exclusively related to each other; this mistaken belief has probably been the direct cause of many deaths in survival situations.

There is danger in over-exertion and the old survival thumb-rule is applicable: "never stand up when you can sit down, and never sit down when you can be resting comfortably on your back." Fatigue often makes one careless and as well, there may be real trouble controlling feelings of apathy and indifference.

But fatigue is also the product of stressors such as hopelessness, dissatisfaction, frustration, or lack of a focussed goal. For many people, fatigue is an escape from a situation which has become too difficult to handle.

Recognizing the sources of fatigue and facing them will help to release enough strength to carry on and become a successful statistic.

Thirst:

Next to the air we breath, water is the most important element in our lives. The human body is composed of about 67% water, and this water is continuously depleted by respiration, perspiration, and waste through our kidneys. We normally lose 2 1/2 to 3 liters of water per day through respiration and through the process of metabolizing food, and about the same again during periods of heavy perspiration.

It takes about 2 liters a day to keep a sedentary human body functioning; while we can survive relatively well for several weeks without food, the survival window without water is not generally much beyond four days in ideal conditions, and diminishes rapidly in very cold and very hot conditions.

It is worth noting that the sensation of thirst lags behind actual hydration requirements; as with pain and cold, thirst is a subjective sensation, and many people have died of dehydration, hypothermia, hyperthermia, and related perils because they counted on thirst to cue them to the appropriate level of hydration.

The most accurate indication of hydration is urinary output, both in terms of volume and color. Urine should be pale yellow and volume about normal or in excess of normal for that individual. Generally, an intake of two to four liters of water is adequate, increasing to between five and seven liters for very hot or very cold conditions.

Hunger:

Usually, one of the first things that enters one's mind after becoming lost, is how small the food supply is; this issue will be viewed variously by survivors from an inconvenience to an abject tragedy depending on the importance they place on eating.

However, as discussed earlier the food situation is not nearly as serious as it may appear, and probably is more of a psychological stressor than a real danger in the short term.

In the longer term, food supplements are usually available; you are surrounded by edible wild plants and animals that will sustain life indefinitely.

Nevertheless, hunger will affect judgement and behavior and it will also increase the effects of cold, pain, and fear.

There are several thumb-rules that should be followed in the catering department:

(1) You probably had a good breakfast or lunch before you took off and this will keep you going for at least 24 hours, so eat nothing the first day.

(2) With normal activity, most bodies can get by comfortably on about 1000 to 2000 Kcals., about what you would get from 2 to 4 Big Macs. Higher levels of activity, as well as cold conditions will increase needs to between about 3000 to 5500 Kcals., or about the same as half of a Pepperidge Farm chocolate cake.

(3) Certain types of food require more water to metabolize, and this may be a consideration in their selection; generally, carbohydrates are more easily and more quickly metabolized than proteins, and use less water in the process.

(4) Meals may well be the highlight of the day; making the best you can of them will have a significant effect on morale.

Loneliness, Boredom and Other Land-mines:

Earlier we talked about the range of human emotions that, when uncontrolled, contribute to the general feelings of misery and serve only to undermine the probability of success. It is worth saying that negative emotions are not "good" or "bad"; they just are. And they can be used to positive ends when taken in perspective. Anger, for example, can directed to produce constructive action as easily as a tantrum.

These emotional land-mines, particularly to the lone person lost in the wilderness, are the amongst the toughest challenges to deal with because they can explode unexpectedly. Ironically, while one would expect these kinds of feelings to be dominant, it is still surprising how pervasive they can be and how profoundly they can affect behavior.

This phenomenon also demonstrates the single most obvious difference between the woodsman out for weekend in the bush, and the survivor who is in the situation by chance rather than by choice; the element of control is removed.

Anticipation of these emotions, and preparation for them by actual experience, is difficult, because it is difficult to simulate the conditions that give rise to them.

However, we do know that certain techniques are effective in dealing with them:

(1) Keep busy; once again, directed action has value in terms of what it will contribute to success, and also for its inherent value: the value of work for work's sake, and a redirection of thought.

(2) Keep clean; personal hygiene has a great influence on how we feel, not to mention the benefit to health (and the comfort of the others in the party).

(3) Keep a fire going; aside from the obvious benefits of fire, we seem to associate it with security, comfort, and community, and it has a remarkably positive effect on morale.

Individual Demands of Survival

Survival depends more on personal abilities and attitudes than upon the type or degree of risk, terrain, or the nature of the emergency. Two people faced with the same situation may experience two entirely different outcomes. As has been discussed, this is due to differences in experience, training, attitudes and, in the final analysis, expectations.

A final few words on personal strengths that will serve the survivor well:

Survival demands a great deal of a person, not the least of which is the ability to make decisions. A good rule to remember is: "The only bad decision is no decision"

Imagination and the ability to improvise are great benefits because most things you will be required to do, will be planned and executed by you alone.

THE CRITICAL THIRTY MINUTES

First Actions

Virtually every survival manual ever written will tell you that your actions in the first few minutes and hours will usually dictate success or failure.

This is because in every successful situation, survivors recognized certain priorities, and began taking appropriate actions immediately.

These priorities are dictated by the stressors discussed earlier, and represent actions to eliminate or minimize their effects.

Many years ago my friend Phil Hay coined a basic survival axiom called the "Rule of 60". It means simply: "accept the fact that you are lost, find a good place to build a camp, and take 60 minutes to completely assess your situation and resources".

Determine the immediate priorities; in general terms, these will always be: fire, shelter, water, food and signals. Circumstances such as weather or injury may change the order of priority, or impose new ones, but the basic five will remain.

An inventory of resources should be taken and should include all group items as well as personal effects. Throw nothing away; with a little imagination many mundane pocket items and airplane parts can be adapted to a new purpose.

Having taken stock, all equipment should be pooled together. Care should be taken to locate a good place for storage of equipment, to protect it from the elements as well as nocturnal visitors, such as rodents. Make sure all of the group is aware of the importance of knowing where each item is stored and of returning it to its proper storage place after use.

Failure to check and inventory survival equipment both before the trip started and after the emergency situation arose has in many cases resulted in just another fatality statistic.

Leadership

Leadership is an important aspect in group survival, and should be addressed in the first actions period. In some cases the leader will be predetermined; in others there will be no obvious choice. Inventory personal skills in the same way as your material resources to determine who might best take charge and begin delegating the various activities. Remember that people skills are at least as important as technical knowledge. And please - avoid that game called "the man with the biggest ego wins"; ego is the one sure killer in the bush.

Many of the problems that face the lone survivor are eliminated in a group but there are many examples of whole groups having succumbed in an emergency.

This is because an emergency does not, as a rule, weld the group together, and in fact frequently creates confusion and disorganization. This is generally a function of lack of leadership, or quality of leadership.

Leadership is management science and art at work; the business is survival of the group, and the manager's job is to organize and use the group's resources to that end.

One of the principal elements of leadership is respect for the feelings and opinions of others. A leader can encourage a high level of morale by making each member feel that the group's well being rests on him. High group morale is an important factor and exists when each member of the group feels himself to be a valued part of the collective, and feelings of security are strengthened in each individual when he realizes that he can depend on the collective.

Friction within the group can be minimized by firm knowledgeable leadership. Delegations should be given directly to the individual best suited to the task. Organize manpower as soon as possible and delegate specific duties to all members; be open to suggestions; criticism should be accepted with a smile and corrections made promptly.

It is also important to keep the group briefed on all activities in the camp. When delegating duties, have the whole group present and don't play favorites. Switch light and heavy duties around and remember to take advantage of the personal qualifications of individuals.

SURVIVAL STRATEGIES

Pre-planning, Kits and Tips

All along, the assumption has been made that survivors took the time to pre-plan for the emergency, and therefore have at least a minimal inventory of survival tools. This leads to the obvious question: what will be the best compromise between bulk and weight, and quantity and type of tools and supplies?

Also, what should be carried on your person, and what should be stowed? A friend of mine, along with two passengers, spent a long, cold, and lonely night after their 185 holed a float and sank, with all of their survival gear on board. Needless to say, he now carries a pocket-full of useful items when he flies.

Your survival strategy should take this type of possibility into consideration, and therefore a "first line" kit should be on your person, and supplemental equipment stowed.

While local conditions and regulations will dictate some customization, the list following has emerged as the best compromise for me.

THE FIRST LINE KIT:

FIRE

Waterproof Matches

The importance of carrying matches on your person cannot be overemphasized; they are cheap insurance, so carry plenty of them, preferably in a plastic or metal container with a striker.

Folding knife

Folding knives have several disadvantages when compared to a straight blade, however in a pinch they will suffice for general utility and fire lighting chores such as making a feather stick.

SHELTER

Space Blanket

Known variously by different trade names, these are large reflective mylar tarps, packaged into a palm size package. While they have no insulative value in and of themselves, they are an effective wind and water barrier, and do reflect body heat or heat from a fire very efficiently effectively. A note of caution however: they are not fire resistant.

SIGNALS

PEN FLARE LAUNCHER
FLARES, WHITE
FLARES, GREEN
FLARES, RED

There are various types of flares available commercially, primarily intended for the marine market. Most sold today are actually a single unit device, with each rocket having its own one-time integral launcher. Remember that flares work best at night; mirrors and smoke signals are usually more effective in daylight.

GENERAL

First Aid Kit

The first aid kit should be basic, since it will be supplemented from the larger kit. You should include a triangular bandage, band-aids, aspirin, a plastic bag and a roll of "kling" gauze.

Compass

The purpose of the compass is aid you in navigating to and from your camp; as time progresses, you may find it necessary to forage farther afield for wood and food. In addition, the camp may be located away from water and your signal area for strategic reasons, making travel a more regular occurrence. The compass is not intended to assist you in attempting to walk out.

Fly Dope

Next to matches, this is your most precious commodity in many parts of the world. Ask any experienced back-country traveller, and insect repellant will always rank in the top three most desirable resources. Whatever brand you choose, be sure it is at least 90% DEET, (the active ingredient).

THE SUPPLEMENTAL KIT

FIRE

Fire construction, for many people, is a poorly understood art. It cannot be learned from a book, because to be proficient at it, one needs to experiment. There are, however, some basic concepts that will help the beginner.

Fire requires three components, in the appropriate mixture: heat, fuel, and oxygen. This is frequently referred to as the "fire triangle", because each "side" must be proportional.

Using this model, a few basic rules can be derived, to address the most common pitfalls:

1) Fuel will normally be wood, but any plant material will burn; generally, the harder the wood, the hotter the flame (and the harder it will be to ignite initially).

2) Dry fuel is easier to light than wet; look for standing dead trees and branches, about wrist thickness, and cut them into stove lengths with a saw. Gather pencil thickness kindling, or use the axe to split the wood into thin strips. Gather grass, moss, dead pine boughs or pine cones to use as the basic kindling.

3) Raise the bed of the fire by placing rocks and stones under a bed of green or wet logs. This is the equivalent of a draft in a stove: you want air drawn into the fire from underneath.

4) Begin laying the fire, starting with the smallest kindling and a small amount of the slightly larger kindling. Light the underside, and as the flame grows, slowly build up the heat by adding progressively larger

pieces. Remember: you are trying to balance air and fuel to provide enough heat to reach the ignition temperature of the next (larger) piece of wood you will add to the fire

5) Don't be afraid to use a small amount of gas or alcohol to help the process along, but do not use it as a substitute for kindling, because it will not burn long enough to ignite a large log.

Multi-fuel Gas Stove - ie. Coleman Pk-1-550 with alternate generators

In many parts of the world, survivors will find an ample supply of firewood, however there are exceptions, such as the high Arctic. In addition it is frequently easier to get a stove going than a fire roaring.

There are dozens of back-pack stoves on the market, and most work well, although each seems to have its own operational quirk. We prefer the Peak One Multifuel, because it will burn avgas and jet grade fuel in addition to naphtha and kerosene. Any reputable outdoor outfitter however, can acquaint you with the options available, so study before you purchase, and learn to use the stove before you really need to.

Sigg Brand Pot Set With Wind Screen

This particular mess kit is very compact, and will contain your stove and some basic supplies in addition to three pots and a handle. Seal the set with duct tape and it will float, as well.

Waterproof Hurricane Matches

Hurricane matches provide a long burning, hot flame and are a real help in windy and wet conditions. Don't throw away the burnt matches; they make good kindling wood.

Bic Lighter or Equivalent

Additional cheap insurance and even if it gets wet, it can be dried out and used; the flint can also be used to ignite flammables such as gasoline or alcohol, in the absence of gas in the lighter.

50 Hour Candle

Candles have a variety of uses, ranging from fire-lighting to heat; one candle, for example, in an adequately insulated shelter will significantly raise the temperature inside. As an example, one candle will raise the temperature in an automobile about 4° C. Be sure to have proper ventilation, though, if are using it inside.

Axe With 28 Inch Handle

You will discover that hatchets and short handled axes are more of a hazard than a help, hence the recommended minimum handle length. Also, the head weight should not be less than 2.5 lbs.

The benefits of having an axe available are obvious, but there are a couple of disadvantages to them as well.

An axe is a dangerous tool and the potential for a serious accident exists every time it is picked up. As well when an axe is available, people often misdirect energy by chopping wood; standing deadfall, cut into stove lengths with a saw is a much cheaper alternative in terms of effort.

Firestarter/stove Pre-heat Paste

Many stoves require pre-heating of the generator before lighting when the stove is used at low temperatures; pre-heat paste is also useful for lighting damp kindling.

Utility Knife

The particular type of knife you include is unimportant so long as it meets one criterion: it will be used as a multipurpose tool, not as a weapon. Will it serve this purpose, and it is durable?

Folding Saw

There are several types of back pack saws designed to be broken down to a compact tube. Most of these saws are of good quality and again here, the outfitter can help.

Wire saws (aka. survival saws) are considerably less efficient and durable, and should only be considered for inclusion in a first line kit.

Shelter

Shelter, technically, is divided into two categories, "micro", and "macro".

The micro-environment describes your clothing, sleeping bag, hand, head, and footwear. The macro-environment refers to your tent or shelter.

There is a plethora of technical information and techniques available on the subject, but basically a few rules apply:

1) Nature likes to have energy in balance; heat will flow to cooler areas until a balance is struck. If your body is attempting to heat the entire great outdoors, (which is an infinitely large heat sink), it's easy to predict the winner.

2) Clothing helps maintain heat by reflecting body heat, or containing it by insulating against convective, and to a limited extent, conductive losses. These very properties however, can actually promote heat loss through perspiration because they also form a vapor barrier, trapping moist air and sweat inside. Wet clothing will promote heat loss at least twenty times faster than dry clothing, so the basic rule is: "the more insulation the better, so long as it is dry". The same applies to a sleeping bag, so if you are fortunate enough to have one, dry it out during the day, and dry your clothes during the night.

Clothing should not be restrictive because this will inhibit the insulative value. Remember the rule: Big, Baggy, and Ugly. Clothing should be loose fitting; if it looks ugly, it's probably about right.

3) The body's main heat loss area is the head and neck, so headgear, such as a toque is a necessity.

4) A wind and water-proof shell is also a necessity, since wind will increase heat loss by convection, (the so-called wind chill factor), and rain will permeate insulation, especially down, and increase heat conductivity away from the body.

5) Macro shelters can be as simple as a tarp hung over a cord, or as complex as an igloo, but generally they will have two aspects in common: they provide a wind and water barrier. Insulative properties will vary with the type of construction material, and with the thickness of the walls and roof. For example, a thick layer of pine boughs will provide considerably more insulation than a tent.

Avoid gullies and depressions in the ground as camp sites, since rain or ground water will probably accumulate in these areas. Also, be sure to check overhead, and pull down any standing deadfall that could fall onto the shelter.

Survival Suit

Survival suits are a relatively new emergence in survival technology. They are constructed of medium weight reflective mylar and packaged quite compactly. Their chief advantage is that they serve well as an outer wind and water repellant shell complete with a full hood, and are a passable sleeping garment in the absence of a sleeping bag.

All-weather Blanket

These tarps are basically a much heavier version of the space blanket, complete with grommets for four corner stays. They are reflective silver on one side and red on the reverse, and therefore double as a conspicuity panel, easily seen from the air.

Sheet, Cheese Cloth

Cheese cloth can serve many purposes, amongst them, as a mosquito net, a dip net for catching bait minnows, and as a water strainer.

Poly Tube Tent

Commercially available, the polyethylene tube tent is just that: a disposable, fire resistant, six foot diameter tube that serves well as a basic shelter

Parachute Cord

One never has enough cord or string it seems, and parachute cord has two distinct advantages over twine and monofilament cord. It has a very high tensile strength for its diameter because it is constructed of three or more strands inside a "mantle" or outer shell. These inner strands can be pulled out and used for example, as fishing line, and the mantle can still be used for utility functions such as stringing tarps.

Duct Tape

The "do-all" tape, also known to some AME's as "100 MPH Tape", its uses are as universal as your imagination. This pilot knows at least one airplane that was flown home (legally) with a control surface repaired using duct-tape, with the subsequent result that it was upgraded to "200 MPH Tape". Be sure it is cloth backed, and not vinyl backed.

WATER

Water Purification Tablets

Boiling your drinking water is still the only guaranteed method of purifying water, however when it is not practical to do so, water filters or tablets such as Halezone, or others containing chlorine or iodine, will suffice. As a tip, remember that swamp water is often safer than lake water, and almost always safer than flowing river water. This is because swamps generally are filled from percolated ground water and rain water; Tannin, leached from the ground may give swampwater a brown (tea) color. However, unlike river and lakewater, the source is known, and while it may not look very potable, filtering or letting it stand will generally improve appearance and odor.

If you do boil the water, allow 5 minutes at full boil at sea level. Higher altitudes will require longer times and boiling is not effective much above 10,000 feet ASL. For chemical treatment, use 2 drops of household bleach per liter. Let it stand one hour before drinking.

Water Bladder

Some sort of a water container will be needed, and the best we have seen is the mylar bladder used inside party casks of wine. They fold up to a compact size and will holdabout 4 litres of water. They are also useful as a bed heater; fill one with warm water and curl up beside it.

FOOD

Lifeboat Ration Bars, 1000 Kcal Each

Most marine dealers and chandlers can provide life boat rations in various types of packaging. They are primarily a grain product, and provide protein and carbohydrate calories in units of 1000 Kcals. per bar. The bars are usually palm size and have a shelf life of five years. Two per person per day are recommended as a minimum.

Dehydrated Soup, Mixed

Include these soups for the variety they provide, rather than for food value. They also make the job of staying hydrated easier, by providing some satisfying flavour to the water. Be aware that these soups usually have a high salt content, and will make you thirsty. If water is scarce, you may want to avoid them.

Tea Packets

Tea bags can be re-cycled longer and more easily than coffee, and can be had cold as well. A note of caution at this point, however, about tea and coffee: Both of these beverages are diuretics, and as such may complicate the hydration process. If water is scarce, you might consider saving them for the celebration when you are rescued.

Sugar, Salt, Pepper And Curry Powder

These acrutrements have been used throughout history to liven up dull meals; curry, in particular, can make the most revolting concoctions at least palatable.

Dried Beans

A variety of dried beans, such as white, lima, and kidney, beans are rich in calories, protein and minerals and provide good bulk and variety. As well, they store well for long periods.

Signals

In addition to the signalling devices we recommend, it is a good idea to set up smoke signals. The internationally recognized distress signal is a group of fires set about 20 yards apart, in the shape of an equilateral triangle. These fires should be set in the same way as was described earlier, but with a supply of green leaves or boughs, and engine oil if available, nearby.

The greenery will generate large quantities of white smoke, and oil will produce black. Remember that white smoke shows up better on a sunny day, while black is more effective on a cloudy day.

Helio Mirror

Heliographic signalling has been used since antiquity, and as long as the sun is shining, it very effective. Commercial mirrors have a sighting mechanism built in to assist in setting the correct angle to hit the target. In a pinch you can use anything that will reflect sunlight, and sight by holding your hand in line between the mirror and the target. But a word to the wise: practice ahead of time; helios are not difficult to use, but they are tricky for the uninitiated.

Flashlight

Any type will do, but please check the batteries occasionally.

Whistle

Sound carries a great distance in the wilderness, and whistles are known to carry a good deal farther than the human voice. Whistles are particularly valuable for guiding wandering sheep back to camp, as well as for assisting ground based rescuers to your location.

GENERAL

Compressed Toilet Tissue

Need we say more?

Field First Aid Kit

The actual contents of this kit will vary according to skill levels; an MD can make use of more equipment, supplies and medications than can a basic first aider. Contents may also vary according to locale; in some areas of the continent, for example, a snake bite antivenom kit would be valuable, and in other parts it would be extra baggage. There are many commercially available back pack kits, each designed to serve special needs and skill levels. They will all have however the basic items, such as dressings, disinfectants, splinting material and so on.

Survival Manual

Military manuals are probably best bets, as they tend to be very complete, and compact. These books and those from other sources are chock full of useful information, tips and ideas. In the final analysis, you will need all the options you can find, and carrying one of these may turn the tables for you.

Diversions

For those times when you just don't want to read any more about survival, carry some diversions, such as a novel, cards, or small games. As previously discussed, keeping busy is important, but that does not mean you must or even can work all the time.

SURVIVAL STRATEGY: A SUMMARY

(A) Stay with the airplane; you probably cannot walk out, and a person is much harder to find than an airplane.

(B) Accept the fact that you are on your own and may not be rescued for several days; inventory everything that you have with you on your person and in the equipment you are carrying. Discard nothing.

(C) Everything in the survival kit should be labelled; instructions should be attached where applicable.

(D) It is critical that you establish and maintain a system of priorities for your activities. These priorities, in order, typically will be:

1) Build a fire or establish a source of heat; failure to maintain body heat is the number one cause of death in the wilderness.

2) Locate and stock water; you will require between 3 and 8 liters of fluid every 24 hours. your urine should be pale yellow at all times.

3) Set up shelter; think in terms of the micro element (you and your clothing), and the macro element (tent or shelter)

4) Inventory your food supply; each ration bar supplies 1000 kcals. You will require between 2000 and 4000 kcals daily, dependant on temperature and activity level. You may supplement this with anything edible that can be found, but balance the energy output against the potential gain. Plant material provides bulk and variety but is typically low in caloric value.

5) Set up your signals; the flare gun and flares should be on your person. Practice with the helio mirror. if practical, lay out three fires in a triangle 6 to 10 meters apart. White smoke is more easily seen on clear days, black on cloudy days.

6) Do not leave your camp except for water, food, or fuel; use the compass to get back to camp, not to walk out of the bush.

(7) If you do travel for food or water, leave a note in camp detailing the time you left, direction travelled and purpose. This is insurance in case you are disabled away from camp, or lost (again).

A Final Note

It is important to know and be able to use the contents of your kit, before the actual event. In addition, label the contents, and include instructions for their use. As a final word, don't forget to inspect the kit from time to time, and replace any damaged, missing or time-lifed components.

CHAPTER 17

Reflections of a Seaplane Pilot Examiner

by Anders Christenson

What's so tough about flying floats? That is one of the questions I might ask an applicant during the oral phase of his seaplane check ride. Over the years that I have been an examiner for seaplane ratings, I've asked myself that question from time to time. There are some cold facts that say that piloting a seaplane safely can be an exacting thing. What is it then that causes the risk to be so high in an otherwise most enjoyable flight experience of power pilots?

I think a great deal of the problem lies right there. It is so much fun. It comes the closest to what we thought flying was going to be before we learned that it is filled with regulations, traffic patterns, radio navigation, etc., and a much greater reliance than we thought possible on other people in the aviation picture. It comes the closest to flying as it was in the barnstorming era. It is just this feeling that causes otherwise excellent pilots to do things in a floatplane that they would never think of doing in a landplane. Let me cite a very common example. A landplane pilot, when approaching for a landing at an airport, will very likely circle the airport above pattern altitude, then enter a downwind leg at a safe altitude, keep a safe altitude on base and have a reasonable distance on final approach. Put this same pilot in a seaplane and he very commonly will disregard downwind altitudes, base leg altitudes and final approach leg distances.

I would like to see the pilot use his imagination. I would like to see him decide where he wishes to touch down on the lake and then imagine a 75 foot wide runway beginning 300 feet before that point and extending for 2,000 feet beyond it. I want him to imagine an airport right there on the lake, then treat it like one, with the normal downwind, base and final legs. If we take all of our safety procedures that have been so well trained into us and use them in our seaplane flying, we will have a much better safety record.

I mentioned imagination. That is difficult to have with minimum experience. However, that is one of the items training should develop. Along that line I might ask an applicant how short a lake he would choose to land on, assuming there was no emergency. After considerable thought he will very likely say "about a half mile". Then I ask him how much lake he would like to have in front of him for a takeoff. The answer, quite commonly I'm pleased to quote, is "one mile". My only concern then, since the problem was no emergency one, is why he would land on a lake that was not what he considered sufficient for a safe takeoff.

How long should a lake be for landing? The Minnesota State Department of Aeronautics requires one mile of effective lake with a one to ten approach slope for the licensing of a seaplane base. Assuming, normally, a fifty foot bank with fifty foot trees surrounding the lake, this means that we need a little over a mile. How can we tell, before landing, if we have that distance? A good method is to fly the long length of the lake as much downwind as possible at an airspeed of 90 mph. If the time is 45 seconds or more, you should have adequate room for a takeoff.

The First Big Rule in Float Flying

So far in my discussion you have very likely seen my hint at the first big rule in float flying. It's the same as in landplane flying- DON'T HURRY! It starts when preflighting the aircraft and floats. You must remember that once you've committed yourself to start the engine, you must have everything completed. That includes not only a thorough preflight of your equipment using a check list, but also just where the aircraft is going to go once the engine is started. Remember, movement is immediate. DON'T HURRY. Think over things such as wind, other boats, people, etc.

Rule Two

Prospective seaplane pilots are always amazed that water spray can seriously damage a propeller. I have seen a perfectly good propeller ruined beyond repair in just 15 minutes of improper handling. But even more important and serious is the number of seaplanes that have capsized due to the same improper techniques. Both conditions can be avoided if the second rule is put into practice. NEVER EXCEED

<u>1,000 RPM UNLESS YOU WISH TO STEP TAXI, STEP TURN, PLOW TURN OR TAKE OFF. In other words, the only time you should exceed 1,000 RPM is when you want to go to full power.</u>

Figure 17.1. Water damage to a composition propeller. Photo by Bill McCarrel.

The Use of Ailerons

There is some misunderstanding about the effective use of ailerons while idle taxiing. I see people terribly concerned with up ailerons and down ailerons. I always remember to always think only of down ailerons. That cuts my remembering problem by one-half. The down aileron is deflected much farther from the horizontal plane than is the up aileron. It may not look that way, but just try it. Turn your control wheel until the underside of the aileron is parallel to the surface of the lake and just see how far up it is from neutral. You very likely remember your flight instructor's stressing the importance of aileron and elevator positions during windy days while taxiing on the airport. The beautiful part of seaplane taxiing is that it is the same. The elevator, however, should normally be held in the up position.

Here is just one more word about that second big rule - the 1,000 RPM limit. It is the combination of excess speed and power while attempting to taxi in a quartering tailwind situation that sets up the classic capsizing problem. If you limit yourself to the 1,000 RPM rule, the airplane will weathercock before you can get into a capsizing situation.

Unless there is a gale blowing, the airplane will not capsize while pointing into the wind. So, if you are taxiing along with a quartering tailwind and find you are no longer able to hold your heading - that is, you are starting to weathercock - close your power. Let it head into the wind and then make other plans. Your plans will not have to be: "How do I get out of this cockpit while I'm upside down?"

On Sailing

Sometime during the flight test I ask the applicant to shut down the engine and sail to a predetermined spot such as a buoy, dock or beach. Not uncommonly, I see a great deal of insecurity at this point. The flaps come down and the rudder is pushed and the ailerons are whipped up and down.

Let's think a moment about what we are trying to do. We are merely trying, to the best of the aircraft's capabilities, to change our sailing direction from straight downwind to either side. Let's just prove that the down aileron position is an effective sail area. With the engine shut down and water rudders and flaps up, neutralize the air rudder - put both feet on the floor - then turn the control wheel or stick to the right. You will notice that the left aileron is down and that the left wing will move back. That is the way it should be when you wish to sail to the right. Then try it to the left - the right aileron comes down and the right wing goes back. That is the way it should be when you want to sail to the left.

Then with the wheel to the left - push your right rudder and see the nose move farther to the right. Now you have the combination for sailing. The way I remember to sail, when the going gets grim, is - TURN THE WHEEL OR MOVE THE STICK IN THE DIRECTION THAT YOU WISH TO SAIL AND PUSH THE OTHER RUDDER - and then have faith. It is much easier for me to remember it that way from one float season to another than to remember such things as "Point the tail where you want to go" or "When you want to sail left, push right rudder and use opposite aileron".

Some manuals mention the use of flaps in aiding your sailing. Think about it. Flaps provide more surface for the wind to act on resulting in added speed. Since both flaps must be lowered, the flap on the up-wind side is providing more drag - just what we don't want. In addition to that, remember that the rudder and ailerons are much more responsive when the airplane's speed is the slowest in relation to the wind's speed. It naturally follows then that by lowering the flaps we are taking away exactly what we want - controlability.

I also find it extremely difficult to see where I'm sailing when some of those big flaps are lowered. However, if I wish only to sail directly backward in the swiftest manner possible, I will lower the flaps and open the doors. If I wish to sail using my power I certianly will use the flaps and even open the doors to control my movement over the water. Whenever you have a problem coming up that will require sailing, think it over very carefully, considereing the wind as it will affect your aircraft. If the problem is a grim one, mentally prepare yourself either to start the engine or to get a little wet in making the aircraft go where you want it. A good float pilot puts his aircraft's safety ahead of his own comfort.

Rule Three

The third big rule to remember is - ALWAYS HAVE MINIMUM RPM AND WATER SPEED WHEN TURNING, INTENTIONALLY OR UNINTENTIONALLY, INTO THE WIND. This rule is no less important than the other two. It is often broken with dire consequences. There are so many circumstances that the pilot can get into where he does not recognize that the rule is being broken. Quite commonly, when I have asked the applicant to show me a left crosswind landing, I will ask him, while we are on final approach, "if I were to ask you to stay on the step after this landing and make a turn - which way would you turn - left or right?" All too often the answer I get is "left". That is the wrong answer. It should be "right".

When centrifugal force and wind force point in the same direction, a powerful capsizing force goes to work. Yet this kind of accident happens. It happens also when taxiing downwind with a quartering tail-wind - the pilot attempts to hold a heading by increasing his power to over 1,000 RPM but the wind is too strong - the plane begins to weathercock (this is an unintentional turn but a turn never-the-less) into the wind. The powerful capsizing force is at work and power must be reduced. Remember, anytime a turn, intentional or unintentional, is happening - when the airplane is turning into the wind, no matter how slight the turn, no power and minimum water speed are the order of the day.

I have been in many bull sessions when the discussion turns to the previous rule. The comment always arises - "If the wind is light, isn't it safe to make such a turn?" My only response to that is, "What do you think is a light wind?" I've had answers ranging all the way from one knot to eight knots. It is one of the variables that, if ignored, forces the new seaplane pilot to make a decision based on experience - experience that he really doesn't have.

I have seen an eight knot wind on one of our local lakes churn the water surface to prominent white caps and two foot troughs. I have seen fifteen knot winds barely make a three inch wave. Much of that depends on the shape, size and depth of the lake and the wind direction.

There are so many variables that my rule number three stands as is. I can't quote the source, but someone once said, "There's nothing that teaches a man a better lesson than having a good scare". True - true, but often those scares take their toll.

On Step Taxiing and Step Turns

I think step taxiing and step turns are mainly a training manuever. I say that because you should be able to fly floats for years without ever having to do any step work. Think of the risks involved. First, we should always think of our landing and takeoff areas as being unimproved airports. Increasingly, there seems to be more debris on and in the lakes and rivers. If you hit a half filled beer can at step speeds, you can damage your floats - hit a plank or something heavier and the chance of damage really increases.

Secondly, the lakes are also becoming more crowded with fishermen, pleasure boats and water skiers. We must always watch out for these people. They tend to feel that what we consider a perfectly safe operation can be nothing but carelessness. There are several good reasons then, to use speeds above idle taxi for takeoffs and landings only.

Rule Four

However, if we are to do step taxi and step turns let us remember the fourth big rule. IF YOU ARE GOING TO INCREASE YOUR RPM ABOVE 1,000, ALWAYS BE HEADED DIRECTLY INTO THE WIND.

Let's assume that you are going to make a crosswind take-off. After you have full power and the nose of the aircraft is at its highest pitch, begin your turn to the crosswind heading. Don't establish a step taxi condition before you make the turn to a crosswind heading. If you are going to make a step turn to the downwind, start your turn when the nose of the aircraft is at its highest pitch. Be sure that you do not turn to more than the exact downwind position.

Takeoffs

I always ask the applicant for a simulated high density altitude, maximum gross weight takeoff. Normally, much of the training has been done at less than maximum allowable gross weight conditions. We simulate this by not allowing full power for the takeoff sequence. I feel that it is a valuable demonstration since all floatplane pilots must, at times, abort a takeoff. They should, at some time in their training, have that experience. It is the attitude that every attempt at takeoff must result in becoming safely airborne that causes seaplane pilots to, at times, end up in the trees.

In any takeoff attempt the most important thing is to gain takeoff speed. That sounds pretty basic, doesn't it, but I have seen good pilots humbled and a little confused when they have failed to reach that flying speed. In each of these cases the pilot failed to attain that necessary item - constant acceleration - that feeling of the body being thrust backward, at times ever so slightly, until flight occurs. Let's review the other feelings a body can feel. They are: 1) Bouncing - this is a water condition, waves, etc. felt as an up and down movement on your seat. That can be stopped, more or less, by forward pressure on the wheel or stick; 2) Porpoise - the fronts of the floats are being held too low - felt as your head and shoulders move forward and back. That can be stopped by applying back pressure to the wheel or stick; 3) Bow Drag - the bows (fronts) of the floats are being held too low - felt by the whole body as brakes are being applied, or, as in less severe cases, as all forces stopping - this is stopped by a slight back pressure on the wheel or stick.

As the aircraft's speed increases, the pilot must change its attitude to accommodate the changing forces. The attitude for fastest acceleration is always just slightly nose up from bow drag. This means that in order to get that fastest acceleration, you must, at times during the takeoff, get just a bit of bow drag so that you know where the least attitude drag is. A takeoff, then, is one of constantly small corrections until the aircraft is airborne.

Glassy Water

The one thing that we do not want on a glassy water landing is a flare-out to a landing. We cannot flare-out because on a glassy water surface we cannot see where the surface is. With that one goal in mind, we must have a procedure that makes the landing possible.

Earlier in these observations, I mentioned that the lake should be at least one mile long. It is important that our procedure fits for that length of lake. I find, quite normally, applicants taking over two miles of lake to get on the water.

We must remember that in order <u>not</u> to have a flare-out, we must have very little attitude change while on final. Let's assume fifty foot banks with fifty foot trees surrounding the lake. In order to have little attitude change on final we will have to be quite close to the tops of the trees as we come over the shoreline - let's say twenty-five feet. This should give us one hundred and twenty five feet to descend to the water's surface. Remembering that we don't want to land on the beach on the far side, we have only about 35 to 40 seconds, once we've passed the shoreline, to get the job done.

How can it be done? First, we must know of any errors in our airspeed indicator at stall speeds using a landing configuration of desired flaps. Secondly, we must be aware of any errors in the vertical speed indicator. These are two very important instruments for the glassy water landing.

Let's start the whole sequence from just after the turn onto final approach until touchdown. At the start of the final, you should be about six hundred feet above lake level - this gives you about 475 feet to descend 'til the shoreline. At an average descent rate of 350 feet per minute - at an airspeed of 1.3 times the stall speed for approach configuration - you will need a minimum of a 1 1/2 mile final before reaching the shoreline.

Remember, control airspeed using the elevator and the rate of descent by the throttle. When you arrive over the tops of the trees, at the shoreline, you should have gradually slowed to 1.2 of your stall speed. From that point to the water's surface, you must descend about 125 feet within a time span of 35 to 40 seconds. In order to get that job done, with a slow descent rate of 25 to 50 feet per minute for the last 25 feet of descent to the surface, you will have to increase your rate of descent for a short time after passing the shoreline. When you are at the shoreline, decrease your power for about three seconds to a power setting that would result in a 500 feet per minute descent rate. <u>Note: We do not want to attain a 500 feet per minute descent rate.</u> We want only a power reduction, for three seconds, that would have resulted, if left unchecked, in a 500 feet per minute descent rate. At the same time of your three second power reduction, increase your attitude to an airspeed of 1.1 times your stall speed.

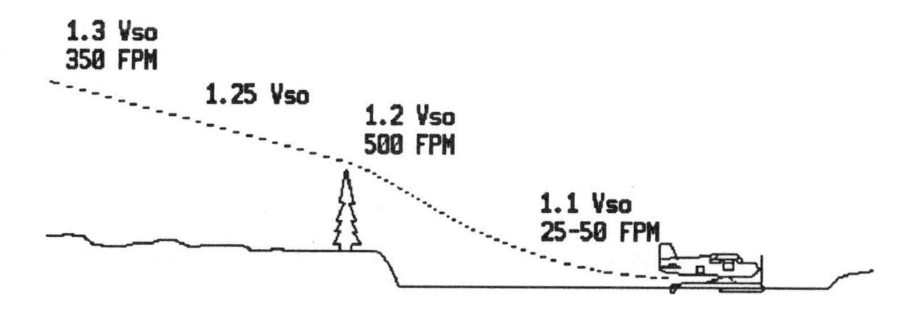

Figure 17.2. The glassy water approach profile.

Then hold your attitude and increase your power for a rate of descent of 25 to 50 feet per minute. Maintain that condition until touch down. After touchdown, close the throttle. The whole profile should look like figure 17.2.

Conclusions

In summary, let me stress that the rules I have suggested are very basic. They are not so complicted that they cannot be remembered from one season to another. They are the rules most often broken that end in accidents. They are the procedures most often done inadequately during flight tests. They can be used as instrument panel placards on seaplanes.

Here they are again:

1. DON'T HURRY.

2. NEVER EXCEED 1,000 RPM UNLESS YOU WISH TO STEP TAXI, STEP TURN OR TAKE OFF

3. ALWAYS HAVE MINIMUM RPM AND WATER SPEED WHEN TURNING INTENTIONALLY OR UNINTENTIONALLY INTO THE WIND.

4. IF YOU ARE GOING TO INCREASE YOUR RPM ABOVE 1,000 ALWAYS BE HEADED DIRECTLY INTO THE WIND.

Mooring

Practicing the four rules just mentioned and the glassy water landing technique should guarantee happy times while flying floats. However, there are two other areas of float flying skills that are absolutely necessary if we are to fly to another lake and stay for a period of time. They are:

1. Beaching, buoying, docking, and

2. Tying down for a stay.

After the choice of area for tying down and its associated problems have been considered, we have to have some procedures to get to the tiedown site. Choice of a tiedown site will be discussed later, but very often an air search for a site prior to landing is much more economical than searching for one while taxiing.

An important point that I want to firmly state -- it is <u>not possible</u> to maneuver the seaplane to <u>any</u> site you may want to go. It's all right to admit that fact. As the pilot gains experience there are <u>more</u> sites from which to select. In gaining that experience, there is one more rule that the pilot must remember. WHEN BEACHING, BUOYING OR DOCKING, ALWAYS BE HEADED INTO THE WIND.

We must keep the wind on the nose of the aircraft if we are to maintain any positive control. An aircraft with the wind on its tail has much less control and it certainly will continue to increase its water speed to nearer the wind velocity. (The only possible exception to this is if the pilot is operating a seaplane on a river where there is a current to consider. Then we have the force of the current as well as the wind force to consider. However, if you have a choice when landing on a river, land into the wind and not the current.

If the wind is blowing toward the dock or beach that you wish to go to, you must stop the aircraft's engine and use your sailing technique. Notice that if things are going badly you can always re-start the engine, pull to safety and try it again. Never get yourself into a situation where you have no desirable options.

If the wind is blowing from the shore and you wish to dock or beach, you have a much easier job. Keep a slow speed -- stopping the engine well before getting to the beach or dock. In this situation the air and water surface are usually quite calm and the last part of your problem should be handled with a paddle.

If there is an on-shore or off-shore crosswind, the problem of docking or beaching can be more difficult. Just remember to plan your approach with the wind as much as possible on the aircraft's nose. Remember always to have a desirable option if things are going badly. DESIRABLE OPTIONS DECREASE WITH THE WIND ON THE TAIL OF YOUR AIRCRAFT.

When you are working up to a buoy you should usually be able to taxi slowly to it from the downwind position. Stop the engine and coast up to it. If you can't do that, the rule still holds -- you will have to sail back to it.

All applicants for a seaplane rating should be trained in how to take care of the aircraft after they have arrived at either the beach or dock. Contrary to popular belief, the float plane is not a boat. It must not be treated as such when one is faced with the problem of safely securing it for any length of time. The plane is very susceptible to wind. The floats are even more susceptible to the lake bottom conditions such as rocks -- both large and small, stones, pebbles and even sand. Wave action caused by wind and boats can rock the aircraft resulting in damage to the floats.

Naturally, the best situation would be a sheltered area with a grass or mud bottom, free of any abrasive materials. These are some of the things the pilot must consider when choosing an area for securing a seaplane. Very seldom will we have the ideal situation, but we should always attempt to get as close as possible to it.

An aircraft float is a fragile thing. For the job it has to do it is fantastically well designed. But, as with all things aeronautical, there are many compromises. A float must be light in order to keep the aircraft's useful load as high as possible. The float that Edo Corporation makes for the Cessna 172 is the 2000 model. Each one weighs about 110 pounds and has the ability to hold 2,000 pounds of weight above the water. In order to stay light the hull is 4/100ths of an inch thick, a compromise to durability.

The sides and bottoms are riveted to bulkheads and the keel. The pounding that the floats take while taking-off and landing in any wave condition is absorbed by the floats' bottoms and sides <u>and</u> the rivets. Basically, the main "shock absorber" is a continuous destruction of the float -- where the rivets hold the structure together. With this very basic information about the construction of a float let us continue with securing procedures. The plane and float must be tied down securely to minimize movement.

Certain amounts of rope are needed for the job. Normally the following number and lengths of 3/8" rope should be available: two 50', two 30', four 15'. Make sure that there is a loop braided into one end of each length and that the other end is prepared so that it will not unravel. Caution - after using, be sure that all knots are out of the lines.

Now, let's tie down the aircraft for the night. Work the tail of the aircraft as far up on the beach as you can - getting the wing's angle of attack as low as possible. Work a wooden post under the keel at the step or under the float aft of the step in order to keep abrasive action of the lake bottom at a minimum. Tie off the tail 45° to each side on shore. This should keep the tail from moving in a wind. Using the loop end of a long length of line, fashion a loop about the wing strut. Pull it up on the wing strut and tie the other end as low and as parallel to the wing as possible.

If enough line remains, tie off the fronts of the floats in the same manner. If you have reason to feel that a bad storm is on its way, it's very acceptable to remove the float covers and flood the front compartments - the resulting lower angle of attack and added weight will make the aircraft even more secure. Naturally, flooding all compartments results in absolute stability.

If the aircraft is to be secured to the side of a dock, the risk of damage to the floats is greater. However, if that is what must be done, be sure that the aircraft is pointed lakeward, and that the side of the float is not rubbing against the dock posts. Some kind of shock absorbing material should be placed between the posts and the floats. If possible, tie off the wings. Once again, the idea is to make the aircraft as secure as possible.

These are the two most common methods of temporary tie-downs. As a parting shot on this topic, also remember that it may not be possible to find a good site near where you want to be. In that case condider the aircraft's safety before your comfort and find a suitable place.

Thoughts for Instructors

Not only the most difficult but also the most important part of training is evaluating the student's progress. As instructors, we must be sure that we have taught a skill that can be evaluated. Any goal we choose has a certain number of problem solving steps associated with it. In evaluating the student's progress on any of these steps we, as instructors, must guard ourselves from instructing. We must be careful to word the problem so that the student will clearly understand it. During evaluation, any communication, other than of a social nature, makes it impossible to evaluate that skill. As the student gets closer to the final flight test, more time should be given to evaluation. The problems assigned should be more complex - the periods of instructor silence, longer.

During the last training period before the flight test, the instructor should act the part of the examiner - remembering to give problems only and no solutions. The most difficult part of evaluating is seeing something going badly and not immediately suggesting a solution to the worsening condition. I do not advocate aircraft damage or personal injury - that is where the instructor's experience is important. The flight test standards for any flight test lists the skill requirements that must be evaluated by both the instructor and the examiner.

Teaching about downdrafts

The most common error resulting in bad accidents is the takeoff and climbout phase. It is that unseen force, the downdraft, that causes much of the problem. In order to demonstrate the viciousness of that force, find a fairly good size lake on a windy day. Approach the lake downwind at normal approach airspeed - set up a constant descent rate of about 200 feet per minute - trim for a hands off condition - set it all up to clear the trees at the shoreline by about 25 feet. With everything set, just sit back and watch the descent rate on the vertical speed indicator after passing the shoreline. Observe everything carefully - it will really make a believer out of the student. It is the best method of demonstrating the effects of downdraft that I have ever used.

After the student has seen the effects of downdraft, his perception of landing and takeoff areas and problems associated with these areas should be apparent in the evaluation process.

Lake size

Much too often, the majority of seaplane training is done on fairly large lakes. When this is done, the student gets almost no chance at solving real problems such as:

1. The real need to make a crosswind landing.

2. The real need to carefully plan the approach and touchdown area.

3. The real need to measure the lake length before landing.

4. The real need to plan the takeoff and departure path.

The ultimate problem to assign a student would be to handle all details from working a weight and balance problem to a tie-down at a predetermined spot on another lake a short distance away.

Life preservers

Even though life preserver jackets are not listed on the equipment check list from either flight test quide, they are required by regulation in Canada. As a good floatplane pilot friend of mine will testify, "It's a good thing they are required". I know from experience that he will not pull away from shore unless all occupants are wearing life jackets. He has good reason for the rule. It is a good idea for each occupant to wear Coast Guard approved life preservers when landing, operating on or taking off from water.

Licensure; points certainly worth mentioning:

1. If the applicant has a Commercial license and wishes a seaplane rating he has a choice of taking the flight test for a seaplane rating limited to Private Pilot privileges or having the rating attached to his Commercial license as Airplane Single Engine Sea.

2. Which license is sought is a matter of proficiency. However, the applicant must declare his intent before the flight test begins.

3. If a Private Pilot ASEL wishes to take a Commercial flight test in a seaplane, at least part of the test would include demonstrating proficiency in complex aircraft. A complex seaplane must have a controllable pitch propeller and flaps.

4. However, applicants for seaplane ratings who have a Commercial license need not demonstrate complex aircraft proficiency since it was already done once before.

5. Likewise, a Private pilot wishing a rating need not demonstrate in complex aircraft.

All of the information I've given you also pertains to the Commercial seaplane rating. However, the appropriate practical test standards must be used while preparing for the flight test.

Hopefully, these observations will give some guidance to the instructor and the student along the watery road to the seaplane rating.

GLOSSARY

Author's note: due to space limitations, it is not possible to do the comprehensive glossary I had in mind. For additional vocabulary, may I recommend the reader to chapter 1 of Chapman(13.1) and the glossary of (13.2).

A

Abeam- a direction at right angle to the keel of the craft. bearing 090 or 270 degrees relative to the craft's nose or bow.
Aft- toward the back of the craft (a direction). Opposite of forward.

B

Bearing- the direction of an object, usually *from* the observer. May be stated in terms of true, magnetic or other values of direction. See 'relative bearing'.
Belay- see page 13-2.
Bend- a knot joining two lines.
Bilge- lowest area of the interior of the float or hull, where water collects.
Bitter end- the inboard end of the anchor rode. Also applies to the mariner's end of any working line.
Block- a pulley.
Boat hook- a short shaft of wood or metal with a hook fitting at one end, designed to extend one's effective reach from the craft.
Bow- the most forward portion of any craft.
Bow line- a mooring line leading from the bow of the craft.
Bridle- a special line, usually prefabricated, to attach from the bow cleats or propeller to a buoy or anchor rode.
Buoy- a floating aid to navigation. Shape and color indicate its purpose.

C

Cast off- see page 13-2.
Catamaran- a craft with two hulls.
Chafing gear- equipment used to prevent abrasion of a line.
Chine- portion of the hull where the bottom and sides meet.
Cleat- fitting of metal or wood with outward curving arms or horns on which lines can be made fast.
Compartment- an interior volume of the float or hull, divided by partitions called bulkheads.

D

Dead ahead- a direction directly in front of the craft.
Dockline- a mooring line used to attach the craft to a dock.
Drag anchor, to- (verb)- to change location of the craft because the anchor is not holding.

E

Ease, to- see page 13-2.
Effective weight- The total of the aircraft's actual (real) weight and the TDF (tail down force). See page 6-2 and bibliography (5.1) for a complete description.
Esker- a narrow ridge of rock, gravel or sand deposited by glacial activity.

F

Fender- a soft object used between the craft and dock or shore to prevent damage to the craft.
Fetch- the distance, across the water, that the wind can work to generate wave action. For any given wind velocity, the greater the fetch, the more severe the wave action will be.
Forward- a direction. Toward the bow (front of the craft).

G

Granny knot- a reef or square knot incorrectly tied. It is not reliable.
Ground tackle- all equipment aboard the craft that is or may be used for anchoring.

H

Halyard- a line, often wire, used to hoist a sail or flag.
Hawser- a heavy line used to moor or tow a large ship.
Heave- see page 13-2.
Heavy weather- conditions which exist when a strong wind is blowing.
Heel- the rear portion of a float, the portion aft of the step or the part near the water rudder attach point, or transom.
Heel up- to bring the floatplane ashore heel first. To rest the heels of the floats on the shore.
Helm- the steering mechanism of the craft.

K

Keel- the major longitudinal structural member located at the lowest point of the float or hull.

L

Leeward- (pronounced loo-ard) a direction away from the wind, reference the observer on the water. Opposite of windward. A lee shore can portend disaster for a drifting craft.
Line- proper marine term for what is called 'rope' ashore.

O

Offshore- a direction, away from the shore, in the opposite direction from the shore.
Onshore- a direction, toward the shore. An 'onshore wind' is blowing from the water toward the shore.

P

Pay out- see page 13-2.
Painter- a short, small line secured to the bow of a small craft, used for making fast or towing.
Pilotage- a method of navigation using landmarks or visible references to establish position and heading.
Port- the left side of the craft

R

Relative bearing- the direction of an object from the observer measured from the craft's forward longitudinal axis.
Rode- a line, cable or chain attached to the anchor.

S

Scope- ratio of length of rode used, to the depth of the water.
Shackle- a U shaped fitting used to connet two loops or fittings. It is closed with a screw pin or spring loaded pin.
Sheet- a line attached to a sail which controls the shape or set of the sail.
Shoreline- a mooring line attached to a point ashore.
Springline- a line leading from the bow aft or from the stern forward to prevent the craft from moving ahead or astern.
Starboard- the right side of the craft.
Standoff- (verb) to remain clear of. Not to touch. (noun) a device used to prevent the craft from touching.
Stern- the rearmost part of the craft.
Stinger- the tailwheel spring or attach point used as the tail tiedown point when 'on floats'.

T

Tackle- a broad term for equipment used aboard a craft. See ground tackle.

Thimble- metal ring or eyelet around which a line is spliced. Its purpose is to decrease wear and spread the load on the loop of the line.
Transom- the nearly vertical structure at the rear of the float. It is often the attach structure for the water rudder fittings.
Trimaran- a craft with three hulls.

W

Windward- (pronounced winnerd) toward the wind. The direction the wind is blowing from, reference the observer on the water. A windward shore gives protection from the wind.

BIBLIOGRAPHY and Other Resources

2.1 Kurt, Franklin T., "Water Flying", Macmillan Publishing, 1974.

2.2 Frey, Jay J., "How to Fly Floats", Edo Corporation, 1972.

2.3 Faure, Marin, "Flying a Floatplane", Tab Books, Inc., 1985.

2.4 "Flight Training Handbook", USGPO, AC-61-21A, 1981.

2.5 WATER FLYING, quarterly periodical plus one annual issue published by the Seaplane Pilot's Association, 421 Aviation Way, Frederick, MD 21701.

4.1 De Remer, Dale, "Seaplane Takeoff Performance: Using Delta Ratio as a Method of Correlation", AIAA Journal of Aircraft, July, 1988.

5.1 Kershner, William, "The Advanced Pilot's Flight Manual", 5th edition, Iowa State University Press, 1986.

8.1 Weflin, Arivd, "External Loads", Water Flying Annual pp. 77-80, 1985.

9.1 Beiser, Arthur, "Modern Technical Physics", 3rd edition, Benjamin/Cummings Publ. Co., 1979, pp. 112-122.

10.1 "Aviation Weather", AC-00-6A, IAP, Inc. or USGPO, 1975.

10.2 "Aviation Weather Services", AC-00-45C, IAP, Inc. or USGPO, 1979.

10.3 Buck, Robert N., "Weather Flying", MacMillan Co. 1978.

11.1 Smithey, Thurman, "Aircraft DR and Sun's Azimuth Program", 56 Center St., Chula Vista, CA 92010.

11.2 Lake & Air Seaplane Catalog, P.O. Box 442244, Eden Prarie, MN 55347

11.3 Map Distribution Center, Surveys & Mapping Branch, 1007 Century St., Winnipeg, MB, R3H OW4, Canada

11.4 FAA-FSDO #61, 3788 University Ave., Fairbanks, AK, 99701

13.1 Maloney, E.S., "Chapman - Piloting, Seamanship & Small Boat Handling", 56th ed., Hearst Marine Books, NY, 1983.

13.2 Snyder, Paul and Arthur, "Knots & Lines Illustrated", Degraff, Inc. Tuckahoe, NY., 1970.

14.1 Downie, Don, "Alaska Flight Plan", Tab Books

15.1 Jacobson, Cliff, "The Basic Essentials of Camping", ICS Books, Merrillville, Ind., 1988.

15.2 Herrero, Steven, "Bear Attacks, Their Causes and Avoidance", Winchester Press. ISBN 0-8329-0337-9

15.3 Forgey, Wm. M.D., "Wilderness Medicine", Indiana Camp Supply Books, Pittsboro, Indiana, 1979.

15.4 Fletcher, Colin, "The Complete Walker III", Knops Publ., 1984.

15.5 "Standard First Aid and Personal Safety", 2nd Ed., American Red Cross, 1979.

15.6 "Cardiopulmonary Resuscitation", 3rd Ed., American Heart Assn., CPR Publishers, Inc., 1986.

15.7 Therm-a-rest, by Cascade Designs, Inc., 4000 1st Ave. So., Seattle, WA 98134.

15.8 Gadabout Chair, Andrews Maclaren, Inc., P.O. Box 2004, N.Y., NY 10017. 212-889-7547.

15.9 L.L. Bean, Inc., Freeport, ME 04033. 800-341-4341. (Catalog available)

15.10 Eureka! Tents, P.O. Box 966,
Binghampton, NY 13902.
607-723-7546. (catalog available)

15.11 REI, P.O. Box C-88125,
Seattle, WA 98188. 800-426-4840. (Catalog available)

15.12 Ramsey Outdoor, 226 Rt. 17N, Paramus,
NJ 07652. 201-261-5000. (catalog available).

15.13 General Ecology, Inc. 151 Sheree Blvd.,
Lionsville, PA 19353. 215-363-7900. (water filter).

15.14 Mountain Safety Research, P.O. Box 3978,
Terminal Station,
Seattle, WA 98124. (MSR stove).

15.15 Campmor, P.O. Box 999, Paramus, NJ 07653.
800-526-4684. (catalog available).

15.16 Backpacker Magazine, P.O. Box 2784,
Boulder, CO 80322.

15.17 Goodchild, Peter, "Survival Skills of the North
American Indians", Chicago Review Press, 1984.

INDEX

A

Acceleration 3-7
    see: net accelerating force
ADF 14-12
Aerodynamics 5-5, 8-4
Ailerons 17-3
Air mattress 15-6
Airspeed
    climb 5-15
    glide 5-16
    max distance glide 5-18
    max endurance 5-7
    max range .... 5-9 to 12
    min sink glide 5-16, 5-18
    stall 5-18
    see also: V speeds.
Alcohol in fuel 12-5
Anchor
    Bruce 13-9, 13-13, 13-14
    design 13-13
    rode 13-2, 13-10, 13-14
    see also: mooring
Anchoring 13-13, 13-15
Apparent precession 11-10, 11-15
Arctic 14-1
    equipment 14-2
    pilot qualifications 14-1, 14-2
    navigation (see)
Astrocompass see: compass
Autogas see: fuel
Automatic direction finder 14-12
    bearing deviation card 14-14
    calibration of 14-14
    errors of 14-12, 14-13

B

Bacon-saver 11-4, 11-5, 14-12
Bears 15-12

Beasts....15-12
Beaver....3-18, 9-6, 9-8, 15-3
Black flies....15-14, 15-16
Brake horsepower see: horsepower
Bugs see: insects
Bug dope see: insect repellant
Bug jacket....15-14

C

Calibration
  ADF....14-14
  compass....11-7
  gyrocompass....11-11
Camping....15-1
  checklist....15-9
  equipment....15-3, 15-5
  site selection....15-10, 15-11
Canada
  autogas use....12-8
  operations in....14-3
Canoe....8-2
Cavitation....3-7
Center of gravity....6-1
  airborne effect....6-1
  effect on water....6-2
Centrifugal force....9-5, 9-7, 9-9, 9-11
Centripetal force....9-7
Cessna 180....5-9, 5-16, 5-17, 6-1, 6-4
Checklists....
  airplane equipment....14-5
  camping....15-9
  survival kit....14-6
Checkride....17-1
Climb....5-11
  rate....5-12
Compass....11-7
  astro....11-10 to 12
  deviation card....11-8 to 9
  gyro....11-9 to 11
  swinging the....11-8
  vertical card....11-9
Control lock....13-11

CPR 15-1, 2
Crosswind....................3-8
CYA....................11-4

D

Dead reckoning see: navigation
Debris....................17-6
Decelerate distance....................3-20 to 23
DEET....................15-14, 16-3
Delta ratio....................3-18, 4-1, 4-2, 4-6, 4-7
    definition of....................4-1
Density altitude....................3-2, 3-4
    high....................3-12, 3-29
Decision-making....................10-1, 5, 8, 11
    intuitive....................10-5, 6
    logical....................10-5, 8
    option test....................10-8
Deviation card....................11-8, 9
Dock see: mooring
    seasonal or short term....................13-17
Downdrafts....................17-14
Drag....................3-10 to 12, 5-2, 5
    aerodynamic (see)
    curve....................3-11, 12, 5-6, 8
    hydrodynamic (see)
    induced....................5-5 to 7
    parasite....................5-5 to 7
    total....................5-6
Drift....................11-10 to 14
    gyro....................11-12, 15
    in flight....................11-12
    stationary....................11-12
Dynamic rollover....................9-4

E

Efficiency
    propeller (see)
ELT....................15-3
Equipment
    aircraft....................14-2, 5, 6

camping (see)
clothing 14-2
outdoor 14-2
survival (see)
Excess thrust horsepower 5-13
External loads 8-1
hazards 8-1

F

Filter
fuel 12-8, 9
water 15-7
Firearms 15-8, 9
First Aid
kit see: checklists
training 15-1, 2
Float flying rules 17-2
Fly dope 16-13
see: insect repellant
Fuel
alcohol 12-5
autogas 12-7, 8
contamination .... 12-1 to 9
dye transference 12-5
hazards 12-9, 11
filtration 12-9
selector valve 13-11
types 12-7
Fueling
hazards 12-9
process 12-9

G

Gascolator 12-2
Glassy water 3-7, 7-6, 9-11, 11-2, 17-8
Glides 5-16
Go, No-go see: No-go
Ground tackle see: mooring equipment
Gun see: firearms
Gyrocompass 11-9, 17, 14-12

see also: compass

H

Headwind....3-8
component multiplier 3-9
Heeling up 13-6, 7
Horsepower
brake 5-2
excess thrust 5-13
required 5-5, 8, 9
thrust 5-2, 4, 5
Humidity 3-13
Hump....3-12
Hydrodynamic drag....3-7, 8, 5-6, 7-1, 9-2

I

ICAO standard atmosphere....3-3
Insects....15-14
Insect repellant....15-2, 14
jacket....15-14
Instructors....17-13
teaching downdrafts....17-14

K

Knots....13-4, 17-12
strength of 13-5

L

Lake
assessment 3-16
large....11-2
length....3-13, 16, 17-14
short 3-17, 4-2, 17-2
Landing
area assessment 3-16, 11-7
Lateral axis....9-1

Licensure....17-15
Life jackets....15-2, 17-14
Lift....5-2
Line....13-2, 17-12
  bitter end....13-10
  characteristics of....13-3
  strength of....13-4, 5
Longitudinal axis....9-1
Lost....11-5
Low drag materials....7-1, 7-8

M

Magnetic
  compass....11-7
  variation....11-8, 15, 16
Moment....9-2
Momentum....9-2
Mooring....13-1, 13, 17-10
  bridle....13-10, 11
  buoy....13-8, 17, 18
  clothesline....13-12
  dock....13-15, 17, 17-13
  equipment....13-19
  heavy weather....13-8, 17-12
  heeled up....13-7
  just off the beach....13-9
  permanent....13-17, 18
  sentinel....13-14
  standoff....13-16, 17
Mosquitos....15-14
  see also: insects
Mosquito coils....15-14, 15
Mousetrap....15-13

N

Navigation....10-6
  ADF....14-12
  dead reckoning....10-6, 7, 11-6
  pilotage....10-6, 11-3, 5, 7
  remote area....14-9

Net accelerating force 3-10, 11
No-go
  flag 3-17, 19, 21
  decision 10-5, 9, 11

O

Obstacle
  farther from the shoreline 3-26
  height 3-25
  higher than 50 feet 3-24
  multipliers for various heights 3-26
  no-obstacle 4-7
Otter 3-18

P

Pelorus see: shadow-pin
Performance 3-1
  takeoff 3-2
  airborne 5-1
Performance, effect of
  center of gravity-airborne .... 6-1 to 3
  center of gravity-on water 6-2
  density altitude 3-12
  headwind 3-8
  humidity 3-13
  new materials 3-10
  other 3-12
  pilot technique see: technique
  pressure 3-1
  temperature 3-2
  weight 3-5
  wind 3-6
Pets 15-16
Pilotage see: navigation
Pitch stability 9-2
Planning 10-1, 11-1
  Alaska 11-21
  Canada 11-21
  flight 10-1
  information 11-20

weather....10-1
wilderness....14-1
POH....3-2
Precession....11-16
apparent....11-10
error....11-17
real....11-15, 16
Preparedness....15-1
Pressure altitude....3-1, 2
Propeller
efficiency....3-12, 5-2, 4, 17-3
fixed pitch....5-3
large....5-3
water damage....5-2, 3, 17-3
Pumping takeoff technique....3-28
Power see: horsepower

R

Rate of climb....5-12
Riblet....7-1
Risk....10-9, 11, 14-1, 17-6
management....10-9, 11-2, 14-1
Rode see: anchor rode
Roll stability....9-3
Rope....13-1, 17-12
see: line
Rudder 17-4
Rule-of-sixty....14-9 to 11

S

Safety procedures....17-1
Sailing....17-4
Section line....11-9
Sentinel see: mooring
Seventh sense....10-10, 14-1
Shadow-pin pelorus....11-10, 17, 18
Shelter....16-12, 15
Short lake see: lake
Shuttling....3-20, 15-4
Sparsely settled areas....14-4

Speed see: airspeed
Stability
in flight 9-2
on land 9-10
on water 9-1, 9-10
pitch 9-2
roll 9-3
yaw 9-9, 12
ultimate 9-1
Standard atmosphere 3-3
Standard day 6-1
Stall speed 5-18
effect of bank angle 5-18
effect of C.G. 5-18, 19, 6-1
effect of weight 5-18
Standoff see: mooring
Steady state 5-2
Step 3-12
taxiing (see)
turns 9-8, 9, 17-6
Stove 15-6, 16-14
Stress .... 16-2 to 8
Survival
equipment 14-6, 7, 15-4
food 16-19
kit .... 14-7, 8, 16-11 to 13
strategy 16-21
training 15-2
Sweet spot 3-10

T

Taildown force 6-1
Taildragger 9-9, 10
Takeoff
area assessment 3-16
high altitude 3-29, 17-7
path length 3-16
performance (see)
technique (see)
time-speed 3-11, 4-3, 6-5
Taxiing 7-6, 9-12, 14-1, 17-3
rules for 17-10

Technique
conventional....4-4, 7-6
flap-change....4-4 to 7, 7-7
float-lift....3-28, 4-4, 6, 7
pilot's takeoff....3-10, 4-1, 6-7, 17-7
various....3-27
Temperature....3-2, 3-4
correction....3-4
Tent....15-5
Thrust....3-12, 5-2, 4, 5
horsepower (see)
required....5-8
TOM....11-6

V

Vertical axis....9-2
Vspeeds see also: airspeed
Vcc....5-14, 16
Vnc....5-14,16
Vobstacle clearance....5-14
Vx....5-14, 15
Vy....5-14, 15

W

Water
drag see: hydrodynamic drag
filter....15-7
loop....9-9 to 11
purifier....15-7, 16-18
rudders....9-11, 13-12
Wave size....3-7
Weather....10-2
mooring in (see)
planning....10-1, 2
windows....10-2
Weight....3-5
actual....5-2
effective....5-2, 6-1
Wilderness Operations....14-1
preparation for....14-1

Wilderness Pilot's Association 15-2
Wind 3-6

Y

Yaw 9-2
    stability 9-9, 12

July 1/92 @ PK

Owned by John Richards &
Shu Oshika